CHILDHOOD TRAUMA AND HIV

CHILDHOOD TRAUMA AND HIV

WOMEN AT RISK

Laura E. Whitmire, Ph.D.
Lisa L. Harlow, Ph.D.
Kathryn Quina, Ph.D.
Patricia J. Morokoff, Ph.D.

BRUNNER/MAZEL
Taylor & Francis Group

USA	Publishing Office:	BRUNNER/MAZEL
		A member of the Taylor & Francis Group
		325 Chestnut Street
		Philadelphia, PA 19106
		Tel: (215) 625-8900
		Fax: (215) 625-2940
	Distribution Center:	BRUNNER/MAZEL
		A member of the Taylor & Francis Group
		47 Runway Road, Suite G
		Levittown, PA 19057
		Tel: (215) 269-0400
		Fax: (215) 269-0363
UK		BRUNNER/MAZEL
		A member of the Taylor & Francis Group
		1 Gunpowder Square
		London EC4A 3DE
		Tel: +44 171 583 0490
		Fax: +44 171 583 0581

CHILDHOOD TRAUMA AND HIV: Women at Risk

1 2 3 4 5 6 7 8 9 0

Printed by Braun-Brumfield, Ann Arbor, MI, 1998.

A CIP catalog record for this book is available from the British Library.

♾ The paper in this publication meets the requirements of the ANSI Standard Z39.48-1984
(Permanence of Paper).

Library of Congress Cataloging-in-Publication Data

Whitmire, Laura E.
    Childhood trauma and HIV : women at risk / Laura E. Whitmire . . . [et al.].
        p.   cm.
    Includes bibliographical references and index.
    ISBN 0-87630-947-3 (CB : alk. paper).—ISBN 0-87630-948-1 (PB : alk. paper)
    1. AIDS (Disease) in women—Risk factors. 2. Child sexual abuse.
RA644.A25W446   1998
616.97′92′0082—dc21   98-35611
                                                                              CIP
ISBN 0-87630-947-3 (case)
ISBN 0-87630-948-1 (paper)

CONTENTS

PREFACE

This book is one outcome of a collaborative team effort that began a decade ago when three of us (Lisa Harlow, Patricia Morokoff, and Kathryn Quina) became concerned that women were being left out of theory and research on HIV risk. A critical and timely topic, nearly all work was being done on men, and the resulting inattention to the issues relevant to women's lives was obvious. Of particular concern, the potential impact of sexual abuse loomed large in our conscience. Over the past decade we have worked with several additional team members, each of whom carved out a special area of interest to pursue. Laura Whitmire led on the writing and analyses addressing this issue, and we are pleased to offer this book as the result.

The book was an equal and full collaboration by all four coauthors, and as such, the magnitude of each of our contributions cannot be adequately differentiated. Laura conducted much of the book's work as her doctoral dissertation at the University of Rhode Island under the mentorship of Lisa. Lisa, who develops quantitative models of psychosocial health, worked closely with Laura throughout all phases of the project and took major responsibility for the chapter on cluster analyses to delineate different levels of psychosocial functioning. Kat, who researches sexual abuse and women's issues, reworked several of the beginning chapters, providing strong, cohesive revisions to our earlier drafts. Trish, a clinical researcher in the field of sexual health, worked a great deal on the last two chapters, producing a beautifully summarized discussion and set of implications. Trish also worked with Laura on creating a set of "clinical composite case studies" that are used to depict various scenarios that could occur with women who have experienced sexual abuse. Given conventional norms for ordering authors, we reluctantly agreed on the given order, while still wanting to acknowledge that the contributions of all four authors were substantial and significant. Without any one of us, the book would have suffered; the joint collaboration with our varying, though intersecting, strengths made the project much richer.

We begin Chapter 1 with an overview of the statistics regarding the exposure risks and prevalence of HIV among women in this country. We discuss the limitations of current prevention options for women within a sociocultural context and present our multifaceted model of HIV risk, which takes behavioral, attitudinal, and interpersonal factors into consideration in the prediction of heterosexual risk behaviors among women. We introduce the proposed relationships between HIV risk and a history of childhood sexual abuse and a negative family-of-origin environment.

In Chapter 2, we discuss the lasting effects of childhood sexual abuse and a poor family environment, with a review of current research findings. Research relating these variables to each other and to HIV risk will be presented.

Chapter 3 establishes the theoretical basis of model development and proposes the model of the relationship between childhood sexual abuse, family-of-origin environment, HIV risk, and potential mediators assessed in our research. A detailed description is provided for the constructs: the predictors (childhood sexual abuse and family-of-origin environment); the proposed mediators (adult sexual abuse, relationship violence, anticipated negative partner reaction, sexual self-acceptance, and sexual assertiveness in refusing unwanted sex and asking about a partner's risk factors); and the reported behavioral outcomes (unprotected sex, perception of HIV risk, and partner-related risk factors).

Chapter 4 focuses on the sample for this research. We identify methodological and ethical concerns and limitations inherent in longitudinal survey research on sensitive topics within an ethnically and culturally diverse community sample of women; our research team's solutions and compromises are discussed. Focus groups we used to address these concerns, including readability and concerns due to the sensitive and potentially intrusive nature of many of the questions, are described. Initial descriptive data about the longitudinal sample are presented, including a description of the sexual abuse and family-of-origin environment histories reported by women in the sample.

In Chapter 5, a system is developed for classifying participants according to the most severe types of sexual abuse they experienced as children, and the conceptual and empirical bases for this classification are presented. Using this classification, four groups of women are compared on a number of measures using Multivariate Analysis of Variance. Significant group differences are discussed along with the implications of the finding that women who experienced the most severe abuse reported the most negative outcomes on a number of the variables in question.

Chapter 6 presents the initial examination of the proposed relationships among the constructs chosen for this study. Assessments of psychometric integrity are presented, including initial data reduction and scale reliabilities. A preliminary, cross-sectional analysis of the proposed model is presented. The good model fit and large proportion of variance accounted for in the dependent constructs suggest that an analysis of the longitudinal relationship among the data is warranted. The results of these longitudinal model analyses are presented in Chapter 7, utilizing structural modeling approaches.

Chapter 8 explores the mediating constructs proposed in the longitudinal model with a series of analyses in which some of the paths are set to zero. The implications of the findings that these mediators are essential to explaining the relationships between the predictors (childhood sexual abuse and family environment) and the three HIV risk outcomes are discussed.

In order to assess the validity of these results, two subsamples of the overall poplulation, the "continuing education" and "community" samples, are compared in a series of analyses. Chapter 9 presents multiple sample analyses showing a number of similarities, and a few differences, between the two samples.

In contrast to the negative impacts addressed in most of this work, Chapter 10 utilizes cluster analyses to examine psychosocial functioning for women across childhood traumas and assesses variables that contribute to better coping and well-being after abusive experiences.

These findings are summarized in Chapter 11, with the implications of the relationships that have emerged in our data. In Chapter 12 we discuss the implications of these findings for interventions, treatment, and future research.

ACKNOWLEDGMENTS

Laura E. Whitmire, Lisa L. Harlow, Kathryn Quina, and Patricia J. Morokoff are all from the Department of Psychology, University of Rhode Island.

This research was based in part on a doctoral dissertation by the first author, and was supported in part by grant MH47233 from NIMH to the second, third, and fourth authors, and grant CA50087 from NCI.

Thanks are extended to Gary Harlow for assistance with the index.

Correspondence concerning this manuscript should be addressed to Lisa L. Harlow, Ph.D., Department of Psychology, University of Rhode Island, Kingston, 10 Chafee Rd., Suite 8, Rhode Island, 02881-0808. E-mail: Lharlow@postoffice.uri.edu; Phone: 401-874-4242; Fax: 401-874-5562.

CHAPTER 1

HIV and Women

Exposure to sexually transmitted diseases (STDs) during unprotected sexual contact constitutes a significant threat to women's health. The most deadly STD, the Human Immunodeficiency Virus (HIV), which causes AutoImmune Deficiency Syndrome (AIDS), is increasingly taking the lives of women and their children. We are not yet able to eliminate the virus itself. But we are at a critical historical moment when we must stop the spread of the virus.

Although there is no miracle cure, there is hope. An exchange of bodily fluids is required to transmit the virus from person to person. That exchange requires behaviors—behaviors that an individual can usually control, and thus can change. To halt the pandemic, we must focus our energy on stopping the behaviors that transmit the virus.

The public has been exposed to another pandemic over the past three decades. Abuse of children, sexual and physical, has become the focus of a considerable amount of scholarly research and mental health practice. Working from the perspective of feminist psychology, we will weave together these two pandemics and the issues the connection raises for women and children. We will describe, using a series of multivariate analyses, the relationship between a history of childhood sexual abuse, a negative family-of-origin environment, and adult HIV risk behaviors among a sample of women recruited from various communities throughout Rhode Island. Throughout this work we demonstrate the significance of powerlessness in understanding the links between these risks for women in our culture.

Research on the long-term effects of childhood sexual abuse suggests that there may be a relationship between sexually traumatic experiences in childhood and sexual behaviors in adulthood, particularly unprotected sexual contacts that place the individual at risk for HIV (e.g., Johnsen & Harlow, 1996; Zierler et al., 1991). Other research indicates that early family experiences, as well as sexual victimization, can have a long-term effect on the sexual experiences of adults (e.g., Kinzl, Traweger, & Biebel, 1995). These long-term effects have been found with women who experience father-daughter incest, especially when accompanied by higher family conflict and lower family cohesion (Lanktree, Briere, & Zaiki, 1991), as well as with women who experience sexual abuse outside of the family, but who also feel that their family failed to offer the necessary support to them (e.g., Witchel, 1991).

We propose and test a longitudinal structural model of the relationship between childhood sexual abuse, family-of-origin environment, and adult HIV risk behaviors, including the role of interpersonal powerlessness factors which we have hypothesized to mediate this relationship: experiences of adult sexual victimization and violence within sexual relationships, sexual self-acceptance, and sexual assertiveness. We do this from a prediction that women who experienced greater childhood trauma, with either or both sexual abuse and a negative family environment, would be more apt to experience difficulties in adulthood, particularly with interpersonal powerlessness and risky sexual behavior.

We then explore these relationships from various perspectives, including comparing different forms of childhood sexual abuse. We contrast clusters of women with differing success in psychosocial adjustment and women from different demographic backgrounds. Finally, we review the findings across these analyses and consider the implications of these data for halting the AIDS pandemic.

☐ HIV Risk and Women

Since the epidemic was first identified, the number of women with HIV and AIDS has increased rapidly, both worldwide and in the United States (Ickovics & Rodin, 1992). In the United States, the proportion of women with AIDS has more than doubled from 7% of the total in 1985 (Ellerbrock, Bush, Chamberland, & Oxtoby, 1991) to 16% in the year ending in December 1997 (Centers for Disease Control [CDC], 1997). Figures from the CDC indicate that the number of AIDS cases is increasing more rapidly among women than men. In states with confidential HIV infection reporting, women represent 25% of the cumulative total and 30% of the cases reported in the year ending December 1997 (CDC, 1997). World-wide, women represent 40% of the total AIDS cases (Mann, Tarantola, & Netter, 1992). Figures released at the 1992 International AIDS Conference project that women will account for more than half of the new HIV infections worldwide by the year 2000 (Altman, 1992).

Attention to these trends in the spread of HIV is particularly important because of the long period during which the virus may be asymptomatic. It may take up to 10 years between exposure to HIV and the development of the opportunistic infections which define AIDS. During those years, every unprotected sexual partner and newborn child of an infected woman will be placed at risk.

Demographics

There is no simple profile of the woman who becomes HIV positive. However, there are populations at greater risk. Among women with AIDS, 56% are African American and 20% are Hispanic. Black women are 16.5 times more likely to be diagnosed with AIDS than White women (who represent 23% of the total women with AIDS). Hispanic women are 6.8 times more likely to be diagnosed with AIDS than White women (CDC, 1997). The majority of women with AIDS are of childbearing age. Seventy-nine percent were between the ages of 20 and 44 at the time of diagnosis (CDC, 1998).

Transmission

The mode of transmission is a crucial component of any discussion of the spread of HIV and AIDS among women in this country. The major transmission modes of the virus are through the exchange of blood or seminal fluids. According to the CDC (1997), in the United States about 32% of women with AIDS were infected by injection drug use (IDU), specifically using an unsterilized needle after an infected individual. Heterosexual sexual exposure is the next most prevalent transmission category, implicated in 38% of the cases of women with AIDS. Included among the heterosexual contact cases is an important subcategory of 11% (nearly a third of that category) who were infected through sexual contact with a male injection drug user. Blood or tissue transfusion and unreported causes account for 4% and 12% of AIDS cases in women, respectively.

It should be noted that the CDC uses a hierarchical definition of risk categorization which may actually underestimate the percentage of cases attributable to heterosexual contact (Holmes, Karon, & Kreiss, 1990). According to this system, if a woman with AIDS has ever injected drugs she will be classified as a case of IDU transmission regardless of the risk status of her sexual partners. Stuntzner-Gibson (1991) reports that women injection drug users are in fact likely to have risky sexual partners, typically other injection drug users. These women are at high risk of exposure to the virus (Cohen, 1991).

In this book, we focus on heterosexual transmission. Mitchell, Tucker, Loftman, and Williams (1992) indicate that HIV is becoming more prevalent within heterosexual non-drug-injecting populations, disproportionately affecting women, minority persons, and teenagers. Heterosexual transmission of AIDS to women has increased in the United States from 13% of women with AIDS in 1983, to 28% in 1988, and to 38% in 1997 (CDC, 1997; Holmes et al., 1990; Mitchell, Tucker, Loftman, & Williams, 1992). This is in contrast to patterns of AIDS cases among men in the United States, only 7% of which are due to heterosexual transmission (CDC, 1997). Mitchell et al. (1992) suggest that such differences may be attributable to two factors: First, the larger numbers of infected men increase the odds that a woman will have an infected partner, and second, male-to-female transmission of the virus may be up to 12 times more efficient than female-to-male transmission (Padian, Shiboski, & Jewell, 1990).

☐ Limitations of Current HIV Prevention Options for Women

Recommended AIDS prevention and safer sex practices for heterosexual women who do not want to conceive include: avoiding the sharing of drug needles, inquiring about the sexual history of partners (not a reliable practice), effectively using condoms and spermicides, and engaging in intercourse-alternative nonpenetrative sexual behavior (Cochran, 1989). These options highlight women's lack of control over sexual decision making (Morokoff, Harlow, & Quina, 1995), as they are options which require male cooperation (Ehrhardt, Yingling, Zawadzki, & Martinez-Ramirez, 1992).

National probability samples (e.g., Catania et al., 1992, 1994) show that among heterosexuals, unsafe sex practices are common. Although public education efforts are aimed at combating these high rates of unsafe sexual behaviors, women and heterosexual men typically do not see themselves as being at high risk for exposure to HIV, despite acknowledging that they engage in unsafe sexual behaviors (e.g., Adler-Cohen &

Alfonso, 1997). Underidentification of risk may be particularly problematic among minority women; although engaging in similar levels of sexual risk behaviors, a sample of minority women reported less perception of risk than a comparison nonminority group (Kalichman, Hunter, & Kelly, 1992). A study of injection-drug-using minority women underscores the danger of such risk minimization. Kline and Strickler (1993) found that these women realistically judged their risk of exposure to HIV via their drug use, but minimized their risk from unsafe sex. Such findings suggest that even if these women were able to stop their drug use, which would be difficult, with limited treatment options for those with dependent children and/or limited means, they would continue to be at risk until they recognized the need to change their sexual risk behaviors and took appropriate steps to implement those changes.

☐ Multifaceted Model of HIV Risk

Over the past decade, our research team has developed and refined the "Multifaceted model of HIV risk" (MMOHR) for women (Harlow, Quina, Morokoff, Rose, & Grimley, 1993). This model is based on three key assumptions.

First, we believe that there are multiple predictors of HIV risk. Theories and research that focus on a single predictor, or a small subset of related predictors, may miss critical information about the complexity of women's behaviors, experiences, attitudes, and relationships. The MMOHR allows us to conceptualize a set of interdependent predictors to obtain a better understanding of the problem, and ultimately to develop a more successful set of interventions. Multivariate approaches give us the empirical tools to take into consideration both the number and the weighting of different components that enter into a woman's HIV-related behavior and decision making.

The MMOHR categorizes predictor constructs into three conceptual categories: behavioral, attitudinal, and interpersonal. Of course, within each of those categories there are many possible constructs. Our work over the past few years has guided our unique selection of constructs. We have focused on two areas of behavior, both of which are directly associated with the behaviors that place one at risk for HIV infection: extent and variety of sexual experiences, and drug and alcohol use experiences. The psychosocial/attitudinal constructs of interest to our work have been self-efficacy for condom use; psychosocial functioning; attitudes about sex, and a construct of sexual assertiveness for initiating desired sex, refusing unwanted sex, and taking pregnancy/STD prevention steps. Each of these has meaning for the individual making choices about her behavior, in particular her sense of control over her choices. Perhaps most unique to this model are the inclusion of interpersonal factors: experiences in prior and current relationships with others. For this research, we find it important to include negative sexual and physical experiences within such relationships (i.e., sexual and physical victimization, and anticipation of a partner's negative response to condom use requests). Each of these constructs will be discussed further in Chapter 3.

The second major assumption is that any research on women's HIV risk must include its relational context. HIV risk involves exchange of bodily fluids, whether it is semen from a husband or blood on a used needle in a crack house. Thus all decisions about HIV risk-taking behavior (about whether to have sex with a partner, whether to use condoms, whether to ask a partner detailed questions about sexual history, whether and how to share a needle) take place in the context of a relationship, whether that occurs within a long-term marriage or involves only a fleeting interaction with an unknown person.

Pivnick (1993) discusses the potential meanings of condom use within the context of a relationship and concludes that efforts to change condom use patterns must be based on increased economic and social opportunities for women. Holland, Ramazanoglu, Scott, Sharpe, and Thomson (1990) suggest that attention be focused on the power relations within which sexual identities, beliefs, and behaviors are constructed. Such a perspective acknowledges the social pressures and constraints which impinge upon women's ability to make decisions in sexual situations. Interpersonal power and powerlessness in sexual relationships are the unifying themes of these perspectives on heterosexual HIV and AIDS risk.

The relational context in which many women make sexual decisions includes concerns about preventing physical abuse, preserving the relationship, maintaining children's relationships with their father, and economic issues, among many others. Once the decision to have sex with a partner has been made, the only ways to protect oneself against HIV infection involve agreement from a partner either to wear a condom or to use a latex barrier, or to engage in nonpenetrative sex, each of which requires an explicit agreement from the partner. In order to reduce HIV risk, interventions must thus also consider the relational context of that risk.

There is an extensive HIV risk literature, based primarily on the study of gay men (e.g., Aspinwall, Kemeny, Taylor, Schneider, & Dudley, 1991), that identifies such predictive factors in risk reduction as self-efficacy (the individual's own perceived power to effect behavior change: Bandura, 1990), cognitive structuring (Ajzen & Fishbein, 1980), and health beliefs (Becker & Joseph, 1988). (For a review of these theories, see Weinstein, 1993.) These variables assume a considerable amount of individuality and, in the case of self-efficacy, of self-determination. We believe, and our data suggest as well, that these variables do not explain the risk-taking behaviors of most women (Harlow et al., 1993). Amaro (1995) has pointed out that "most models . . . fail to consider the broader cultural and social context of sexuality. . . . Although current theoretical models could be adapted to investigate gendered behavior . . . , their basic conceptualization is devoid of gender as a central determinant of sexual behavior" (p. 440).

Following a similar line of reasoning, we consider interpersonal power to be essential to an understanding of the interactions that structure relationships. This leads to the third major assumption in our work, that a gendered form of interpersonal power infuses each aspect of HIV risk. Two aspects of the relationship of interpersonal power and autonomy to HIV risk are a woman's ability to insist on condom use and her ability to refuse sex she does not want. To understand relationships, and in particular HIV risk, we must also acknowledge the role of interpersonal power in interactions between women and their partners. And to understand interpersonal power, we must understand the multiple dynamics of being a woman in our culture, which include many conflicting messages about female sexuality. Such dynamics affect a woman's ability to make autonomous decisions within sexual relationships; we consider the ability to make autonomous decisions about sexual behaviors to be crucial to a woman's capacity to protect her health. Thus, in this study, we attend to this dynamic and use it to shape our understanding of the patterns revealed within these data. We discuss the nature of these dynamics in our interpersonal power theory (Quina, Harlow, Morokoff, & Saxon, 1997).

Stuntzner-Gibson (1991) reports that women often feel pressured to acquiesce to their partners' demands for unsafe sex, fearing angry or violent responses, rejection, or abandonment. She suggests that battered women may be at especially high risk for exposure to HIV because of their poor self-esteem and their inability to negotiate with their partners. Research with young women indicates that a wide range of pressures to engage in risky sexual behaviors, from verbal persuasion through sexual assault, are experienced within relationships (Holland et al., 1990). Although women are not without power to identify and resist these pressures, they may not necessarily want to do so when love, romance, and the fear of losing a partner are critical issues (Holland et al., 1990). These issues have led our team of researchers to attend to the multiple factors that may affect a woman's ability and motivation to protect her health within sexual relationships.

Our interpersonal power theory requires that for each independent variable, and each dependent measure of relational risk, we must evaluate not only the specific measure but also the meaning of that variable to the individual in the context of her relationships. Explicit agreement from a partner is more difficult in a relationship where power is unequal, and there is ample evidence that women hold less decision-making power in sexual relationships than men. Even when women feel they are capable of taking an active role in initiating and controlling a sexual relationship, they may not be comfortable doing so, because of the threat of negative social responses to openly expressed sexuality (e.g., Peplau, Rubin, & Hill, 1977). McCormick (1994) points out that although "women do not have a weaker, paler sexuality than men... culturally learned scripts for who does what to whom in a sexual relationship often hold us back" (p. 16).

Women's sexuality is held back by past experiences with gender- and power-based inequities as well. For example, sexual victimization epitomizes the experience of powerlessness in the loss of sexual autonomy and control by the victim. That experience may subsequently affect the way a survivor characterizes her choices with other partners, even when nonabusive. Furthermore, because sexual abuse affects more women in our culture than men (Quina & Carlson, 1989), women are conditioned to attend to the potential for abuse within any sexual interaction. Such conditioning, reinforced by a culture where "normal male-female interactions are expected to maintain differences in power and strength [and] where men and women are trained to act out sexual roles of aggressive pursuer and submissive pursued" (Quina & Carlson, p. 12), can potentially affect all women, not only those who have been victimized within relationships. Finally, these gender roles culturally prescribed for women are somewhat victim-like (passive, weak, cooperative), and thus victimization may confirm role-expectancies (and lead to a nonassertive sexual style) rather than helping women break out of unhelpful behaviors.

In this research we focus on sexually transmitted HIV risk. However, we believe the principles we present here are applicable to needle-based HIV risk, since similar contexts can affect drug use practices. For example, women are more likely to share needles, which is the factor that puts them at risk (Clark, Calsyn, Saxon, Jackon, & Wrede, 1992; Hinden, Bigelow, Vickers-Lauti, Lewis, & McCusker, 1992, cited by Castro, Valdiserri, & Curran, 1992). It is reasonable to assume that the person who uses the needle first, thus not placing himself at risk, is the user with the most social, economic, and physical power.

In this study we consider the widespread sexual and physical victimization of women to be one manifestation of the inequitable power relations that structure gender interactions in our society. We are guided by a concern for the ways in which traumatic childhood experiences, particularly childhood sexual abuse, are related to indicators of lower interpersonal power, and the extent to which being in such a position vis a vis her sexual partners places her at risk for exposure to HIV.

Childhood Sexual Abuse

Studies of the prevalence of childhood sexual abuse have shown that significant proportions of adult men and women report childhood victimization (e.g., Finkelhor, Hotaling, Lewis, & Smith, 1990; Russell, 1986). Data from large national probability samples best illustrate the scope of the problem. From such a sample, Finkelhor et al. (1990) report that 27% of women and 16% of men reveal victimization experiences in childhood. Probability samples of local populations reveal comparable findings (e.g., Murphy, et al., 1988; Russell, 1983). In a more targeted sample of community women, Wyatt (1985) found that 45% reported previous sexual abuse.

One factor limiting the comparability of such research findings is the lack of a standardized operational definition of childhood sexual abuse. In general, childhood sexual exploitation refers to the "misuse of power and authority by adults or older children to obtain sexual gratification from a child" (Rew, 1989a, p. 230). Operational definitions used by researchers of childhood sexual abuse range from exhibitionism to touching, and extend to intercourse. Researchers often define an experience as abuse if the age difference between the perpetrator and victim is at least 5 years. Such criteria are employed in order to demonstrate the power differential between the child and the abuser. Regardless of age difference, an experience is considered abusive if force or coercion is used.

Additional methodological issues cloud the interpretation of this research. While most studies use written surveys to elicit prevalence rates and correlates of childhood sexual abuse, others have used telephone or face-to-face interviews. As discussed by Wyatt and Peters (1986), however, such methods are not equivalent. Research participants are in fact more likely to disclose information about sensitive topics such as childhood sexual abuse in an interview, rather than on a paper-and-pencil survey. Because these different methodologies have been demonstrated to lead to different findings, it is difficult to compare such studies.

Although accurately and reliably determining the prevalence of childhood sexual abuse is an important research goal, another focus of much of the research in this field has been to describe the characteristics and problems in living of adults who were sexually abused as children. Saunders, Villeponteaux, Lipovsky, Kilpatrick, and Veronen (1992) refer to childhood sexual assault as a major public health problem (e.g., Peters & Range, 1995) which is a significant and preventable mental health risk factor that occurs in up to one third of all women. We will argue that it is also a serious health risk factor through its association with HIV-risky behavior.

☐ Childhood Sexual Abuse as a Risk Factor for HIV

Little research has addressed the relationship between childhood sexual abuse and sexual risk-taking behaviors in adulthood. In a sample group identified as being at some risk of exposure to HIV, Zierler et al. (1991) found a significant relationship between a reported history of childhood sexual abuse and engaging in HIV-risky behaviors. More significantly, among these participants, childhood sexual abuse was also significantly associated with HIV seropositive status. Specifically, in this high-risk sample, survivors of childhood sexual abuse were 4 times more likely than nonabused participants to report having worked as a prostitute during their lifetime, and women survivors were at 3 times the risk of nonabused women of not finishing high school, primarily due to higher teenage pregnancy rates. In addition, women in this sample reporting childhood sexual abuse were significantly more likely than nonabused women to report engaging in sexual activities with casual acquaintances.

Zierler, Witbeck, and Mayer (1996) examined the association between HIV infection in women and prior sexual assault experience. They found that among HIV infected women, sexual assault history was associated with a variety of risk factors, including a greater number of sexual partners, more unprotected sex involving drugs, more sexually transmitted diseases, and earlier use of injection drugs.

Working with a population of HIV positive men and women, Allers and Benjack (1991) assessed the incidence of childhood sexual and physical abuse and found that a large proportion (65%) reported childhood physical and/or sexual abuse. These researchers interpreted these findings to suggest that unresolved childhood abuse may increase the likelihood of engaging in behaviors such as sexual compulsivity or substance use which increase the risk of exposure to HIV. Such behaviors may in turn lead to a vulnerability to further victimization in adulthood. Allers and Benjack discussed the implications of their work in terms of how to work therapeutically with those who are already infected with the virus, but their work also suggests the potential importance of working with survivors of sexual abuse to reduce their sexual risk behaviors and prevent further negative outcomes.

Although not specifically addressing HIV risk, Wyatt, Guthrie, and Notgrass (1992) present findings relevant to the association between sexual victimization and HIV-risky sexual behavior. In a representative sample of European American and African American women, Wyatt et al. (1992) found that unintended pregnancies and abortions were significantly associated with sexual revictimization in survivors of childhood assault. Women in this sample who reported more than one sexually abusive incident in childhood and adulthood were also significantly more likely to report having multiple partners and brief sexual relationships. Wyatt, Newcomb, and Riederle (1993) further identified intrafamilial abuse as the most serious risk exposure. Severity of intrafamilial childhood abuse and adult rape were both associated with more unintended pregnancies. In contrast, women with more severe extrafamilial abuse (which also tended to be single-incident rather than multiple) were less sexually active as adolescents and were more likely to be using effective contraception. However, across all three kinds of abuse, the greater the severity of abuse, the more adult sexual contact these women reported and the more likely they were to have had an abortion. Such findings support the conceptualization of childhood sexual assault, particularly in a negative family environment, as a risk factor for engaging in unprotected and risky sexual behaviors in a representative community sample.

Several studies have reported that incest and sexual abuse survivors may engage in behaviors described as sexual "compulsivity" (Browne & Finkelhor, 1986; Courtois, 1988), including "stylized" sexual behavior (Herman, 1981). Allers and Benjack (1991) reported sexually compulsive behaviors in 50% of their sample of 34 men and women with AIDS or symptomatic HIV infection who also reported sexual and/or physical abuse.

An association between childhood sexual abuse and unprotected sexual behavior can also be found in studies of adolescent pregnancy. Since pregnancy rates increase with age, the links between sexual abuse and pregnancy are primarily discussed in the research literature with respect to adolescents. Among pregnant and parenting teens, a disproportionate number report prior sexual abuse (Boyer & Fine, 1992; Butler & Burton, 1990; Stevens-Simon & Reichert, 1994). Among three studies with a total of 1,221 adolescent women, previous forced sexual intercourse was found among 32% (Lanz, 1995), 33% (Gershenson et al., 1989), and 44% (Boyer & Fine, 1992). Boyer and Fine (1992) found this disproportionate abuse rate was especially true of white adolescents (70%), as compared to African American (42%) or Hispanic (37%) teens.

Lodico and DiClemente (1994) examined HIV risk behaviors in high school students and found that adolescent women who had been sexually abused were 1.7 times more likely to be sexually active, and 2.4 times more likely to have ever been pregnant, compared to those reporting no prior abuse. Condom use was very low among all groups.

Further support for an association between sexual abuse history and HIV risk comes from studies of women with serious mental disorders and gay and bisexual men at a treatment clinic for STDs. Within this latter sample, a history of sexual victimization in childhood or adolescence was associated with a variety of poorer adult outcomes relative to nonabused men (Bartholow et al., 1994). Men who had been sexually victimized in childhood or adolescence reported more depression, suicidality, substance use including IDU, and more unprotected anal intercourse. Thus, these abused men were engaging in more behaviors that could put them at risk for exposure to HIV relative to the nonabused men at the same facility. Among poor urban women with serious mental disorders, Goodman and Fallot (1998) found an association between child sexual abuse and HIV risk behaviors.

Cunningham, Stiffman, and Dore (1994) found in a national sample of youths ages 13–18 that a history of physical abuse, sexual abuse, or rape was related to a variety of HIV risk behaviors including IDU, prostitution, and more unprotected sex, as compared to nonabused youths. Furthermore, their research suggested that the deleterious effects of such experiences were cumulative, increasing over time among those participants who were followed longitudinally.

Two studies examined the association between a history of childhood sexual abuse and reported HIV risk behaviors in college women. Loferski, Quina, Harlow, and Morokoff (1992) demonstrated a significant association between reported sexual abuse in childhood and/or adulthood and more fear of AIDS and less reported self-efficacy for HIV prevention. In this sample, sexual abuse was also significantly associated with poorer psychosexual attitudes.

Johnsen and Harlow (1996) compared a group of college women who reported childhood sexual abuse with women not reporting abuse on a number of measures of sexual attitudes and behaviors, including reported HIV risk behaviors. As compared to nonabused women, women who reported childhood sexual abuse reported significantly less assertiveness in refusing unwanted sexual activity and less assertiveness about the use of birth control, including condoms. Women with a history of childhood sexual abuse also reported being significantly less sure of their partner's HIV status, as well as anticipating a more negative partner response to HIV prevention activity; they reported perceiving themselves at significantly higher risk for exposure to HIV, engaging in significantly more risky sexual behaviors, and using significantly fewer HIV preventive behaviors than women in the nonabused comparison group. Finally, women with a history of childhood sexual abuse reported significantly more lifetime sexual partners and a significantly younger age at first intercourse than nonabused women. Although not conclusive, such evidence suggests that a significant association exists between a history of childhood sexual abuse and HIV risk.

☐ Assessing Long-Term Consequences of Childhood Sexual Abuse

Comprehensive reviews of the serious and long-term psychological consequences associated with childhood sexual abuse can be found in the literature (e.g., Browne & Finkelhor, 1986; Cahill, Llewelyn, & Pearson, 1991; Courtois, 1988; Glod, 1993; Gregory-Bills & Rhodeback, 1995; Quina & Carlson, 1989; Roesler & McKenzie, 1994). In general, studies exploring sequelae of childhood experiences work retrospectively from adults who are experiencing difficulties. The various problems identified among adults, then, should not be interpreted as necessarily frequent nor common sequelae of child abuse. In addition, it should be recognized that as a rule, several factors increase the likelihood of experiencing problems and the severity of these problems: number of abuse incidents, amount of physical violence or harm, relationship to abuser, age of child, and concomitant physical abuse (see Browne & Finkelhor, 1986; Quina & Carlson, 1989; Wind & Silvern, 1992; Wyatt et al., 1993). Intrafamilial abuse is more likely to involve multiple offenses and trust violations, and not surprisingly, long-term effects are often observed to be more severe.

Most research that has examined these long-term effects has been correlational in nature, so a causal relationship between the experience of the abuse and subsequent problems cannot necessarily be concluded. Nevertheless, Briere and Runtz (1990) suggest that in addition to the temporal sequence of abuse and subsequent problems in living, the significant covariation they have observed between specific abuse characteristics and subsequent problems lends support to the conclusion that childhood sexual abuse does influence later psychological functioning (see also Browne & Finkelhor, 1986; Murphy, et al., 1988).

A methodological limitation of much of the research that examines the long-term effects of childhood sexual abuse is the widespread use of clinical samples. In a clinical sample, all members have the target characteristic, for example, the experience of childhood sexual abuse or presentation for psychotherapy at a particular facility. Meaningful comparisons across such studies are made difficult because of the vastly different populations from which their samples are drawn. Whereas research on prevalence typically uses nonclinical participants who are randomly selected from local populations, the clinical samples from which many of the long-term effects of abuse are inferred consist of abuse survivors, many of whom have presented for psychotherapy. These participants presumably differ in at least some ways from people who have not sought psychological services. This distinction is an important one that must be noted in any review of the child abuse literature.

Although the findings of studies using clinical samples have been important in identifying the common adult correlates of childhood sexual abuse, and useful in suggesting directions for future research, Browne and Finkelhor (1986, p. 75) recommend sampling from the general population, including the community or other "natural collectivities," such as high school or college students, in order to avoid the bias involved in studying exclusively those abuse survivors who seek treatment.

The use of such populations presents its own set of methodological problems, however. Bias in terms of higher socioeconomic status and levels of functioning can be expected within such samples, particularly among college student samples. The highest quality data, from which inferences to the relevant populations can be made, result only from random selection from the population of interest.

Despite these methodological issues, enough evidence has accumulated to conclude that childhood sexual abuse is correlated with serious and long-term consequences in a significant proportion of those who experience it (Browne & Finkelhor, 1986). Finkelhor (1985) presents a conceptual framework for understanding the long-term effects of childhood sexual abuse. He has identified four factors that underlie the trauma of the sexually abused child: traumatic sexualization, stigmatization, betrayal, and powerlessness.

Traumatic sexualization refers to the process by which a child's perceptions of sexuality are shaped by inappropriate experiences. Sexuality and sexual experiences become associated with frightening or confusing memories which can lead to sexual dysfunction in the adult. Stigmatization occurs as a child learns to associate her or his experience with negative feelings toward the self; shame and low self-esteem can result, which increase the risk of drug and alcohol use or suicide. Betrayal results from a child's realization that trust in the abusing adult has been misplaced. When the abusing adult is a family member, the effects of the betrayal can be even more damaging. Mistrust of others or increased risk of further victimization are potential consequences. The final factor conceptualized by Finkelhor is powerlessness. Children who have been sexually abused often experience a loss of control over their bodies. One potential outcome of this powerlessness is the development in adulthood of a need for control, possibly manifested in the form of substance use problems or risky sexual behavior. Finkelhor and Baron (1986) emphasize powerlessness as the core manifestation of the trauma and suggest that other negative effects may be mediated by the feelings of powerlessness which result from the abusive experiences.

☐ Family-of-Origin Environment

Family functioning, or family-of-origin environment, deserves special consideration as another contributor to adult HIV-risky behavior. Belsky (1980) calls for a multidisciplinary, ecological perspective as crucial to an understanding of complex phenomena such as the lasting effects of childhood sexual abuse. Within such a framework, it is not enough merely to study the correlates of childhood sexual abuse; rather, one must try to clarify the relationships between and among relevant variables such as family, community, and cultural characteristics. One important application of this imperative has been the examination of the characteristics of families of origin.

Several studies (e.g., Briere & Runtz, 1988; Kinzl et al., 1995; Lanktree et al., 1991) that have focused on adult correlates of childhood sexual abuse have considered the effects of family variables on the individual's outcome. The conclusion is that the incidence of sexual abuse is, in fact, associated with certain family characteristics regardless of whether the perpetrator of the abuse was or was not a family member (Alexander & Lupfer, 1987).

Peters (1988) proposes a model in which the experience of childhood sexual abuse interacts with the family environment to increase or decrease the likelihood of problems in adulthood. She argues that in order to understand these relationships and interactions, it is important to describe not only individual differences between those with a history of childhood sexual abuse and those without, but also the family characteristics of both.

Because research shows that perpetrators, victims, and nonparticipating family members are within normal range on standardized tests of psychopathology (Scott & Stone, 1986), we are justified empirically in focusing attention on the patterns of interaction in the family and the values that are endorsed therein, rather than on the psychopathology of individual family members, even for intrafamilial childhood sexual abuse.

☐ The Relationship Between Childhood Sexual Abuse and Family Environment

General measures of family functioning have shown that the families of origin of survivors of childhood sexual abuse are remembered as being more dysfunctional than those of comparison groups not reporting childhood sexual abuse (e.g., Kinzl et al., 1995). Of course, as with any retrospective measure, significant sources of bias can result when subsequent events influence perceptions. The traumatic and emotionally charged experience of sexual abuse and its sequelae could greatly affect an adult's perceptions of her family of origin.

Most of the studies in this area have focused on families in which the sexual abuse was committed by a family member. For example, among women in a clinical sample, Jackson, Calhoun, Amick, Maddever, and Habif (1990) found that those who experienced intrafamilial sexual abuse reported a significantly less cohesive family environment than participants in a nonabused control group. In this context, "cohesion" refers to the degree of emotional bonding and the degree of individual autonomy that family members experience. These findings were also noted in a child outpatient sample investigating family variables linked with childhood sexual abuse between a father and his daughter (Lanktree et al., 1991).

In a community sample of women, Harter, Alexander, and Neimeyer (1988) demonstrated that those with a history of childhood sexual abuse by a family member reported on a standardized measure that their families of origin were significantly less cohesive and adaptable than those of a nonabused control group. In this study, "adaptability" refers to the extent to which the family is flexible and has the capacity to change. Alexander and Lupfer (1987) found similar results in a community sample of adults victimized as children; people who were victimized as children, either by family members or by individuals outside the family, described families of origin that were significantly less adaptable and cohesive than the families of a nonabused comparison group.

Interestingly, however, the association between abuse and negative family perceptions may not be limited to familial abuse survivors. By comparing women who were victimized in childhood by more than one perpetrator with singly victimized women and with nonabused controls, Long and Jackson (1991) present a somewhat different picture of the relationship between family characteristics and childhood sexual abuse and its aftermath. Nonabused and singly victimized women did not describe their families differently, but those who reported multiple victimization reported significantly poorer family functioning, including less cohesion and expressiveness, and more conflict and control. In addition, those who were multiply victimized were significantly more likely to have been the victim of intrafamilial sexual abuse than those who were victimized by only one perpetrator. These researchers strongly recommend that additional research should explore and clarify this relationship, especially in light of work, previously cited, which suggests that subsequent victimization may be associated with a history of childhood sexual abuse.

In a later study, Long and Jackson (1994) found that regardless of who the perpetrator was, women who were sexually abused as children reported their families as being more disorganized and less support oriented than did women who were not sexually abused as children. Research by Witchel (1991) confirms that a lack of trust, openness, and support from the family is associated with later difficulties for survivors of childhood sexual abuse.

Another aspect of family functioning that has been associated with a history of childhood sexual abuse is a lack of closeness with one's parents (Finkelhor & Baron, 1986). This lack of closeness is conceptualized as being beyond the expected interpersonal difficulties with the actual perpetrator of the abuse. In her clinical sample, Gold (1986) found that victims of childhood sexual abuse reported less closeness with parents than nonvictims; a limitation of this study is that the type of abuser (intra- versus extrafamilial) was not specified.

In another study, Fromuth (1986) found that perceived emotional unavailability on the part of the parents (rated together), as opposed to the actual presence or absence of an abuse history, explained most of the differences in psychological and sexual functioning between abused and nonabused participants. In contrast, Greenwald, Leitenberg, Cado, and Tarran (1990) used perceived parental emotional support as a covariate in a community sample and continued to observe significant differences between abused and nonabused participants on several psychological variables; differences in current sexual functioning were accounted for by the covariate, however. The type of abuse and relationship of the perpetrator to the victim were not considered in these analyses.

The amount of emotional supportiveness received from parents has also been found to be associated with childhood sexual abuse and the adult sequelae of such abuse. Finkelhor and Baron (1986) report a significant relationship between a lack of maternal warmth and increased childhood sexual victimization, a relationship that holds regardless of whether the perpetrator is a family member or not. Peters (1988) reports that a lack of maternal warmth is specifically associated with increased psychological symptomatology in adults who are victims of childhood sexual abuse. This relationship appears to be a robust one; although a lack of maternal warmth was the strongest predictor of sexual abuse in her sample, controlling for it did not eliminate the significant differences in psychological functioning between abused and nonabused participants.

Research on childhood sexual abuse has also demonstrated a significant association between childhood sexual abuse and extremely punitive discipline or child abuse (Finkelhor & Baron, 1986). In Gold's (1986) sample, women who had been sexually abused as children were significantly more likely than controls to have been physically punished by their parents and to have witnessed family violence. In their work, Briere and Runtz (1990) demonstrated unique and overlapping effects on adult psychological functioning of childhood sexual, physical, and psychological abuse, suggesting that their co-occurrence should be assessed in future research.

A final observation regarding the family characteristics of victims of childhood sexual abuse is that they are likely to be more male dominated than families of nonabused control subjects. Jackson et al. (1990) found that a clinical sample of intrafamilial sexual abuse victims were more likely to report that fathers made all family decisions than members of the comparison group. Such findings are additionally relevant to the previous discussions (in Chapter 1) of the relationships of victimization to a sense of interpersonal powerlessness.

In their community sample, Alexander and Lupfer (1987) found that survivors of childhood sexual abuse (intra- and extrafamilial) were significantly more likely to rate their families as espousing traditional, patriarchal views than those in the comparison group. Further analyses suggested that most of these differences were due to the attitudes and beliefs of those who had experienced intrafamilial abuse. Examples of such beliefs are that children should be subservient to adults and that women should be subservient to men. This relationship is important conceptually to a feminist analysis of childhood sexual abuse, but as yet has not received clear empirical support.

☐ Proposed Mediators of the Relationship Between Childhood Sexual Abuse and HIV

This section will review the potential mediators linking childhood sexual abuse to subsequent HIV risk. A number of these factors may mediate the hypothesized relationship between a history of childhood sexual abuse and heterosexual HIV risk behaviors in adulthood. We will be guided by the MMOHR (Chapter 1), and consider the three major kinds of factors: behavioral, psychosocial/attitudinal, and interpersonal. These agree well with the three major areas in which survivors of childhood sexual abuse experience difficulty relative to their nonabused peers, discussed by Cahill et al. (1991): (a) sexual problems; (b) negative emotional reactions and self-perceptions, including increased depression, lower self-esteem, and more guilt and self-blame; and (c) relationship problems, including difficulty trusting others and a greater tendency to be victimized in later relationships. In the behavioral category we would include substance abuse.

Behavioral Mediators

Testa (1996) proposed and tested a model predicting adult sexual victimization from childhood sexual victimization, mediated by (a) increased risky sexual behavior and (b) increased alcohol and drug use. Results with 191 young community women at moderate risk for HIV infection showed that childhood sexual victimization predicted adult sexual victimization, but not risky sexual activity or adult substance use. However, both risky sexual activity and adult substance use predicted severity of adult victimization. Thus, the relationship among these variables may be indirect and not directly predictive. Furthermore, as Wyatt et al. (1993) observed, the relationship may depend on whether the abuse was intra- or extra-familial.

Sexual Behavior

The literature on unprotected sexual behavior was reviewed earlier in this chapter. Wyatt et al. (1993) suggest a mechanism for the links to childhood sexual abuse they observed. Sexual abuse may cause discomfort and shame regarding one's own body. Such negative feelings may make it difficult for sexual abuse survivors to carry out the bodily contact required to use many birth control devices.

One important reminder is that we should avoid the negative label ''promiscuous'' when referring to frequent or risky sexual behavior (Schaefer & Evans, 1987). No comparable term exists for describing the sexual behavior of the majority of heterosexual men, and the use of such terms suggests an inappropriate judgmental stance reserved primarily for women.

Substance Abuse

Rainey, Stevens-Simon, and Kaplan (1995) found greater rates of weekly alcohol use, and of having ever used drugs, among previously abused adolescents, a finding supported by Boyer and Fine (1992) and Hernandez (1992). Lanz (1995) noted in particular a higher rate of crack/cocaine use. Lodico and DiClemente (1994) reported the rate of IDU was nearly 3 times greater among adolescent survivors, although overall rates were small (under 1%) in their sample.

Few studies using community and college student samples have found significant differences in substance use between abused and nonabused adults. This lack of a relationship may be due to the low base rates of substance abuse problems among these groups. However, researchers using clinical samples have found more substance abuse among abused than nonabused adults (Rew, 1989b). Briere and Runtz (1993), Browne and Finkelhor (1986), and Peters (1988) documented 17% to 27% rates of alcohol abuse and 21% to 27% rates of other drug use among survivors, compared to 4% to 11% and 2% to 12%, respectively, among women not reporting abuse. In their sample of HIV-infected men and women, Allers and Benjack (1991) found that 88% reported alcohol or other drug abuse, which accounted for infection in nearly half of them.

Substance abuse problems, reviewed by Goodman, Koss, and Russo (1993), have been attributed to poor coping strategies, along with a range of poor health habits which show a pattern of not caring for oneself. Other researchers point to substance use as a way of masking the pain caused by abuse, particularly in the context of sexual relationships that, without the substance, may be emotionally difficult (Schaefer & Evans, 1987).

Psychosocial/Attitudinal Mediators

Across a range of studies, the concept of powerlessness emerges as a general outcome of childhood sexual abuse. As discussed in Chapter 1, existing models of HIV risk define psychosocial variables in individualistic terms, e.g., health beliefs (Becker & Joseph, 1988), reasoned action (Ajzen & Fishbein, 1980), and self-efficacy (Bandura, 1990).

In keeping with Amaro's (1995) call for gendered approaches to identifying the psychosocial variables relevant to HIV risk, we have identified three potential groups of psychosocial mediators that, while still representing individual attitudes, are much more in line with both the sexual abuse outcome literature and the issues facing women: sexual self-acceptance, sexual assertiveness, and psychosocial functioning (focusing on self-esteem, purpose in life, and demoralization).

Empirical research has linked psychoattitudinal functioning (e.g., hopelessness, demoralization, meaninglessness, stress) with HIV risk (Harlow et al., 1993). Counterintuitively, this research found that college women with poorer psychoattitudinal functioning were less likely to have a partner who was at risk for HIV. It is possible that this link can be explained by the fact that highly distressed individuals would be less apt to be in any relationship, regardless of the HIV risk status of the partner. It could also suggest that, in this younger sample of women who are generally associating with a lower-risk set of peers and partners, high psychoattitudinal functioning signals an optimistic bias, that one is perhaps invincible to negative outcomes, toward sexual or any other behaviors. In the present research, we included indices of attitudes more specific to sexual functioning along with the more general measures.

Sexual Self-Acceptance

Briere (1992) suggests looking at psychosocial attitudes and beliefs specific to sexuality in order to examine more meaningfully the lasting effects of childhood sexual abuse. Such specificity is essential to the identification of the relationship between a history of childhood sexual abuse and adult sexual functioning that has been observed in women (Browne & Finkelhor, 1986).

In our preliminary studies with college women, a measure of sexual self-acceptance developed by Harlow (1991a) has been shown to be significantly related to the experience of childhood sexual abuse. Specifically, women who reported childhood sexual abuse reported significantly more negative psychosexual attitudes and significantly fewer positive psychosexual attitudes than a comparison group of women not reporting childhood sexual abuse (Johnsen & Harlow, 1996). In follow-up analyses using structural equation analyses (Johnsen, Harlow, Morokoff, & Quina, 1994), a significant relationship between sexual abuse and HIV risk was both direct as well as mediated by psychosexual attitudes.

Sexual Assertiveness

An individual's ability to assert herself in a given situation is a function of that situation and of the interaction between the individual and the situation (Rakos, 1991). Many situational dimensions affect the individual's desire and opportunity to exhibit assertiveness, including: intimacy with the other person, the status of the other person, and the formality and location of the setting (Rudy, Merluzzi, & Henahan, 1982).

In a review of assertiveness training, Rakos (1991) notes that interpersonal variables, including the relative status of the participants, are primary determinants of assertive behavior. Rakos further notes that although more research is needed to determine which factors are most salient, it is clear that relationship variables including power, status, intimacy, and expected behavioral outcomes, are primary determinants of assertive behavior.

Our research group has applied the concept of assertiveness to sexual behavior. The ability to refuse unwanted sexual behavior and to discuss and insist upon condom use is crucial to the health of women in light of the current epidemic of STDs, including AIDS.

We have developed a conceptual and empirical assessment of sexual assertiveness, demonstrating a fairly reliable self-perception of one's style in sexual situations (Morokoff et al., 1997). In our view, sexual assertiveness includes attitudes and practices regarding refusing unwanted sex, initiating wanted sex, insisting on condom use, and communicating with partners regarding their HIV risk status (Deiter, 1993; Morokoff et al., 1997). To the extent that men occupy a position of higher status in our culture than women, a male partner's status may influence the level of sexual assertiveness women are able to exhibit within heterosexual encounters.

Harlow et al. (1993) found that within a sample of undergraduate women, assertive sexual initiation was significantly correlated with higher AIDS risk behaviors. Such relationships demonstrate the varying benefits and hazards of different types of assertiveness in our culture.

Interpersonal Mediators

It is important to recognize the limitations of approaches that attend exclusively to the individual and ignore the context in which that individual exists. Although a range of potential interpersonal dynamics may occur after sexual abuse, we have chosen to focus primarily on negative relationship variables, particularly subsequent sexual and physical victimization, since these are areas in which direct interventions are both necessary and possible.

Sexual Victimization in Adulthood

Previous research has shown that women who were sexually abused as children report significantly more abuse, both physical and sexual, as adults. Himelein, Vogel, and Wachowiak (1994) found that among incoming college women, both childhood sexual abuse and previous consensual sexual experience were significant risk factors for sexual victimization in dating situations. In a sample of university women, Alexander and Lupfer (1987) found evidence of a significantly higher rate of subsequent sexual assault among women sexually abused as children as compared with nonabused women. Although they did not address issues of prevalence, Murphy et al. (1988) demonstrated that women who were sexually abused in childhood and later revictimized as adults report significantly higher levels of psychological distress than survivors of either childhood or adult sexual abuse alone. In their clinical sample, Briere and Runtz (1987) found that adult women sexually abused as children were significantly more likely to report victimization in a subsequent adult relationship (sexual assault or battering) than women who had not been sexually abused as children. Letourneaux, Resnick, Kilpatrick, Saunders, and Best (1996) interviewed rape victims in a hospital emergency room, and found that two thirds of them had a prior sexual assault, compared to 16% of a nonraped comparison group. Prior victims were twice as likely (80% vs. 44%) to have been engaging in unprotected sex.

Mandoki and Burkhart (1989) surveyed 282 female undergraduates concerning childhood sexual abuse and adult victimization. Although childhood victimization did not directly predict adult victimization, the number of victimization experiences in both childhood and adulthood was directly related to the number of adult consensual sexual partners. These authors criticize previous research on revictimization and suggest that high revictimization rates reported in earlier studies may simply reflect high base rates of victimization, rather than cycles of revictimization.

Countering this assertion, however, Gidycz, Coble, Latham, and Layman (1993) report in a prospective study of college women that childhood sexual victimization is a risk factor for adult sexual victimization, and furthermore, that it is also associated with significant negative psychological outcomes. In another longitudinal study of college women, Himelein (1995) found that sexual victimization in dating relationships before college was the best predictor of sexual victimization while in college.

Relationship Violence

Relationship violence may also affect a woman's ability to protect herself from exposure to HIV. Women in abusive relationships frequently have low self-esteem and feel powerless to change their situations (e.g., Follingstad, Rutledge, Berg, Hause, & Polek, 1990). Aguilar and Nightengale (1994) demonstrate that women subjected to emotionally controlling abuse (e.g., being forbidden to work or to see people outside the home) experience significantly more feelings of powerlessness and hopelessness than nonbattered women and women subjected to other types of abuse. Thus, it can be seen that a variety of abusive relationships can greatly undermine a woman's ability to protect herself and leave a dangerous situation.

The relationship between battering and sexual victimization in childhood remains unclear, however. Dutton, Burghardt, Perrin, Chrestman, and Halle (1994) found no evidence of additional symptomatology among battered women who had experienced childhood or adult sexual abuse as compared to those who had not been sexually victimized. These researchers do suggest, however, that more research is needed to disentangle the impact of multiple victimization experiences.

Anticipated Partner Negative Responses

Expected partner response is an important aspect of the decision to use HIV-protective behaviors in sexual encounters. Research with young women indicates that a wide range of pressures to engage in risky behavior, from verbal persuasion through sexual assault, are experienced within relationships (Holland, Ramazanoglu, Scott, Sharpe, & Thomson, 1990; Stuntzner-Gibson, 1991).

Thus, based on her past experiences, a woman's expectations of a partner's reaction to refusal to engage in sex or to have sex without a condom may range from minor concerns about the partner's happiness to fear of violent retribution. Regarding social expectations, Lewin (1985) applied a cost-benefit analysis of college women's decisions on whether or not to refuse unwanted sexual behavior to reveal a double bind for about half the women. For this group, neither course of action, refusing or acquiescing to unwanted sex, offered a positive outcome. Because of their concerns for the feelings of their partners, submitting to unwanted sexual advances became the (interpersonally) less costly alternative for these women. The results of this study are also consistent with Rakos' (1991) conclusion that a woman's level of assertiveness is directly correlated with her partner's support of assertive behavior.

At the other extreme, studies of relationships in which there is physical violence also demonstrate a high level of sexual violence, perpetrated by the same partners (see, for example, Finkelhor & Yllo, 1987; Walker, 1984).

☐ Other Abuse Outcomes

There are a number of somatic and psychological outcomes associated with childhood sexual abuse in the extensive literature, which are not directly considered in our research. These are reviewed below, with possible associations to HIV risk and ideas for further research provided for the interested reader.

Problem Behaviors

Adolescent and adult survivors appear to be more likely to come in contact with the law in negative ways (Rainey et al., 1995), including delinquency and running away (reviewed by Lanz, 1995). The primary means of survival for runaways are selling drugs and prostitution, and many are involved in both drugs and sex work (Weisberg, 1984). Young people living on the streets are vulnerable targets for sexual assault; some opt to live with older men for "protection." Unfortunately, these are also the situations most risky for HIV infection. Zierler et al. (1991) demonstrated a strong connection between childhood sexual abuse, drug involvement, prostitution, and HIV infection.

   Adult survivors also demonstrate poorer health behaviors in general, including increased levels of smoking and alcohol use (as opposed to abuse) and poorer eating habits (Goodman et al., 1993). This lack of attention to personal health appears to extend to sexual health as well, with survivors of intrafamilial abuse being less likely to use any form of birth control (Wyatt et al., 1993). Rainey, et al. (1995) shed more light on this phenomenon. Among 200 sexually active adolescent women, the 20% who reported prior sexual abuse were not more likely to be engaging in unprotected sex. However, they did report greater concerns about fertility and more reported they were trying to conceive. In addition, boyfriends of the previously abused women were significantly older and were reported as desiring the pregnancy. The power differential that this age difference can create has been discussed by Boyer and Fine (1992).

Dissociative Symptomatology

Links between childhood sexual and physical abuse and various dissociative symptoms, ranging from nightmares to serious personality disorders, have been observed in a number of studies (Briere & Runtz, 1987; Elliott & Briere, 1992; Putnam, 1993; Ross & Joshi, 1992; Sanders & Giolas,

1991). *Dissociation* has been discussed as a coping strategy that allows the victim to distance herself from the reality of the abuse while it is happening, and that allows the survivor to cope with traumatic memories by distancing herself from the anxiety they bring. Incest survivors who undergo repeated assaults often report specific tactics they have developed to cope during the abuse, which sometimes involve active or passive dissociations (Herman, 1992).

One disruptive set of adult reactions commonly linked to child sexual abuse falls under the rubric of posttraumatic stress disorder (PTSD). Resnick, Kilpatrick, Dansky, Saunders, and Best (1993) found that one third of their sample of adult rape and aggravated assault survivors met criteria for PTSD. Several common symptoms of PTSD are associated with avoidance and helplessness: recurrent dreams of the traumatic event, intrusive thoughts, hallucinations and/or dissociative flashbacks, psychological or physical reactivity to cues that recall the trauma, efforts to avoid thoughts, places, activities, or people that recall the event, inability to recall significant aspects of the traumatic event, feelings of detachment or estrangement from others, restricted range of affect, and a sense of foreshortened future (American Psychiatric Association, 1994).

Resnick and Seals (1995) point out that the abuse survivor who is actively avoiding thinking about the traumatic experience may also actively avoid thinking about other frightening things, including HIV risk. Thus she may engage numbly in behaviors without considering their implications. This would be compounded by feelings of helplessness to alter the course of one's behavioral outcomes.

The extent of dissociative symptoms following childhood sexual abuse may vary with the population under study. Germano (1995) examined the relationship between abuse histories and dissociative experiences in college women, most of whom are high functioning. Using the Dissociative Experiences Scale (Bernstein & Putnam, 1986), Germano found significant relationships between depersonalization/derealization and child abuse and trauma, family conflict and neglect, and punishment, but not with sexual trauma. Dissociative experiences of absorption/trance or activities were not related to prior abuse. Chu and Dill (1990) found that scores on the Dissociative Experiences Scale were significantly greater in female psychiatric inpatients who had been victims of child sexual abuse by a family member, and when both sexual and physical abuse co-occurred. Dissociation was not higher for extrafamilial child sexual abuse survivors.

Among women identified as having severe dissociative symptoms, particularly those diagnosed with Dissociative Identity Disorder (known formerly as Multiple Personality Disorder), rates of reported sexual abuse are disproportionately high, leading some to consider childhood abuse to be a primary cause of adult personality disorders (e.g., Braun, 1984; Kluft, 1985). Coons, Bowman, Pellow, and Schneider (1989) found reports of child sexual abuse in 80% of patients diagnosed with Dissociative Identity Disorder.

Severe dissociative symptomatology has direct implications for HIV-risky behavior. Sexual abuse survivors, in particular, find sexual situations stressful. If the individual reacts to stress by directing her thoughts and emotions away from her present situation, perhaps even adopting an entirely different persona, she is not able to react effectively to protect herself. In addition, the "alter," or alternate persona, may be a disinhibiting mechanism allowing a person to engage in acts she otherwise would not. Several clinicians have described a sexually assertive woman as a common alter among women with multiple personalities (Peterson, 1992). In this case the sexual abuse survivor is at particularly high risk, since she later may not even be aware of her risky behaviors.

A concern about the diagnosis of Dissociative Identity Disorder has been raised by Spanos (1994), who argues that multiple personalities are actually socially constructed "identity enactments." Spanos suggests that both the alternate identities and the stories of child sexual abuse are products of others' expectations, an issue not resolvable with existing retrospective data. Regardless of the "reality" of the alternate identities, however, Spanos agrees with others that, for the individual, the behavioral result is the same: An individual acts as if, and may believe they are experiencing, a separate personality, with respect to her risk of exposure to HIV, that, unfortunately is sufficient to endanger her health.

Sexual Dysfunctions and Chronic Pain

A range of sexual problems have been linked to child sexual abuse (Becker, Skinner, Abel, & Cichon, 1986; Briere & Elliott, 1993). Romans, Martin, Anderson, Herbison, and Mullen (1995) surveyed a random sample of 138 community women and found more frequent reports of sexual dysfunction among those reporting abuse (37% of the total sample). These include disorders such as inhibitions of desire, orgasmic difficulties, and a range of somatic problems. Kinzl et al. (1995) found that women reporting sexual desire and arousal disorders also reported chronic sexual pain. In fact, reports of sexual disorders were greatest for women with multiple abuse histories, but still significantly greater for women with even a single incident than for women reporting no abuse. Several research studies have linked adult somatic pain, notably chronic pelvic pain (CPP), to earlier sexual abuse (reviewed in Leserman and Drossman, 1995). In a nonclinical population of college women in Austria, Kinzl et al. (1995) found a 21.8% overall prevalence of child sexual abuse. Reports of sexual pain disorders were higher in women with multiple incidents of child sexual abuse (which were also more likely to be committed by family members) than in women with single sexual abuse experiences (almost always by a stranger or distant relative or family acquaintance) or women reporting no abuse. Among 200 female ambulatory patients, half with CPP, Walker et al. (1995) found 14 with severe child sexual abuse histories; of these 14, 12 had experienced CPP. Many of these women have a documented physical source of pain, often adhesions or scarring caused by a pelvic infection. Whether the infection was acquired during the abuse and caused subsequent damage including scarring (Anderson, 1995) or was acquired during subsequent unprotected sex with multiple partners, or whether vaginal tissue exposed to early contact is more sensitive to infection, has not been researched and remains an important question. Women with other sexually transmitted diseases may have a heightened receptivity to HIV, so CPP may be an important cue to further vulnerability.

Another problem raised in the literature is a predominance of sexual abuse among women diagnosed with "premenstrual syndrome" (PMS). Peterson (1993) lists PMS as a risk factor for HIV-related behavior, because of the sufferer's more labile premenstrual emotional state and sexuality, and heightened sensitivity to the effects of alcohol. Although the American Psychiatric Association has determined that there is insufficient evidence to include PMS as a diagnosable mental disorder, Premenstrual Dysphoric Disorder is included in the current Diagnostic and Statistical Manual of Mental Disorders (4th edition; American Psychiatric Association, 1994) as a provisional research diagnostic category. In fact, the symptoms required for a premenstrual "syndrome" are not well defined or supported by scientific research (Caplan, 1995), and there is little evidence for a widespread incidence of premenstrual dysfunction among women (e.g., Fausto-Sterling, 1985). Among 968 women ages 12–56, Miccio-Fonseca, Jones, and Futterman (1990) reported that overall severity of retrospective ratings on 88 negative "premenstrual experiences" were significantly higher for 151 women who had experienced rape, incest, or molestation. Reports were significantly higher on the cognitive/attentional symptom subscale, but not on emotionality or physical complaints, premenstrual eating behaviors, or water retention. The authors suggest that the difference may lie in coping responses to physical symptoms, which may be less effective in survivors.

Hamilton and Gallant (1990) shed light on this issue with their work relating psychological symptomatology to symptoms associated with PMS. Their data suggest that any relationship between PMS and childhood sexual abuse may be due to their mutual associations with a variety of negative psychological symptoms.

A Model for the Relationship Between Childhood Sexual Abuse and HIV Risk

The preceding chapters have documented that childhood sexual abuse, the long-term consequences of which are complex and may be mediated in a number of ways, is related to a number of problems in adult living. HIV risk behaviors are equally complex and multiply determined. Given the literature that suggests their association, we propose that the relationships among these constructs merit further exploration.

One promising way to examine these sets of relationships is by conceptualizing them within the context of a theoretical model. This would provide a framework in which to make predictions, conduct analyses, make interpretations, draw conclusions, and finally offer suggestions for future research in this area. Meehl (1997) emphasizes the need to examine strong models that are stated so specifically that they can be rigorously tested and potentially refuted. If an explicit model is rigorously tested and is able to withstand attempts at rejection, there is evidence that the model offers a contribution and that it can be retained.

Models can take several forms, including a verbal description, a pictorial diagram, and a mathematical set of equations. It can be argued that incorporating all of these forms into the development of a model would allow for clear tests of the verisimilitude of such a model. That is, a model that can be verbally articulated, diagrammatically depicted, and mathematically specified would provide a clear framework within which potentially to refute or support a theory. Furthermore, when several competing models can be rigorously specified and tested, there is an opportunity to fine-tune the theory, thus offering more clarity to the field.

29

In this chapter, we specify a theoretical model of childhood sexual abuse, family-of-origin environment, and HIV risk, mediated through several additional constructs. We will describe the constructs in more detail, and then several versions of the model will be specified in order to help provide clarity on the presence and nature of constructs that might mediate this relationship.

In subsequent chapters, model testing is conducted using the methodology of structural equation modeling. Structural equation modeling allows for the testing of an overall theoretical model in a path analysis framework (Bentler, 1995). It can be used to examine the relationships among variables, taking into account any measurement error within the variables, and any leftover prediction error within a dependent construct. Several relevant statistical and theoretical benefits of structural equation modeling are evident. From a statistical perspective, structural equation modeling allows the use of more than one measure per latent factor. For complex behavioral and attitudinal constructs, this offers a more complete assessment, or "capturing," of the construct. An additional benefit of the use of more than one measure per construct is the possibility of assessing and accounting for measurement error in variables. Additionally, the regression component of structural equation modeling offers an estimation of prediction error, or unexplained variance, in dependent constructs.

From the standpoint of theory testing, structural equation modeling offers the possibility of examining both direct and indirect relationships among latent constructs. In our modeling approach, childhood sexual abuse and family-of-origin environment can be conceptualized either as having a direct relationship with HIV risk or as being mediated by experiences of sexual assault in adulthood, psychosexual attitudes, sexual assertiveness, or family-of-origin environment.

Finally, by using multiple measures of a construct, structural equation modeling can provide relatively unbiased estimates of the regressions among latent constructs.

☐ Model Constructs

A large survey of over 200 items was constructed that tapped women's knowledge, attitudes, and behaviors regarding past and present relationships, sexuality, AIDS risk behaviors, substance use, history of abuse, family-of-origin environment, and psychosocial characteristics. A subset of these questions was used in this study (see the Appendix). Many of the scales in this survey were adapted from previous research (Harlow, 1991). As will be elaborated in Chapter 4, items were modified extensively for readability and the format was modified to make the survey more "user-friendly" (Quina et al., in press). Internal consistencies for all scales used in this study are reported later, in Table 6.2.

Interpersonal Constructs: Abuse History

Childhood Sexual Abuse

Seven items adapted from Wyatt (1985) were used to assess a history of childhood sexual abuse. Items were constructed to ask about specific experiences before age 14 and ranged from exhibitionism ("Did anyone older ever show their genitals to you?") to rape ("Did anyone older ever put his penis in your mouth, vagina, or rectum?"). Items were scored on a 4-point scale, with 1 = "no," 2 = "once," 3 = "a few times," and 4 = "many times." A final question asked participants to check, from a list, who the abusers were. Response choices ranged from a person not known at all to a close family member. For the purposes of most analyses, items for the construct of childhood sexual abuse were grouped to form three composite means assessing unwanted exhibition, unwanted touching, and unwanted penetration.

Family-of-Origin Environment Scale

The Family-of-Origin Environment Scale (Harlow, 1989) consists of six items that focus on individuals' perceptions of the atmosphere in their family-of-origin while growing up. Sample items include "When I was growing up, people in my family were upset a lot of the time" and "When I was growing up, I made choices my family liked." A 5-point response scale was used, ranging from 1 = "never" to 5 = "very often." When describing the construct of family environment as a whole, negatively worded items were reverse-scored so that higher scores indicate a more positive family-of-origin environment. For the purpose of most analyses using the family-of-origin environment construct, items were grouped to form three two-item composite means assessing understanding family, helpful family, and happy family.

Adult Sexual Victimization Scale

Twelve items were adapted from the Sexual Victimization Scale (Koss & Oros, 1982) which assesses the extent to which a woman has been sexually coerced in previous adult relationships. Responses ranged from 1 = "definitely yes" to 4 = "definitely no." Two subscales were formed from these items, one assessing coercion, the other assessing force.

Adolescent Sexual Abuse

A single item, adapted from research at Bradley Hospital, Providence, RI, was used to assess a history of sexual abuse in adolescence (ages 14–18). Responses were coded on a 4-point scale ranging from 1 = "no" to 4 = "yes, many times."

For most analyses, three averaged composites were formed to assess adult sexual victimization: adult coercion, adult force, and adolescent intercourse.

Relationship Violence

Two items that were adapted from research at Bradley Hospital ask the participant about her and her partner's typical behaviors during an argument. Responses were coded on a 5-point scale such that 1 = "gives in"; 2 = "try to settle things"; 3 = "ignore my partner or leave"; 4 = "yell at partner"; and 5 = "becomes violent." Eight other items were adapted from the Conflict Tactics Scale (Straus, 1979) in order to assess how frequently violence occurs within a participant's sexual relationships. Examples of violent behaviors assessed include: "How often has a sex partner threatened to hit you or throw something at you?" and "How often has a sex partner slapped you?" Responses were coded on a 5-point scale ranging from 1 = "never" to 5 = "very often."

For most analyses, the construct of relationship violence is assessed with three composite means assessing argument violence, throw violence, and hit violence.

Anticipated Negative Partner Reaction

Three items assessed expected partner reaction to sexually assertive refusal behavior; responses were on a 4-point scale such that 1 = "accept my decision," 2 = "accept my decision but be upset," 3 = "insist that I do it anyway," and 4 = "force me to do it anyway."

The three items assessed a woman's anticipated negative reaction from a partner: if refuse to do oral sex, if refuse to touch partner, and if refuse sex without a condom.

Psychosocial Attitudes

Sexual Self-Acceptance

Six items, adapted from the Sexual Self-Acceptance Scale (Harlow, 1991a), assessed attitudes regarding one's sexuality and sexual behaviors.

A sample item is: "Sex is a positive part of my life." Items were coded on a 5-point scale from 1 = "never" to 5 = "always." For most analyses using this construct of sexual self-acceptance, three averaged composites of two items each were formed assessing: sexual meaning, sexual control, and sexual esteem.

Sexual Assertiveness

Two 6-item subscales were adapted from the Sexual Assertiveness Scale (Morokoff et al., 1997) to assess refusal and condom-use sexual assertiveness. Responses were coded on a 5-point scale (1 = "never" to 5 = "always"). An additional subscale of six items was added (Deiter, 1993) which assessed communication sexual assertiveness regarding sexual partners' HIV risk factors.

For most analyses using this construct, three averaged composites of two items each were formed to assess sexual assertiveness for communication, refusal, and condom use.

Psychosocial Functioning

Four psychosocial functioning scales were used in the cluster analyses in Chapter 10: (a) A four-item Self-Esteem Scale (Harlow et al., 1993); (b) a Demoralization Scale (Harlow, 1990) with two reliable six-item subscales of subjective competence and distress; (c) a five-item Powerlessness Scale (Newcomb & Harlow, 1986); and (d) a Psychosexual Scale (Harlow et al., 1993) consisting of the 12 demoralization items and the 5 powerlessness items that were worded specific to sexuality. These subscales are discussed further in Chapter 10.

HIV Risk Measures

Recent research from our project (Burkholder & Harlow, 1996) emphasizes the importance of assessing multiple aspects of HIV risk in order to fully understand and address this area. In this volume, we operationalize HIV risk with several multiple-indicator constructs described below.

Unprotected Sex

Participants were asked to report the number of times they had engaged in vaginal, oral, and anal sex without a condom over the past 6 months.

To facilitate recall, a grid format was employed in which sexual activities engaged in with each partner (with columns for up to 15 partners) were reported and then summed across partners. For most analyses using this construct, three summed composites were formed assessing unprotected vaginal, oral, and anal sex.

Perceived HIV Risk

Two items were averaged that assessed how sure the participant was that she had not been exposed to HIV and how sure she was that her sex partners had not been exposed to HIV, with "absolutely sure" = 5 through "not at all sure" = 1. Additionally, two subscales from the AIDS Risk Behaviors and Attitudes Survey (Harlow, Quina, & Morokoff, 1990) assessed participants' perceived risk of AIDS and AIDS preventive behaviors. Responses to items such as "I feel that I am at risk of getting AIDS at this time in my life" and "I try not to get into situations where I might get AIDS" were coded such that "definitely yes" = 5 through "definitely no" = 1.

For most analyses using the construct of perceived HIV risk, three averaged composites were formed assessing how sure of safety, perceived risk, and preventive behavior.

Partner-Related Risk Factors

Using the same grid format as for measures of unprotected sex, partner risk factors were assessed for each sexual partner reported by participants. Responses to such questions as: "Does your partner have sex with other women?" or "Does your partner use IV drugs?" were coded as: "no" = 0, "not sure" = 1, and "yes" = 2. A composite partner risk status score was formed by averaging these responses across partners. A second measure, reported number of sexual partners over a woman's lifetime, was also used in this category to evaluate partner risk.

For most analyses, the two indicators of partner status and number of partners were used to anchor the factor of partner risk.

☐ Demographics

A number of items assessed demographic information from the women in our sample. For analyses that include demographics, six measures were used assessing age, education, income, religiosity (on a 1–5 Likert scale), number of pregnancies, and a rating of extent of health problems (from 1 = "no problems" to 5 = "very severe problems lasting over one year").

☐ Research Hypotheses

The present study extends previous work in this area by examining not only the relationship between a history of childhood sexual abuse, family-of-origin environment, and HIV sexual risk behaviors in adulthood, but also by including several possible mediators of this relationship. Mediating factors were drawn from the subset of attitudinal and interpersonal factors from the MMOHR (Harlow et al., 1993) discussed previously in Chapter 1. Factors that are examined for a possible mediating role between childhood sexual abuse and HIV risk include: adult sexual victimization, relationship violence, anticipated partner reaction, sexual self-acceptance, communication sexual assertiveness, refusal sexual assertiveness, and condom use sexual assertiveness.

The overall model to be examined is illustrated in Figure 3.1. This full model will be examined, as well as several submodels that individually test the merit of each of the mediators. Each of the models will be evaluated using the following criteria: (a) Overall model appropriateness will be assessed with a χ^2 significance test, in which smaller χ^2 values relative to the degrees of freedom are preferred; (b) Supplemental fit indices will assess how much of the variation and covariation in the data is being explained by the model, e.g., Bentler's (1990) comparative fit index (CFI), with values greater than .90 preferred, and the average absolute standardized residual (AASR; Bentler, 1995), with values less than .06 preferred; (c) Predictive variance (i.e., R^2) will be examined for each dependent construct, with values indicative of large effect sizes ($> .25$; Cohen, 1992) expected; and (d) Specific hypothesized associations will be tested by z-ratios, with values greater than 1.96 demonstrating statistical significance at $p < .05$.

It is expected that the following relationships will occur:

1. Childhood sexual abuse is expected to be:

A. negatively related to positive family-of-origin environment;
B. negatively related to refusal sexual assertiveness;
C. negatively related to communication sexual assertiveness;
D. negatively related to condom-use sexual assertiveness;
E. negatively related to sexual self-acceptance;
F. positively related to adult sexual victimization;
G. positively related to relationship violence;
H. positively related to anticipated partner negative reaction.

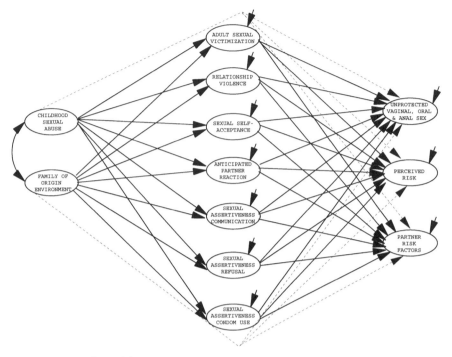

FIGURE 3.1   Full Model.

2. Positive family-of-origin environment is expected to be:

A. negatively related to childhood sexual victimization;
B. negatively related to adult sexual victimization;
C. negatively related to relationship violence;
D. negatively related to anticipated partner negative reaction;
E. positively related to refusal sexual assertiveness;
F. positively related to communication sexual assertiveness;
G. positively related to condom-use sexual assertiveness;
H. positively related to sexual self-acceptance.

3. Frequency of unprotected sex is expected to be:

A. positively related to childhood sexual abuse;
B. positively related to adult sexual victimization;
C. positively related to relationship violence;
D. positively related to anticipated partner negative reaction;
E. negatively related to positive family-of-origin environment;
F. negatively related to refusal sexual assertiveness;
G. negatively related to communication sexual assertiveness;
H. negatively related to condom-use sexual assertiveness;
I. negatively related to sexual self-acceptance.

4. Perception of risk is expected to be:

A. positively related to childhood sexual abuse;
B. positively related to adult sexual victimization;
C. positively related to relationship violence;
D. positively related to anticipated partner negative reaction;
E. negatively related to positive family of origin environment;
F. negatively related to refusal sexual assertiveness;
G. negatively related to communication sexual assertiveness;
H. negatively related to condom-use sexual assertiveness;
I. negatively related to sexual self-acceptance.

5. Partner risk is expected to be:

A. positively related to childhood sexual abuse;
B. positively related to adult sexual victimization;
C. positively related to relationship violence;
D. positively related to anticipated partner negative reaction;
E. negatively related to positive family-of-origin environment;
F. negatively related to refusal sexual assertiveness;
G. negatively related to communication sexual assertiveness;
H. negatively related to condom-use sexual assertiveness;
I. negatively related to sexual self-acceptance.

☐ Analyses

After describing our sampling goals and resulting sample of women in Chapter 4, Chapters 5–10 address six major sets of analyses for these data.

In Chapter 5, analyses are conducted to assess differences among groups of women with varying levels of sexual abuse. These analyses involved comparing different ways of classifying childhood sexual abuse, and then investigating whether women with different levels of abuse were related to a set of relevant experiences, attitudes, and behaviors.

In Chapter 6, preliminary analyses are conducted to verify each of the model constructs. First, principal components analyses (PCAs) were conducted on each of the 12 scales to verify their structures. It was expected that subscales would be unidimensional or would form conceptually based factors. For example, the Sexual Assertiveness scale was expected to form three factors of refusal, condom use, and communication. Composite scores were formed for each subscale by averaging across items with loadings greater than or equal to .35. Second, coefficient alpha was calculated for each subscale. It was expected that all subscales would show high internal consistency, with alpha values from the .70s to .90s. Third, descriptive statistics were calculated for all subscales. These included means, standard deviations, ranges, skewness, and kurtosis. Descriptives were calculated for the whole sample obtained at Time 1, and then for the sample from whom longitudinal data were available. Fourth, a cross-sectional structural equation model (see Figure 6.1) was examined in order to get a preliminary assessment of our proposed longitudinal model of childhood sexual abuse and HIV risk.

In Chapter 7, a series of longitudinal structural equation model analyses is examined to investigate the nature of relationships among sexual abuse and other interpersonal factors, attitudes, and behaviors. Structural equation model analyses are evaluated using several criteria, including χ^2, degrees of freedom, AASR, and CFI to assess overall fit, and z-ratios to examine the significance of parameter estimates. Longitudinal analyses were conducted on the sample of women from whom longitudinal data were available and were evaluated for overall fit and significance of parameter estimates as well as for parsimony (see Figure 7.1).

In Chapter 8, nested comparisons are conducted on the longitudinal data in order to evaluate the performance of the independent constructs and of the proposed mediating constructs in predicting HIV risk outcomes. Nested analyses test a subset of the larger set of hypothesized relationships; comparisons between the full and the nested analyses evaluate the importance of the parameters excluded in the nested analyses. Using a χ^2 difference statistic, the importance of a nested subset can be statistically compared to the full set; if the χ^2 difference statistic is significant, we conclude that the parameters eliminated in the nested subset should be retained to explain the set of relationships. For example, one nested analysis, which estimates no direct path between childhood sexual abuse and HIV risk and only estimates paths mediated through sexual self-acceptance, sexual assertiveness, and relationship violence, was evaluated. A significant χ^2 difference between this and the full set, with all paths estimated, would suggest that the direct relationship between childhood sexual abuse and HIV risk behaviors may be important to include.

Chapter 9 presents cross-group comparisons conducted in order to evaluate whether the proposed relationships were comparable in the two subsamples (representing two different recruitment strategies, one among adult women at a college of continuing education, the second among women from the wider community) that comprise the full longitudinal sample. Analyses with increasing degrees of restrictiveness were evaluated and compared to a congeneric analysis in which all parameters are free to vary across both subsamples. Cross-group equality constraints that were evaluated include factor loadings, error variances, factor variances and covariances, and regression weights between factors. A final analysis with implausible equality constraints removed was also evaluated.

Chapter 10 determines whether the women can be statistically separated into clusters that differ on levels of psychosocial functioning. Cluster analyses were conducted on two approximately equal subsamples of the data that are stratified by type of sexual abuse. After finding a cluster solution that replicated in the two subsamples, group differences among the clusters were examined for each of the major model constructs using Multivariate Analyses of Variance (MANOVAs) and χ^2 tests. This chapter provides information that could inform tailored interventions, depending on a woman's level of psychosocial functioning.

Finally, in Chapter 11, we discuss the overall findings, and in Chapter 12 we present contributions, limitations, and implications for interventions.

Methodological
Considerations and
Compromises

Our research team had previously worked with traditional-age women college students to establish the general approach and to collect data on this important but less vulnerable group (Harlow et al., 1993). For the present research, we worked with women from the community, many of whom who were not college educated. Furthermore, we were determined to recruit, and to make our instruments relevant to, a diverse population, including different ethnic backgrounds, which requires more than superficial adaptations (Landrine, Klonoff, & Brown-Collins, 1992). To make these transitions, we had to consider methodological, measurement, practical, and ethical issues.

These issues arise in any community-based research project, but are particularly crucial in a sensitive topic area such as HIV risk behaviors (Mays & Jackson, 1991). We chose to make this adaptation of our research a systematic and comprehensive process, one which engaged the entire team in a great deal of consultation with others, including members of the populations from whom we would recruit. We utilized other researchers' expertise and experiences, focus groups, multiple qualitative and quantitative assessments of our survey materials, and ethical self-questioning. In this section we will first describe the approach we developed for preparation of the survey instrument itself. Then we will briefly describe some of the challenges we identified, and the solutions—often only compromises—that we ultimately chose for this project.

Small focus groups were brought together to discuss specific changes to the survey. This approach has been adopted by other researchers using focus groups to refine survey instruments (Flaskerud & Nyamathi, 1989; Fuller, Edwards, Vorakitphokatorn, & Sermski, 1993). The methodology of focus groups is primarily qualitative; in-depth views of participants are elicited on specific topics in order to understand individual perspectives. Focus groups can be helpful in developing instruments to assess sensitive and personal matters in community samples (Morgan, 1993) and in learning the vocabulary of diverse participants (Krueger, 1988). Various researchers have used focus groups in addressing sexual behavior and decision making, where existing measures might miss important information (e.g., Fullilove, Fullilove, Haynes, & Gross, 1990; Steckler, McLeroy, Goodman, Bird, & McCormick, 1992).

Two of the populations from whom participants would be recruited for the large survey, diverse from each other, were targeted for the focus groups: a General Equivalency Diploma (GED) and support program for single mothers at a community literacy training agency serving primarily minority women; and non-traditional-age students recruited through an urban extension of a university continuing education (CE) program, serving predominantly nonminority women. Fourteen and sixteen women from these agencies, respectively, participated in six small focus groups, filling out the survey with the understanding that their answers would not be seen or collected by the researchers. The GED women took the survey with two researchers present and gave immediate feedback about the items and their experiences in answering them. The CE women filled out the survey at home and came together with two researchers to discuss their reactions. Each group gave detailed and thoughtful responses and expressed gratitude that the researchers were sincerely listening to their concerns. Although demographics were not collected, nearly every woman spontaneously reported low family incomes and a variety of life experiences and stresses.

☐ Survey Development

To evaluate and prepare our survey instruments we developed and applied a systematic "process model" (Quina et al., in press) containing six major revisions based on various forms of input:

1. The research team reviewed previously used instruments for obvious problem areas, including readability and format;

2. Literacy educators and community-based researchers were consulted for specific suggestions regarding format, terminology, and sensitive personal issues;
3. Two sample groups representative of populations targeted for the research program filled out the survey in focus groups and gave feedback about all aspects of the survey and the process of filling it out;
4. Four additional focus groups gave feedback on the resulting revised survey;
5. After first-wave data were collected, quantitative assessments of psychometric integrity were performed;
6. Participants were invited to write comments about the survey and the research process at various places in the questionnaire.

During this process, virtually every item on the survey was reworded, and a number of changes were made to enhance comfort with the questions and decrease the likelihood that the participant would misunderstand the response options. Even after the study began, two minor adjustments were made for the second and third survey administrations based on this multiple feedback approach.

This process had three particularly important benefits to participants and to our research team. First, participants had been included in the design of a publicly funded project that would be sampling from their communities; they expressed appreciation and shared that information with peers. Second, the process heightened our awareness of the personal issues that shaped the lives of these women who would be typical of our participants. Ultimately, we emerged feeling a greater sense of connection to the women we were studying.

☐ Challenges and Solutions

Some problems could be solved with a bit of hard work, some were actually easy. Some of the larger issues, however, could not be readily resolved. Each of these decisions was made in the context of teamwork, involving up to seven or eight researchers. We caution against assuming that our choices were the best, the most logical, or the most practical. Guided by our feminist ethical principles, we made the decisions we felt were best for our participants, in the context of the existing constraints and opportunities.

Sampling and Recruitment

Several problems arose regarding sampling. We needed a large sample for statistical validity (at least 400), and that size did not allow for individual contact or recruitment. We felt that to be truly ethical, we would need to provide women with childcare and taxi fare and offer flexible hours. Thus we opted for a mailed survey with self-addressed return mail envelopes enclosed. Because participants might need privacy from family or others to fill out the surveys, all mailings were in plain manila envelopes, and plenty of time was made available for their response.

We wanted to reach a wide-ranging community-based population. Fortunately, several of us had worked within established community agencies and were able to make new contacts with other agencies. These agencies helped us formulate a recruitment plan that was tailored to their clients and their needs. We recognized there would be language barriers for non-English-speaking and for nonreading populations, some of whom are at high risk for HIV. Ultimately, however, because of the need to operate with mailed surveys, we compromised by developing and refining a survey that was readable at a 6th-grade reading level (a process described later in this section).

The funded project was explicitly focused on HIV risk through heterosexual contact. To maximize the number of contacts from women who met the risk criteria and to avoid misunderstandings and unnecessary mailing costs and payments to women whose data could not be used, we set up a checklist of criteria for participation. This list was sent to each woman with her informed consent to participate, before we sent out surveys. This approach was easy to follow ("If you answered 'yes' to all of these questions, you are invited to participate") and virtually eliminated unusable data from ineligible participants.

The University Institutional Review Board requirements, the state child sexual abuse reporting requirements, and the unwillingness of community agencies and schools to provide research access to minors, even anonymously, made it virtually impossible to assess issues of sexual abuse in subjects under the age of 18. Thus we adopted a criterion of being 18 years or older for participating, which was clearly described on the criterion sheet and in the informed consent.

Volunteers in sexuality-related research are likely to be more sexually active than non-volunteers (Morokoff, 1986), particularly when the questions may lead to a suggestion of HIV risk (e.g., Catania, Gibson, Chitwood, & Coates, 1990). Thus we may have recruited a more risky sample than the full population meeting our criteria. Since we were seeking a higher risk sample, this was not a serious problem, but we advise caution in generalizing the data given this bias, which is a constant feature of voluntary research programs.

Finally, this was a longitudinal study. We needed to minimize dropout from women even though we were asking them to fill out a lengthy survey at three time points over a year. We were guided by a respect for the participant's time. We reviewed every item and eliminated items that were redundant or not critical to the overall research goal. We offered payments in increasing amounts ($5, $10, and $15) for returning surveys at the three time points, and awarded a substantial bonus amount ($250, $500, and $750) to two participants at each time point. Finally, we mailed reminder letters and resent survey packages to participants at the second and third time points. This approach seemed reasonably successful, with a retention rate over the three time periods of about 70%.

Measurement Issues

We devoted considerable attention, especially during the early phases of the project, to developing a survey instrument that would be readable by a wide range of respondents while retaining good psychometric properties. Most of the survey instruments were developed and previously used by members of our team or by other published researchers, so much of our effort was in evaluating and revising existing instruments and subsequently assessing their psychometrics. This work is detailed in Quina et al. (in press), so only the basic changes are addressed here.

The first issue was mechanical. With younger college populations, who are used to computer-scored multiple-choice tests, one can rely on using standard multi-item computer-scored response sheets which can then be optically scanned for immediate data collection. These sheets were highly confusing to community participants. Thus we revised the entire survey, providing clear response options on an item-by-item basis (repeating words instead of using numbers, e.g., 1–5). The resulting packet was much longer (increasing from the original 10 pages to 25 pages) and required more research assistants to carry out hand-scoring (and reliability checking), but was much more accessible to participants and less prone to subject error.

Another major problem was readability. The survey instruments we had wanted to use were developed and validated with college students. A check using Flesch's (1948) readability formula (built into the Microsoft Word processing program) confirmed our suspicions that most of the items, and all of the scales, were designed for more advanced readers. Some required reading levels of 12th grade and higher. We reviewed every item and rewrote most of them to meet a criterion of 6th-grade level. Subsequent assessments demonstrated that these changes did not in fact harm the psychometric properties of our scales to any significant extent. Comparable analyses were conducted on the initial (premodification) versions of nine scales, using data from over 400 college women and the revised (postmodification) versions, using first-wave data from the present sample (in Quina et al., in press). Using Cronbach's (1951) coefficient alpha, internal consistencies were quite good and highly comparable between pre- and postmodification scales, averaging .81 and .80, respectively, and even improving for two scales. Principal component extraction and Promax oblique rotation verified consistent factor structures on all scales across the two large samples, and multiple sample confirmatory factor analyses provided evidence for a good model fit between the two versions of the survey. Further analyses demonstrated equality of covariances among items within each of the scales across the two samples, again confirmed by multiple sample comparisons. The few exceptions were found for demographic subsamples and posed no serious threat to data interpretation.

A third problem was that scales designed for general use have less predictive power than measures that are specific to the dependent variables, in this case women's sexuality and HIV risk. Yet this area of research was new enough that specific measures had not been developed. We adapted several scales, including those developed by team members, to refer specifically to HIV risk. For example, the Self-Efficacy Scale was worded specifically for HIV risk reduction, Sexual Assertiveness for Birth Control was altered to focus on condom use (pregnancy/STD prevention), and a scale measuring psychosexual functioning was developed out of the original Psychosocial Functioning measure (which was also included).

A large problem area was assessment of sexual behaviors. Here four issues arose. One was the recognition that women may act very differently with different partners, so general answers about frequency of behaviors would limit our understanding of their behavior. A second was a well-placed concern that accuracy may be compromised in self-report. We provided the participant with a behavioral matrix (see Appendix), which guided her through a set of items asking her to list numbers of different sexual acts (protected and unprotected) with each separate partner, followed by information about potential risk of that partner. This type of matrix reduces response bias, has been shown to be fairly accurate for retrospective work, and allows us to assess behavior by partner (Catania et al., 1990; Morokoff, Harlow, & Quina, 1991).

Third, we recognized that different individuals would use different terms for sexual acts and body parts. The possible terms ranged from those that would shock some to those that would not be comprehensible to others. After consultation and work with focus groups, we settled on one clear definition of "sex" and "sexual," in basic terms (e.g., "his penis in your vagina;" "your mouth on your partner's genitals"). This definition was repeated at the top of any page or section in the survey using these terms.

Fourth is another issue that has not often been considered in research on women's sexuality; namely, that even women at heterosexual risk are not necessarily having sex exclusively with men. While some questions in our survey were specific to penile-vaginal contact, all items were reviewed carefully for heterosexist bias, and where possible items were reworded. For example, instead of "condom" we used "condom or latex barrier"; and we included the response option "partner is female" on the behavioral partner matrix.

☐ Ethical Challenges

Of less consequence methodologically, but more concern ethically, were a series of problems that arose in carrying out our stated empirical objectives.

Anonymity

In this project, even knowing that a woman was participating could identify her as at some risk for heterosexual transmission or suggest to the knower that the participant was sexually "promiscuous." (Even though that was not necessarily the case, it was a concern.) Thus we were concerned about names appearing in any place accessible to others. The longitudinal design required us to keep in mail contact with participants, but also made anonymity impossible. We developed a tightly controlled system of double-coding ID numbers and kept all records containing names and addresses on a floppy disk locked at all times and handled only by one specific individual (with one designated backup).

Payment of Subjects

At first, university accounting processes, responding to federal guidelines, required us to pay by check but did not allow us to send out a check to an unnamed individual. Once a check was issued to an individual from the university, the identity would be available (although tracking specific data would be difficult). After extensive negotiations we were allowed to make the checks out to "cash" with the double-coded subject ID number in the memo line. This satisfied auditor's requirements and minimized the access to identity (although a signature on the back of the check still existed, it could be claimed that someone else had signed it). We fortunately had virtually no problems with this system.

Inquiring about Illegal Behaviors

The attorney general's office in the state in which the data were collected has a right to request information about illegal acts self-reported by participants. While this was highly unlikely, it was very discomforting to ask questions about illegal drug use or trading sex for money or drugs. When the state refused to grant us an exception for immunity, we consulted with other comparable research projects who felt the likelihood was minuscule. Nevertheless, we decided that we would use whatever legal means necessary to protect the confidentiality of our participants.

HIV Status

We were advised that if an HIV seropositive woman knew about her status, that knowledge would change so much about her profile that her data should probably not be included in the analyses. This was a difficult dilemma, since we did not initially wish to inquire about HIV status. However, we ultimately chose to include a question asking if the woman knew she were seropositive. However, the description of the study as one of risk no doubt influenced the participation rate of seropositives.

Emotional Effects of Taking the Survey

A number of our items were intrusive and perhaps shocking to someone not anticipating such detail. We also asked potentially painful questions about sexual abuse, partner violence, a wide range of sexual behaviors, and psychosocial problems. We reviewed this issue carefully with focus groups and came up with several solutions which, according to the focus group participants who reviewed them, seemed to provide a sufficient range of options for a participant upset by any of the survey materials. These included:

- Multiple cautions about the nature of the survey, in the informed consent and other pre-survey materials.
- Reminders throughout that a participant could quit at any time with no negative consequences. If she chose to return a partially filled out survey, she was still paid for participation (since data were never linked up to names, we never knew who ultimately did this, but we received very few incomplete surveys).
- Wording of the instructions to incorporate caring, concerned comments, to stress that we were not attempting to judge the participant (e.g., about sexual or drug behaviors).

- An item-by-item review to reduce negative reactions to questions. For example, when focus group participants raised concerns about asking for number of occasions of abuse, we reworded to more general response options such as "never," "seldom," etc. which were deemed more comfortable.

- Installing a toll-free 800-line number (since some of the calls to our laboratory would be toll calls) and an answering machine with a welcoming message, and appointing a clinical psychology team member to monitor and respond to requests for information or referral.

- Including with every mailing a small business-sized pink card printed with the research laboratory 800 number and a list of community agencies offering crisis help, developed with members of the community to include the agencies they were most likely to utilize. These agencies were also listed at the end of the survey as an immediate reminder that help could be obtained.

☐ Abuse Experiences of Women in the Sample

Longitudinal data from 519 women were collected over a 1-year period, each data collection point six months apart. More detailed information about demographic and other data from this longitudinal sample will be presented in Chapter 7. Women in this sample averaged 31.4 years and, reflecting the ethnic and racial composition of the area, consisted of 83% European American, 9% African American, 2% Hispanic, 1.2% Native American, .5% Asian, and 3.3% other.

As the central predictive constructs within this study, a brief description of the abusive experiences reported by women in this sample is reported in this section. A more detailed discussion of the sexual abuse experienced by women in this sample as well as the consequences associated with different types of abuse will be presented in Chapter 5. The specific experiences reported by women in this sample are presented in Table 4.1. As expected, rates of endorsement of specific items were relatively high and are similar to data reported from samples obtained in other parts of the country. Also as expected, rates of endorsement of specific items fall as the severity of the experience escalates. Together, these observations provide evidence that the assessment method used in this study offers a valid means of examining issues associated with childhood sexual abuse.

Based on an argument developed more fully in Chapter 5, women were categorized into four groups based on the most severe type of sexual abuse they experienced as children. Two hundred twelve women reported no

TABLE 4.1   Childhood sexual abuse experiences reported by women in this longitudinal sample (N=519)

Abuse experiences before age 14	Frequency (N=519)		Percent by response	Percentage never/ at least once
Did anyone older ever show their genitals to you?	Never	275	53.0	Never: 53.0%
	Once	88	17.0	
	A few times	111	21.4	At least
	Many times	45	8.7	once: 47.0%
Did you ever see anyone older touch their genitals in front of you?	Never	333	64.2	Never: 64.2%
	Once	61	11.8	
	A few times	94	18.1	At least
	Many times	31	6.0	once: 35.8%
Did anyone older ever touch your breasts or genitals?	Never	298	57.4	Never: 57.4%
	Once	70	13.5	
	A few times	108	20.8	At least
	Many times	43	8.3	once: 42.6%
Did anyone older ever try to make you touch their genitals?	Never	353	68.0	Never: 68.0%
	Once	55	10.6	
	A few times	77	14.8	At least
	Many times	34	6.6	once: 32.0%
Did anyone older ever rub their genitals against your body?	Never	339	65.3	Never: 65.3%
	Once	50	9.6	
	A few times	92	17.7	At least
	Many times	38	7.3	once: 34.7%
Did anyone older ever TRY to put his penis in your mouth, vagina, or rectum?	Never	423	81.5	Never: 81.5%
	Once	24	4.6	
	A few times	43	8.3	At least
	Many times	29	5.6	once: 18.5%
Did anyone older ever PUT his penis in your mouth, vagina, or rectum?	Never	445	85.7	Never: 85.7%
	Once	19	3.7	
	A few times	30	5.8	At least
	Many times	25	4.8	once: 14.3%
When you were 14–18 years old, were you ever forced to have sex with anyone?	Never	400	77.1	Never: 77.1%
	Once	66	12.7	
	A few times	36	6.9	At least
	Many times	17	3.3	once: 22.9%

abusive experiences as children; 54 women were victimized by an exhibitionist as children; 156 women experienced childhood sexual abuse that involved physical contact or touch; and 97 women experienced actual or attempted penetration as children younger than 14 years.

Adult sexual victimization was also highly prevalent in this sample, with the specific experiences reported by women in the sample presented in Table 4.2. Again, it can be seen from these data that women in this sample report a variety of sexual victimization experiences in adulthood, with more than a third of women reporting having been raped. Although alarmingly high, such reports are consistent with regional as well as national, probabilistic data (e.g., Russell, 1984).

TABLE 4.2   Adult sexual abuse experiences reported by women in this longitudinal sample (N=519)

Sexual abuse experiences (have you ever...)	Frequency	(N=519)	Percent by response	Percent definitely no vs. all other
had a man mistake how far you wanted to go with sex?	Definitely yes	240	46.2	Definitely no: 17.5%
	Probably yes	138	26.6	All other:
	Probably no	50	9.6	82.5%
	Definitely no	91	17.5	
been with a man who got so turned on that you couldn't stop him, even though you didn't want to have sex?	Definitely yes	180	34.7	Definitely no: 35.5%
	Probably yes	78	15.0	All other:
	Probably no	77	14.8	64.5%
	Definitely no	184	35.5	
had sex with a man even though you didn't want to because he said he would break up with you?	Definitely yes	43	8.3	Definitely no: 69.7%
	Probably yes	52	10.0	All other:
	Probably no	62	11.9	30.3%
	Definitely no	362	69.7	
had sex with a man when you didn't want to because he argued and put pressure on you?	Definitely yes	125	24.1	Definitely no: 40.1%
	Probably yes	125	24.1	All other:
	Probably no	61	11.8	59.9%
	Definitely no	208	40.1	
found out that a man talked you into sex by saying things he didn't mean?	Definitely yes	144	27.7	Definitely no: 30.1%
	Probably yes	141	27.2	All other:
	Probably no	78	15.0	69.9%
	Definitely no	156	30.1	

TABLE 4.2   (continued)

had a man use force (twist your arm, hold you down, etc.) to make you kiss or feel him when you didn't want to?	Definitely yes Probably yes Probably no Definitely no	160 55 33 271	30.8 10.6 6.4 52.2	Definitely no: 52.2% All other: 47.8%
had a man TRY to have sex with you when you didn't want to by saying he would use force, but then sex didn't happen?	Definitely yes Probably yes Probably no Definitely no	83 42 61 333	16.0 8.1 11.8 64.2	Definitely no: 64.2% All other: 35.8%
had a man USE force to make you have sex when you didn't want to, but then sex didn't happen?	Definitely yes Probably yes Probably no Definitely no	77 41 63 338	14.8 7.9 12.1 65.1	Definitely no: 65.1% All other: 34.9%
had sex with a man when you did not want to because you thought he would use force (twist your arm, hold you down, etc.)?	Definitely yes Probably yes Probably no Definitely no	76 55 54 334	14.6 10.6 10.4 64.4	Definitely no: 64.4% All other: 35.6%
had vaginal sex (penis in your vagina) with a man when you didn't want to because he USED force?	Definitely yes Probably yes Probably no Definitely no	129 34 39 317	24.9 6.6 7.5 61.1	Definitely no: 61.1% All other: 38.9%
had anal or oral sex (penis in your rectum or mouth) with a man when you didn't want to because he used threats or force?	Definitely yes Probably yes Probably no Definitely no	77 28 32 382	14.8 5.4 6.2 73.6	Definitely no: 73.6% All other: 26.4%
been raped?	Definitely yes Probably yes Probably no Definitely no	124 39 32 324	23.9 7.5 6.2 62.4	Definitely no: 62.4% All other: 37.6%

Differential Effects of Childhood Sexual Abuse

In this chapter we examine our data to understand better the effects of childhood sexual abuse on variables that may be associated with HIV risk. There are many levels and forms of abuse perpetrated on children under the age of 14. Do levels of behavioral and psychological functioning among adult women survivors differ for different types of abuse? Different perpetrators? What is the most effective way for researchers to assess differences for other analyses?

In Chapter 2, we reviewed the various ways in which women who survive childhood sexual abuse have poorer adult functioning overall than women who report no abuse. In our previous research, we documented more sexual risk taking, poorer sexual self-esteem, and more sexual victimization in adult relationships among college women reporting childhood abuse than among peers who had not experienced childhood victimization (Johnsen & Harlow, 1996). However, differences among the various types of sexual abuse were not explored.

Several authors have conceptualized sexual victimization during adulthood as forming a continuum, from verbal harassment through violent rape-murder (e.g., Lott, 1987; Quina & Carlson, 1989). In this view, categories of sexual victimization represent increasing levels of physical contact and force, from none to extreme (most simply described as harassment, coercive sex, rape, and rape-murder), but have important common underlying themes. For example, Quina and Carlson note some startling similarities in the underlying experience of coercion and the emotional reactions of the survivors. In addition, across the continuum, the potentially causal roles of gendered expectations for male power-fulness and female submissiveness are noted by different scholars study-ing these different forms of assault (e.g., Groth, 1979; Koss, Goodman, Browne, Fitzgerald, Keita, & Russo, 1994; Quina & Carlson, 1989).

In spite of their commonalities, most researchers and clinicians observe more serious adult problems for the more intrusive and more violent forms of assault which lie at the upper end of this continuum. As dis-cussed in greater detail in Quina and Carlson, sexual victimizations in-clude elements of trauma, criminal victimization, and sexual invasion. As with other traumas such as fire or hurricanes, and with other forms of criminal victimization such as assault, greater physical harm and violence create stronger fear and feelings of loss of control. Sexual invasion, which can be considered a violation of one's intimate self and dignity, is present across the continuum, but is most extreme with penetrative abuse.

Several researchers have found data to suggest a similar pattern with childhood abuse survivors. Most sexual assaults on children do not in-volve a great level of physical force; psychological coercion and the child's trust are usually sufficient to engender the child's compliance. Thus, for children, the continuum can better be conceptualized as based on the level of physical intrusion on, and thus harm to, the child. On such a continuum the levels of victimization would range from exposure to sex-ually explicit materials or activity, to sexual contact ("molestation" or "fondling"), to penetration. The level of physical intrusion of the coerced sexual act has been found to differentially affect a variety of adult symp-toms (e.g., Briere & Runtz, 1988). Of particular interest are the findings of Wyatt et al. (1992), who found that severity of childhood sexual abuse was strongly associated with subsequent revictimization in adulthood re-gardless of who the perpetrator was.

With child sexual abuse victims, differences are also often noted be-tween incest survivors and survivors of nonfamilial abuse. Much of the child sexual abuse literature has focused on incest; for example, Courtois (1988) and Herman (1981) noted severely negative outcomes among adult survivors of incest, particularly among clinical samples. When abuse is perpetrated by an adult family member, a number of destructive forces enter into the dynamic, including the loss of an opportunity to learn normal, respectful relationships and trust from the abusive parent. Freyd (1996) has discussed this dynamic in terms of "betrayal trauma" and underlined the importance of the betrayal of trust in shaping the child's memory of the event.

Several studies have indicated that the psychological effects of abuse by a family member are more severe than a survivor abused by a nonfamily acquaintance or a stranger (e.g., Browne & Finkelhor, 1986), a finding backed up by reports from clinical populations. For example, Briere & Runtz (1988) found higher levels of anxiety, somatization, and dissociation among adult survivors of familial abuse, compared to nonfamilial abuse survivors. Wind and Silvern (1992, p. 274) noted that "the frequency and duration of the abuse, the subject's ratings of the emotional significance of the perpetrator, the perpetrator being a father figure, the severity of the abusive acts, and whether physical force was used" were all associated with symptoms such as trauma, self-esteem, depression, and sexual enjoyment. Of these, the perpetrator being a father figure was the characteristic most consistently associated with symptoms, and remained so even after the interrelated factors of frequency, duration, and emotional significance of perpetrator were considered.

For the present research, we were concerned with (a) finding a predictor variable or variables that efficiently described differences among our participants for use in model building; and (b) understanding the impact of childhood sexual abuse on HIV risk and associated behavioral and psychosocial variables. We used the SAS (1989) computer program for all analyses in this chapter.

We explore the issues of differentiating types of abuse in this chapter. First, we compare two classification schemes for type of abuse, assessing which scheme best fits a statistical modeling approach. Our comparative assessment of these two classification schemes then serves as a basis for analyzing group differences by type of abuse, as we use the preferred four-group scheme to investigate whether women experiencing different levels of physical intrusiveness during abuse experienced different outcomes. Then we will evaluate the importance of other factors, including the relationship of the perpetrator to the victim and the relevance of other factors specific to the victimization experience.

☐ Classifying Types of Abuse

One problem of particular interest to a number of researchers in this area is the classification of sexual abuse. For example, Briere and Runtz (1988, p. 332) pose the question: "Can maltreatment be conceptualized as a continuous (as opposed to dichotomous) variable?" They point out that an abuse/no abuse dichotomy is seriously insufficient to the task of classifying the majority of incidents of maltreatment. As an alternative to a quantitative continuum, we will explore a multigroup ordinal classification approach.

In this section we offer a comparison of two ways of classifying sexual abuse, assessing the reliability and validity of each scheme. Although it is not difficult to see a conceptual difference in assaults across the contin-uum, it remains to be explored whether comparisons of survivor effects can be adequately made with the dichotomous categories of "abused" versus "not abused" (or perhaps most accurately, not reporting abuse), or whether we would best be served by a more thorough differentiation of four categories arranged ordinally across level of physical intrusion (not abused, sexual exposure, sexual contact, or sexual penetration).

Regardless of type of abuse, perpetrator, or other situational factor, any abuse experience can be extremely traumatic, and thus may result in severe consequences. The severity of trauma is most likely influenced by prior emotional status, social support, and personal coping strategies, and each individual responds from her unique circumstances.

The first classification scheme was obtained through a PCA of all of the items which comprise the Childhood Sexual Victimization Scale (see Appendix). The resulting scale revealed three conceptually distinct forms of victimization: (a) exhibitionism, (b) sexual abuse involving physical touch, and (c) actual penetration or attempted rape. Using such a catego-rization, women could be placed in one of four groups depending on the most severe form of abuse they had experienced prior to age 14. Of the 519 women participating in this study, 212 reported no abuse (Group 1); 54 reported exhibitionism but no other abuse, labeled "exhibition abuse" (Group 2); 156 reported sexual abuse involving physical contact, which we have labeled "touch abuse" (Group 3); and 97 reported attempted penetration or actual rape, or "penetration abuse" (Group 4). This was contrasted to a simple dichotomous scheme, created by dividing women into those reporting no abuse ($n = 212$) and those reporting any abuse, of any kind ($n = 307$).

Because questions regarding childhood victimization were repeated across the three administrations of this survey, it was possible to assess the reliability of any classification scheme across the three time points at which data were collected, each 6 months apart. The more consistently a participant responds to the items assessing childhood sexual victimiza-tion, the more credence can be placed on any relationships revealed be-tween childhood sexual abuse experiences and adult functioning. Furthermore, the more reliable the particular classification scheme is, the more useful that scheme is in estimating true differences among the categories of women.

Within these current data, correlation analyses revealed that the four-category description of abuse experiences suggested by the statistical anal-yses was in fact more reliable, i.e., consistent across time, than a two-category division of the data (no reported childhood abuse and any re-ported abuse). Correlations across time for the four categories ranged from .74 to .77, whereas correlations across time for two categories ranged from .66 to .69, indicating that there is more consistency of categorization across time in the more specific classification scheme.

Following these correlation analyses, a series of MANOVAs were conducted using both the four- and two-category classification schemes in order to compare the validity of these methods of categorization. Results are presented in Table 5.1. Although the two-category classification scheme revealed many significant differences in the various sets of dependent variables assessed in this study, it can be seen that more and clearer differences among the groups were revealed with the four-category classification scheme.

Among demographic variables, the four-category classification scheme revealed more clear distinctions among groups than the two-category classification scheme; using four categories of abuse, significant differences were noted for the racial/ethnic background of participants, type of current employment, current marital status, and religion. Within the two-category classification scheme, significant differences based on abuse status were revealed only for racial/ethnic background of participants and for current marital status. Among other demographic variables, similar patterns of group differences were revealed regardless of classification scheme used. In several of the analyses of relevant dependent variables, the pattern of group differences was similar regardless of classification scheme used; these include analyses of adult sexual victimization, psychosexual attitudes, sexual assertiveness, family-of-origin environment, relationship violence, unprotected sex, and perceived risk of HIV infection. Among the partner risk variables assessed in this study, more significant group differences were revealed among the four-category classification scheme than between the abused/nonabused groups used in the two-category classification scheme.

This set of analyses substantially verified the conclusion that a four-category classification scheme is recommended for differentiating among the consequences of childhood sexual abuse in this community sample of women. More variance in the dependent variables assessing adult behaviors and functioning was consistently accounted for by the four-category classification scheme than by the two-category scheme. The average effect size in analyses using the four-category classification of childhood sexual abuse experiences was .09, whereas in the two-category classification scheme, the average effect size was .04. Consequently, it was concluded that the detailed questions about childhood sexual abuse asked in this study offer a valid and reliable method for assessing the degree and type of childhood sexual abuse in women and for investigating any long-term effects of such abuse. Subsequent results to be presented will reflect this conclusion, and group differences discussed will be based on four

TABLE 5.1 MANOVAs and ANOVAs for two-group vs. four-group childhood sexual abuse classification schemes

Factor (MANOVAs) Variables (ANOVAs)	Two categories (some abuse, no abuse)			Four categories (none, exhibition, touch, penetration)		
	F(df)	p	η^2 R^2	F(df)	p	η^2 R^2
Demographics	$F_{(5,513)}=2.72$	.020	.026	$F_{(15,1539)}=3.00$	***	.083
Age	$F_{(1,517)}=3.17$	NS	.006	$F_{(3,515)}=1.13$	NS	.006
Education	$F_{(1,517)}=1.53$	NS	.003	$F_{(3,515)}=10.12$	***	.056
Income	$F_{(1,517)}=0.72$	NS	.001	$F_{(3,515)}=0.99$	NS	.006
#Children	$F_{(1,517)}=9.31$	.002	.018	$F_{(3,515)}=5.72$	***	.032
#Pregnancies	$F_{(1,517)}=11.80$	***	.022	$F_{(3,515)}=5.86$	***	.033
Family Environment	$F_{(2,516)}=25.37$	***	.089	$F_{(6,1030)}=13.31$	***	140
Neg. perceptions	$F_{(1,517)}=50.71$	***	.089	$F_{(3,515)}=26.15$	***	.132
Pos. perceptions	$F_{(1,517)}=30.00$	***	.055	$F_{(3,515)}=18.87$	***	.100
Adult sexual victimization	$F_{(3,515)}=11.17$	***	.061	$F_{(9,1545)}=11.57$	***	.189
Adult coercion	$F_{(1,517)}=28.22$	***	.051	$F_{(3,515)}=26.08$	***	.132
Adult force	$F_{(1,517)}=16.07$	***	.030	$F_{(3,515)}=14.15$	***	.076
Adolescent sex	$F_{(1,517)}=22.47$	***	.042	$F_{(3,515)}=28.47$	***	.142
Relationship violence	$F_{(3,515)}=3.61$	.013	.021	$F_{(9,1545)}=3.10$	***	.053
Argument violence	$F_{(1,517)}=7.00$	.008	.013	$F_{(3,515)}=4.70$	.003	.027
Throw violence	$F_{(1,517)}=2.57$	NS	.005	$F_{(3,515)}=4.25$	.006	.024
Hit violence	$F_{(1,517)}=4.94$	.027	.009	$F_{(3,515)}=4.88$	.002	.028
Antic. neg. reaction	$F_{(3,515)}=1.62$	NS	.009	$F_{(1,1545)}=1.94$	.042	.034
If refuse oral sex	$F_{(1,517)}=1.63$	NS	.003	$F_{(3,515)}=2.12$	NS	.012
If refuse touching	$F_{(1,517)}=2.00$	NS	.004	$F_{(3,515)}=0.98$	NS	.006
If refuse sex	$F_{(1,517)}=4.65$	.031	.009	$F_{(3,515)}=3.87$	.009	.022

TABLE 5.1 (continued)

	F	p		F	p	
Sexual self-acceptance						
Positive attitudes	F(2,516)=4.73	.009	.018	F(6,1028)=2.66	.014	.031
Negative attitudes	F(1,517)=3.82	NS	.007	F(3,515)=2.28	NS	.013
	F(1,517)=9.46	.002	.018	F(3,515)=4.12	.007	.023
Sexual assertiveness						
Communication	F(3,515)=0.46	NS	.003	F(9,1545)=1.20	NS	.021
Refusal	F(1,517)=0.48	NS	.001	F(3,515)=0.98	NS	.006
Condom use	F(1,517)=0.29	NS	.001	F(3,515)=0.45	NS	.003
	F(1,517)=0.31	NS	.001	F(3,515)=2.69	.046	.015
Unprotected sex						
Vaginal	F(3,515)=0.74	NS	.004	F(9,1545)=0.58	NS	.010
Oral	F(1,517)=1.69	NS	.003	F(3,515)=1.18	NS	.007
Anal	F(1,517)=0.69	NS	.001	F(3,515)=0.55	NS	.003
	F(1,517)=0.96	NS	.002	F(3,515)=0.76	NS	.004
Perceived risk						
How sure of safety	F(3,515)=5.58	***	.013	F(9,1545)=4.12	***	.070
Perceived risk	F(1,517)=7.08	.008	.014	F(3,515)=4.73	.003	.027
Preventive behavior	F(1,517)=15.58	***	.029	F(3,515)=9.57	***	.053
	F(1,517)=5.12	.024	.010	F(3,515)=3.40	.018	.019
Partner risk						
Partner status	F(2,516)=5.63	.004	.021	F(6,1030)=4.12	***	.047
Number of partners	F(1,517)=10.94	***	.021	F(3,515)=5.76	***	.032
	F(1,517)=1.22	NS	.002	F(3,515)=3.53	.015	.020

NOTE: *** p<.001 unless otherwise noted; NS=nonsignificant; η^2 = Pillai's trace for MANOVAs; R^2 = Proportion explained variance for follow-up ANOVAs.

categories of childhood victimization experiences: no abuse, exhibition abuse, touch abuse, and penetration abuse.

☐ Case Examples

Three clinical composite case examples of women whose childhood experiences of victimization meet these descriptions will be presented to illustrate the issues to be discussed below. Any identifying information has been changed in order to protect the woman's privacy.

Case History of Penetration Abuse (Group 4)

Jill is a 40-year-old woman who was raped as a child. She recalls that her mother had a boyfriend. Sometimes when her mother was not there, the boyfriend would hold her on his lap and touch her, or he would sleep in bed with her and touch her. One day her mother went to work and left her home alone with the boyfriend. While the mother was gone, the boyfriend forcibly penetrated her vagina. Jill was 8 years old at the time. The boyfriend threatened to harm her if she ever told anyone. Despite her fear, Jill told her mother, but her mother did not believe her. The same thing happened once or twice again. Eventually, the boyfriend got in some type of trouble and he moved away.

In high school Jill experienced further sexual victimization in a relationship with a man who was 7 years older than she was. Jill later dropped out of high school, but has now completed her high school equivalency requirements and is taking some continuing education courses. At this time Jill is unemployed and staying home to care for her children. She reports having been raped when she was in her 20s. She was married to a physically abusive husband who is the father of her three children. She also had one pregnancy that ended in miscarriage and one pregnancy that ended in abortion. She left this relationship 10 years ago and is currently involved with a man she is living with but is not married to. Jill is concerned that he is engaged in sexual relations with other women and is not sure of whether she is currently at risk for HIV or other STDs. She is also concerned because her partner has in the past used injection drugs.

Jill has sought psychotherapy several times, first to help her leave her abusive relationship and more recently to help her "get her life together." This has been a positive experience in helping her to pursue her educational goals and evaluate relationship issues.

Case History of Touch Abuse (Group 3)

Jennifer is a 32-year-old woman who had the experience of being touched inappropriately by her grandfather. Periodically throughout her childhood she remembers being asked to sleep with her grandfather. On one occasion when she was 11 she remembers falling asleep and waking up to the sensation of someone touching her genitals and rubbing against her. It was her grandfather. Jennifer did not feel she could tell anyone about this experience, even though it was very upsetting to her and made her dread visiting her grandparents. Her grandfather never acknowledged this occurrence and it did not happen again.

One reason that Jennifer did not feel she could bring this up to her mother was that she did not feel supported and understood in her family. It always seemed that whatever she did was the wrong thing and that other family members were upset with her a lot of the time. Jennifer was quite unhappy as a child and this experience became somewhat symbolic for her of her victimization and lack of care.

Jennifer was able to complete college and then married. She is currently not employed. Although her marriage is not perfect, she has stayed in the relationship for 10 years and she now has one child. Despite the fact that she has been monogamous, she still has concerns that her husband may have affairs and worries that she may be exposed to HIV or other STDs.

Jennifer has never entered psychotherapy, although she has a friend who has suggested that doing so might help her relationship with her husband and help her to "make peace" with her family.

Case History from Exhibition Abuse (Group 2)

Lara is a 35-year-old woman. She recalls that when she was 8 years old she was approached by a teenage boy when she was walking home from school. When she got close to him she realized that his pants were undone and he was holding his penis. While she was watching, he ejaculated, although at the time, she did not know what that was. She never told anyone in her family or at school about the incident because she was embarrassed and ashamed that she had looked. This was the only time she had an experience like this and she never saw the teenage boy again.

She reports that in general her family was supportive to her and she enjoyed relationships within her family. She completed college and is working in a job that she enjoys. She married 2 years ago and has no children. She trusts her partner to remain monogamous and does not worry about sexually transmitted disease.

Lara reports having attended a support group during college and having tried psychotherapy once in her mid-20s to help with relationship problems.

Following the presentation of statistical findings about group differences will be a discussion of these case histories.

☐ Group Differences Among Survivors of Four Types of Childhood Sexual Abuse

In this section, the group differences among women reporting penetration abuse, touch abuse, exhibition abuse, and no abuse will be presented for all variables of interest in this study (see Table 5.2) using χ^2 analyses and MANOVAs.

Demographic Data

A MANOVA using the category of childhood sexual abuse as a grouping variable revealed significant differences among a set of demographic variables: age, education, income, number of children, and number of previous pregnancies, with Wilks' $\Lambda = .91$, $F(15,1539) = 3.00$, $p < .0001$. Follow-up ANOVAs reveal that women who experienced different types of abuse do not significantly differ in age or income; they do, however, differ significantly in years of education, with $F(3, 515) = 10.12$, $p < .0001$. Tukey tests reveal that at $p < .01$, penetration abuse (Group 4) survivors report significantly less education than women in Groups 1, 2, or 3; these latter groups did not differ significantly from one another. Follow-up ANOVAs also reveal that women who experienced different levels of abuse differed significantly in the number of children they have $[F(3,515) = 5.72, p < .001]$ and in the number of prior pregnancies they report $[F(3,515) = 5.86, p < .001]$. Tukey tests reveal that women in the penetration abuse group report significantly more children as well as higher number of prior pregnancies than women in the no abuse group (at $p < .01$). Other groups do not significantly differ in these follow-up analyses.

χ^2 analyses were next conducted on participants' responses to the following categorical demographic variables: racial/ethnic background, current marital status, whether the participant had a regular sex partner, current living arrangements (with or without a partner), sexual orientation, and religion. A summary of these results can be found in Table 5.3.

TABLE 5.2 Demographic differences among four abuse groups (N=519)

Variables	Group 1 (No abuse)	Group 2 (Exhibition)	Group 3 (Touching)	Group 4 (Penetration)	X²(df)	p
Race/ethnicity					22.3(15)	.10 NS
White	193	48	128	72		
African Amer.	13	4	14	12		
Native Amer.	1	0	2	2		
Asian Amer.	0	0	1	2		
Hispanic	2	0	4	4		
Other	3	2	7	5		
Race/ethnicity (recoded)					18.9 (6)	.004
White	193	48	128	72		
African Amer.	13	4	14	12		
All other	6	2	14	13		
Current marital status					24.5 (9)	.004
Single	140	31	93	39		
Married	17	11	17	17		
Separ./Div.	50	11	43	36		
Widowed	5	1	3	5		
Regular sex partner NS					2.63 (3)	.45
No	52	19	43	28		
Yes	160	35	113	69		
Current living arrangement (w/ sex partner)					5.19 (6)	.52 NS
No	129	37	85	56		
Sometimes	34	5	28	13		
Yes	49	12	43	28		
Sexual orientation					10.3 (6)	.11 NS
Only w/ men	200	50	140	81		
Bisexual	8	2	10	11		
Only w/women	4	2	6	5		
Religion					24.7 (12)	.016
Catholic	104	26	69	49		
Protestant	41	4	33	10		
Jewish	11	5	7	1		
Muslim/eastern other	34	8	24	27		
None	22	11	23	10		

Note: NS=Nonsignificant.

In this sample, non-White women were significantly more likely to have experienced the more severe types of childhood sexual abuse, with $\chi^2(15)$ = 26.2, $p < .05$. Significant group differences emerged regarding religious orientation, with $\chi^2(18) = 36.1$, $p < .01$. Women in Groups 3 (touch) and 4 (penetration) were significantly more likely than women in Groups 1 (no abuse) and 2 (exhibition) to report "none" or "other" as their religious affiliation. The type of childhood sexual abuse experienced was unrelated to participants' current marital status, whether she had a regular sex partner, current living arrangements, or sexual orientation.

Family-of-Origin Environment

MANOVAs were conducted on the remaining set of dependent variables, with results also presented in Table 5.3. These analyses revealed significant differences among the four groups on the set of family-of-origin environment variables, with Wilks's $\Lambda = .86$, $F(6,1030) = 13.31$, $p < .0001$. Follow-up ANOVAs revealed significant group differences on reports of both positive and negative family-of-origin environment [$F(3,515) = 26.15$ and 18.87, respectively, both $p < .0001$]. Tukey tests were used to follow up significant one-way ANOVAs. Groups 1 and 2 (no and exhibition abuse) did not significantly differ in reports of positive family-of-origin characteristics, but both reported a significantly more positive environment than those in Group 3 (touch abuse) who, in turn, reported a significantly more positive environment than those in Group 4 (penetration abuse). Tukey tests also revealed that Group 4 (penetration abuse) reported significantly more negative family-of-origin characteristics than the other three groups. Groups 2 (exhibition) and 3 (touch), who did not significantly differ from each other, reported a significantly more negative family-of-origin environment than those in Group 1 (no abuse).

Adult Sexual Victimization

Women who experienced different types of sexual abuse as children differed significantly in the amount of adolescent and adult sexual victimization they reported, with Wilks's $\Lambda = .81$, $F(9,1545) = 11.57$, $p < .0001$. Follow-up ANOVAs reveal significant differences for each of the dependent variables: adolescent sexual abuse, adult sexual coercion, and adult sexual abuse [$F(3,515) = 28.47$, 26.08, and 14.15, respectively, all $p < .0001$]. Follow-up Tukey tests evaluated at $p < .01$ reveal that Group 4 women, who experienced actual or attempted rape, report significantly

TABLE 5.3   Means and Tukey results for four abuse categories on set of variables

Factor Variable	Group 1 (no abuse)	Group 2 (exhibition)	Group 3 (touching)	Group 4 (penetration)	Tukey $p<.01$
Demographics					
Age	30.4	32.2	31.8	32.4	NS
Education	4.43	4.83	4.37	3.94	4<1,2,3
Income	1.87	2.07	1.97	1.84	NS
#Children	0.67	0.81	0.89	1.28	4>1
#Pregnancies	1.25	1.50	1.67	2.13	4>1
Family environment					
Neg. perceptions	2.81	3.03	3.40	3.87	4>3,2,1; 3>1
Pos. perceptions	3.61	3.53	3.26	2.85	1>3>4; 2>4
Adult sexual victimization					
Adult coercion	2.21	2.12	2.45	2.80	4>3,2,1
Adult force	1.54	1.53	1.82	2.43	4>3,2,1
Adololescent sex	1.18	1.26	1.29	1.95	4>3,2,1
Relationship violence					
Argument violence	2.38	2.48	2.46	2.70	4>1
Throw violence	1.98	1.85	2.06	2.37	4>1
Hit violence	1.37	1.40	1.44	1.70	4>1
Anticipated negative reaction					
If refuse oral	1.37	1.28	1.48	1.45	NS
If refuse touch	1.42	1.43	1.51	1.53	NS
If refuse sex	1.40	1.41	1.50	1.70	4>1
Sexual self-acceptance					
Pos. attitudes	3.86	3.65	3.77	3.55	NS
Neg. attitudes	1.85	1.94	2.07	2.17	4>1
Sexual assertiveness					
Communication	4.41	4.52	4.34	4.28	NS
Refusal	3.98	4.02	3.95	3.88	NS
Condom use	3.36	3.78	3.32	3.37	NS
Unprotected sex					
Vaginal	37.3	29.9	27.6	37.0	NS
Oral	18.9	14.5	16.1	19.0	NS
Anal	0.66	0.36	0.42	0.67	NS

TABLE 5.3   (continued)

Factor Variable	Group 1 (no abuse)	Group 2 (exhibition)	Group 3 (touching)	Group 4 (penetration)	Tukey $p<.01$
Perceived risk					
How sure	2.09	1.98	1.98	1.71	1>4
Perception of risk	2.26	2.23	2.60	2.79	4>1,2; 3>1
Preventive behavior	4.80	4.70	4.74	4.57	1>4
Partner risk factors					
Partner status	1.23	1.36	1.45	1.72	4>1
Number partners	23.0	20.1	22.2	47.0	No follow-up Tukey tests significant

Note: NS=follow-up ANOVA was not significant (see Table 5.1 for details).

more sexual victimization in adolescence than women in the other three groups, including those who report no sexual victimization prior to age 14. Reports of adolescent victimization by women in these three groups do not differ significantly. Follow-up Tukey tests for the amount of adult sexual coercion and victimization reveal comparable results: Women in Group 4, those experiencing actual or attempted sexual penetration, report significantly more of both forms of adult victimization than women in the other three groups. No significant differences in adult victimization were revealed among these latter three groups: those whose most severe abuse involved touch only, those whose most severe abuse was exhibitionism, and those who reported no sexual victimization in childhood.

Relationship Violence

Significant differences among groups were also revealed on the set of variables that assessed experiences of relationship violence, with Wilks's $\Lambda = .95$, $F(9,1545) = 3.10$, $p < .001$. Follow-up ANOVAs show significant group differences on all three measures of relationship violence: threats of violence within a relationship $[F(3,515) = 4.70$, $p < .01]$, use of violence within a relationship $[F(3,515) = 4.25$, $p < .01]$, and style of conflict resolution $[F(3,515) = 4.88$, $p < .01]$. Follow-up Tukey tests reveal an identical pattern among all three dependent constructs; for each measure of relationship violence, women in Group 4 (penetration abuse) report experiencing significantly more threats of violence, more violence actually used against them, and an approach to relationship conflicts which is more likely to include violence than women in Group 1 (no abuse). No other significant differences were revealed in these follow-up analyses.

Anticipated Negative Partner Reaction

No significant group differences were revealed in a set of measures asking about anticipating a partner's negative reaction to assertiveness about HIV prevention since the original MANOVA was not significant at a stringent $p < .01$ level.

Sexual Self-Acceptance

Significant differences were revealed among the four groups on the set of sexual self-acceptance variables, with Wilks's $\Lambda = .97$, $F(6,1028) = 2.66$, $p < .01$. Follow-up ANOVAs show that group differences exist on both positive sexual self-acceptance [$F(3,515) = 2.28$, $p < .05$] but on negative sexual self-acceptance [$F(3,515) = 4.12$, $p < .01$]. Follow-up Tukey tests revealed no significant differences among groups on positive sexual self-acceptance, while Tukey tests reveal that Group 4, those experiencing penetration abuse, had significantly higher scores on negative sexual self-acceptance than Group 1, women reporting no childhood victimization.

Sexual Assertiveness

No significant group differences were revealed in a MANOVA using the three sexual assertiveness constructs: assertiveness to refuse unwanted sex, to use condoms to prevent STDs, and to communicate with partners about sexual risk status.

Unprotected Sex

MANOVAs revealed no significant group differences in the reported frequency of engaging in unprotected vaginal, oral, or anal sex.

Perceptions of Risk

A MANOVA revealed significant group differences on the set of variables assessing participants' perceptions of their risk of exposure to HIV or other

STDs, with Wilks's Λ = .93, $F(9,1545)$ = 4.12, $p < .0001$. Follow-up ANOVAs revealed significant group differences on each of the three risk perception variables: how sure they were that their sexual partners have not exposed them to HIV or other STDs [$F(3,515)$ = 4.73, $p < .01$], their perception of risk of HIV [$F(3,515)$ = 9.57, $p < .0001$], and use of HIV preventive behaviors [$F(3,515)$ = 3.40, $p < .05$]. Follow-up Tukey tests clarify the nature of these group differences and reveal that those in Group 1 (no abuse) report being significantly more sure that their sexual partners have not exposed them to HIV or to an STD than women in Group 4 (penetration abuse). Other groups are not significantly different for this variable. Tukey tests also revealed several differences among groups on perception of risk of exposure to HIV: Group 4 (penetration) women reported significantly higher perceptions of risk of exposure to HIV than Groups 1 (no abuse) and 2 (exhibition), whose reports of risk perception were not different. Those in Group 1 also reported significantly less perception of risk than those in Group 3 (touch). Follow-up Tukey tests did not reveal significant group differences in the use of risk-reducing behaviors.

Partner-Associated Risk Factors

Significant group differences were next revealed in the set of variables assessing number and risk levels of sexual partners, with Wilks's Λ = .95, $F(6,1030)$ = 4.12, $p < .001$. Follow-up ANOVAs show group differences in each variable: number of partners [$F(3,515)$ = 3.53, $p < .05$] and partner risk factors [$F(3,515)$ = 5.76, $p < .001$]. Tukey tests reveal no statistical differences among women in the four groups on the number of partners they report. However, these follow-up tests show that women in Group 1 (no abuse) report that their sexual partners have significantly fewer risk factors than women in Group 4 (penetration abuse) report for their partners. No other significant differences were revealed for partner risk status.

☐ Relationship Between Perpetrator and Victim

The next step was to examine whether the relationship of the perpetrator of the childhood sexual abuse to the woman (e.g., whether the perpetrator was a family member or not) exerts an independent effect on the various measures of adult functioning or whether the type of perpetrator interacts with the type of abuse to influence adult functioning. A series of MANOVAs examined the independent effects of type of abuse (exhibition, touch, or penetration) and type of perpetrator (familial versus nonfamilial), as well as the interaction between these. Because the no abuse group is not distinguished by the independent variable "perpetrator," women reporting no abuse were dropped from this analysis. In addition, note that analyses for the independent variable type of abuse are redundant with the comparisons of Groups 2, 3, and 4 reported in the previous section, and thus details of those results will not be repeated here. Results of these analyses are presented in Table 5.4.

Across most of the 12 MANOVAs, which involved five demographic indices, 21 measures used as predictors in the model, and six HIV risk measures, the relationship to the perpetrator was not significantly related to most of the outcome measures. In none of these analyses were the eta values, which represent the proportion of variance accounted for, greater than 4.5%; in 33 of 39 analyses, the perpetrator relationship accounted for less than 1% of the variance. Perpetrator was related to adult outcomes in only three group-difference analyses: demographic data, adult victimization experiences, and family environment. Analyses of the Sexual Powerlessness Scale also revealed an interesting, though nonsignificant, trend. Results from these factorial MANOVAs will be discussed only for the three analyses in which the type of perpetrator was significant.

Demographic Data

The factorial MANOVA revealed significant differences for both independent variables, type of abuse and perpetrator, among a set of demographic variables: age, education, income, number of children, and number of previous pregnancies. The interaction between the independent variables was nonsignificant, while the main effects were significant for both type of childhood abuse experienced [Wilks's $\Lambda = .89$, $F(10, 574) = 3.42$, $p < .0002$] and the perpetrator relationship [Wilks's $\Lambda = .96$, $F(5,287) = 2.69$, $p < .02$]. Follow-up ANOVAs for the main effect of type of abuse has been discussed in the previous section. Following up the significant main effect for perpetrator of abuse revealed significant differences in the amount of education reported [$F(1, 292) = 9.70$, $p < .002$] and a difference approaching significance in the age of the participant [$F(1, 291) = 5.90$, $p < .016$]. Women reporting sexual abuse by a family member were slightly older and more educated than women reporting abuse by a nonfamily abuser, but none of the follow-up Tukey tests in these analyses reached significance.

TABLE 5.4   Two-way MANOVA results with abuse category (exhibition, touch, or penetration) by type of perpetrator of abuse (family or nonfamily member) (N=307).

Effect Tested	Perpetrator			Abuse type x perpetrator		
Factor Variables	F	p	η^2	F	p	η^2
Demographics	2.69	**.021**	.045	1.23	.270.	.042
Age	5.90	**.015**	.020	0.79	.456	.005
Education	9.70	**.002**	.028	1.49	.223	.008
Income	3.29	.071	.011	0.49	.612	.003
#Children	0.01	.955	.000	3.56	.100	.015
#Pregnancies	1.09	.105	.003	16.01	**.009**	.031
Family environment	1.33	.265	.009	0.20	.933	.003
Negative perceptions	4.69	**.031**	.016	0.20	.820	.001
Positive perceptions	2.91	.089	.007	0.20	.816	.001
Adult sexual victimization	0.75	.525	.007	2.41	**.026**	.049
Adult coercion	2.00	.159	.006	0.22	.801	.001
Adult force	4.90	**.027**	.014	1.58	.207	.009
Adolescent intercourse	0.01	.945	.001	3.25	**.040**	.019
Relationship violence	0.29	.831	.003	1.46	.191	.030
Argument violence	0.01	.934	.000	2.37	.096	.016
Throw violence	0.18	.669	.001	1.91	.149	.012
Hit violence	0.47	.495	.001	0.54	.586	.003
Anticipated partner negative reaction	0.50	.681	.005	0.40	.881	.008
If refuse oral sex	0.04	.833	.000	0.41.	664	.002
If refuse touch	0.02	.893	.000	0.09	.914	.001
If refuse sex	0.91	.340	.002	0.01	.992	.000
Sexual self-acceptance	1.05	.350	.007	1.68	.154	.023
Pos. attitudes	0.73	.394	.002	0.88	.415	.005
Neg. attitudes	0.34	.558	.001	0.50	.605	.003
Sexual assertiveness	0.25	.861	.003	0.65	.689	.013
Communication	1.16	.281	.004	0.55	.580	.003
Refusal	0.25	.618	.001	0.74	.477	.005
Condom use	0.39	.535	.001	1.06	.348	.007
Unprotected sex	0.72	.538	.007	0.69	.659	.014
Vaginal	1.56	.212	.005	1.37	.256	.009
Oral	0.61	.435	.002	0.50	.607	.003
Anal	0.01	.913	.000	0.88	.417	.006

TABLE 5.4   (continued)

Effect Tested	Perpetrator			Abuse type x perpetrator		
Factor Variables	*F*	*p*	η^2	*F*	*p*	η^2
Perceived risk	0.07	.974	.001	0.81	.564	.017
How sure (of safety)	0.09	.763	.000	1.02	.363	.005
Perception of risk	1.14	.287	.004	1.98	.140	.013
Preventive behaviors	0.32	.570	.000	1.12	.328	.003
Partner risk factors	0.15	.858	.001	0.82	.510	.011
Partner status	0.14	.709	.001	0.11	.898	.001
Number of partners	0.99	.321	.003	1.60	.204	.011

Note: Participants not reporting childhood sexual abuse (*N*=212) were deleted from these analyses; see Table 5.1 for main effect results for type of abuse category. Significant differences (*p* < .05) are in bold.

Adult Sexual Abuse

A factorial MANOVA with type of childhood sexual abuse experienced and relationship of perpetrator as independent variables revealed significant group differences on the set of adult victimization measures (sexual abuse in adolescence, and sexual coercion and sexual assault in adulthood) reported by participants. The interaction between these two independent variables revealed significant group differences, with Wilks's Λ = .95, $F(6, 578)$ = 2.40, p < .03. Follow-up ANOVAs revealed significant interaction effects for two of the three dependent variables: adolescent sexual abuse [$F(5, 291)$ = 10.39, p < .0001] and adult sexual abuse [$F(5, 291)$ = 10.30, p < .0001]. The nature of these interactions are that: (a) for those who experienced penetration abuse as children younger than 14, those whose perpetrators were family members report more adolescent and adult sexual assault than those whose abusers were not family members; and (b) for those who experienced touch sexual abuse as children younger than 14, those whose perpetrators were family members report more adult sexual abuse than those whose perpetrators were nonfamily members. For those whose most severe form of abuse prior to age 14 was exhibitionism, there were no significant differences in the amount of adult or adolescent sexual abuse reported based on who the childhood perpetrator was.

An evaluation of the main effects in this analysis revealed no significant group differences based on the perpetrator of the abuse. Significant differences were revealed, however, across the three types of abuse participants reported, with Wilks's Λ = .83, $F(6, 578)$ = 9.71, p < .0001. The findings from the follow-up ANOVAs and Tukeys have been discussed for all abuse groups in the previous section of this chapter.

Perceptions of Family-of-Origin

On the family-of-origin environment MANOVA, the main effect of type of abuse was significant [Wilks's Λ = .92, $F(4, 580)$ = 5.87, $p <$ .0001], but not the main effect of type of perpetrator or the interaction. For positive family-of-origin environment follow-up analyses, the penetration abuse group was significantly different from both other groups, while the touch and exhibition comparison was not significant. Although the main effect for type of perpetrator was not significant, the follow-up Tukey test for type of perpetrator was significant at $p <$ .01, with the women abused by a family member evaluating their family-of-origin environment as less positive.

For negative family-of-origin environment, the main effects of both type of abuse and perpetrator were significant on the followup ANOVA [for type of abuse, $F(2, 291)$ = 13.40, $p <$ .0001; for perpetrator, $F(1, 291)$ = 4.69, $p <$ .03)]. As with analyses already discussed, Tukey analyses on the three abuse groups showed a pattern similar to the positive environment scale, with women who had experienced penetration abuse differing from both other groups (exhibition and touch). Tukey analyses on the two perpetrator groups showed that women abused by a family member evaluated their family-of-origin environment as significantly more negative ($p <$ .01) than women abused by someone outside of their family.

Sexual Functioning

Although the perpetrator variable was not significant in any of the Tukey analyses, for the variable "sexual powerlessness," there was a consistent pattern of higher powerlessness scores for all family-perpetrated abuses, with a trend towards significance [for main effect of perpetrator, $F(3, 289)$ = 2.34, $p <$ .074].

☐ Other Potential Distinguishing Factors

Rather than carry out multiple analyses, it seemed important to assess the most important factors for our attention as predictor variables in the model-building process. Furthermore, it seems likely that various characteristics of child sexual abuse would be interrelated. In this section, we identify relationships among the various aspects of child sexual abuse that could be potentially important predictors of adult outcomes.

The first question, given the lack of significance in most of the analyses above of type of perpetrator, is the association between type of abuse and perpetrator. Indeed, there is a significant association (χ^2 (2 df) = 15.09, $p < .001$). Exhibition and touch abuses were far more likely to be perpetrated by a nonfamily member (77% and 73% of the total, respectively). In contrast, penetration abuse was almost as likely to be perpetrated by a family member (48.45%) as a nonfamily abuser (51.55%). In fact, nearly 50% of all abuses by family members involve penetration, in comparison to only 25% of those by nonfamily abusers.

Type of abuse and perpetrator are not the only factors suggested as having an effect on the severity of negative outcomes. Another is the number of incidents of assault. Not surprisingly, multiple assaults result in more severe adult symptomatology (Wyatt et al., 1992). These factors may be interrelated to a large extent; Wyatt et al. (1992) observed that survivors of intrafamilial abuse were more likely to be assaulted extrafamilially as well.

Both type of abuse and perpetrator appear to be associated with number of abusive experiences. Women whose most intrusive experience was exhibition abuse almost always reported only one experience (82.5%), and none reported "many" incidents. Women who experienced touch abuse often also reported exhibition abuse (68%), but again the majority (60.4%) reported only one incident of touching, and only 5% reported "many" incidents.

In contrast, nearly two thirds of the women reporting penetration abuse reported multiple incidents. Of these women, 27% reported the penetration happened "many" times, and another 40.4% reported it happened "a few" times. Ninety-seven percent reported exhibition abuse and 99% reported touch abuse in addition to the penetration.

Perpetrator type appeared to be related systematically to the number of abuses, but the χ^2 analysis of number of abuses (once, a few, many) $\times$ perpetrator (family or nonfamily) was not significant (χ^2 (df = 2) = 4.285, $p = .117$). Nevertheless, the pattern was consistent in that family members were more likely to commit multiple abuses (76.4% reported "a few" or "many") than to commit the abuse only one time (23.5%). Although women abused by nonfamily members still reported more multiple abuses (58.4% reporting "a few" or "many"), almost twice as many as those abused by family members reported only one abuse (41.5%). From another view, those women abused only once were more likely to have been abused by a nonfamily abuser (64.7%) than a family member

(35.3%), while those women abused "many times" were more likely to have been abused by a family member (60.71%) than a nonfamily abuser (39.3%). Thus, in spite of the lack of significance, the overlap among these categories is important to recognize in interpreting the findings on these variables.

Not considered in the present analyses is the age at which the abuse occurred. It is possible that familial sexual abuse begins at earlier ages than nonfamilial abuse because access to younger children is more limited for nonfamilial perpetrators.

☐ Discussion of Case Histories

The women presented in this chapter were selected because their childhood sexual abuse experiences typify those of women who are seen by physicians and psychotherapists. It is clear from their stories that neither Jill nor Jennifer have adequate resources to change their vulnerability at the present time; both are unemployed and both have dependent children. Each is in a relationship in which they are not sure that their partners are not exposing them to HIV or other STDs, but their options for protecting themselves while at the same time maintaining relationships that meet at least some of their needs are limited. Discontinuing sexual relations may be the equivalent of ending the relationship, and thus not an acceptable option. On the other hand, the introduction of condoms into an ongoing relationship in which they previously were not used may communicate unacceptable information to their partners. The limited options for disease prevention place women, particularly women such as Jill and Jennifer, in a situation with few real solutions.

It is crucially important for health care providers to understand the circumstances that limit options for self-care by women such as Jill and Jennifer. The fact that they are both at risk of exposure to HIV will be missed by the practitioner who does not ask about the womens' current sexual behaviors and concerns over their partners' risk factors. The complex relationship between each woman's victimization (and revictimization) history and thus consequent opportunities to intervene will also be missed by the practitioner who does not take a thorough sexual history.

☐ General Discussion and Interpretation

The results presented in this chapter suggest that using an instrument that assesses the specific sexually abusive behaviors experienced by women reveals a more clearly defined picture of the lasting effects of childhood sexual abuse. The most consistent finding revealed in these analyses is the poorer functioning of women who report the most severe childhood sexual abuse. Women who have experienced actual or attempted rape as children younger than age 14 report poorer functioning in a number of areas of adult functioning, poorer not just than women without a history of childhood victimization, but also, in general, poorer functioning than women who as children were victims of exhibitionism or who reported abuse involving some physical contact.

These results are important to consider in the context of previous research on the lasting effects of childhood sexual abuse, much of which has attempted to provide answers to the question of whether or not childhood sexual abuse effects adult functioning. Because we had access in this study to a more specific and reliable description of the various types of abuse experiences reported by a large group of women, we could begin to address the question: Do these various experiences of sexual abuse in childhood differentially effect adult functioning? Is childhood sexual abuse a uni- or multidimensional construct? The differential effect of the various types of abuse identified within this sample strongly suggests that childhood sexual abuse is in fact multidimensional and further suggests what those working with survivors of abuse would intuit, namely, that all survivors are different and that the severity of abuse is an important variable to consider in designing any intervention designed to ameliorate the lasting, negative effects of childhood sexual abuse. The case examples presented here illustrate these themes; these women, who have had very different experiences as children, report great variety in their adult functioning.

It is important both to HIV-related research and to understanding the issues of sexual abuse recovery that for the outome variables we were concerned with—revictimization, sexual functioning, sexual risk behavior, psychosocial attitudes—who perpetrated the abuse was not as important as how physically assaultive the abuse was. When the abuse involved penetration and, for some outcome variables, sexual contact, effects were more severe for both familial and nonfamilial abusers. This is in keeping with the finding reported in Wyatt et al. (1992), as stated earlier in the chapter, that the severity of the abuse was the significant predictor for similar outcomes involving sexual behavior and related attitudes.

However, it is also important to recognize that these categories overlap and that family members were much more likely to attempt or complete penetrative rape than nonfamilial abusers. Furthermore, it is important to appreciate that we addressed only one part of the large spectrum of potential outcomes of sexual abuse, and that research reviewed in Chapter 2 has indicated that adults with psychological difficulties are more likely to have experienced incest.

Comparisons between incest and nonfamilial abuses are sometimes muddied by the fact that the perpetrator may not be related to his victim but may be living in her or his family as a stepfather or other authority figure. In addition, abuse by a family member who lives next door and is seen frequently may provoke different reactions than abuse by a similarly related family member who is rarely seen. While we have used familial categories, these finer distinctions are important to recognize in clinical applications.

One of the implications of such findings, that different levels of severity of childhood sexual abuse are associated with differing levels of adult functioning in a wide variety of areas, is that we can begin to conceptualize a continuum of abusive interpersonal experiences. The relationship between such a continuum of abuse and other factors that are hypothesized to relate to risk taking within sexual relationships can then be examined in the proposed model or set of relationships among constructs presented in Chapter 3.

Preliminary Model Analyses

Before testing aspects of our proposed longitudinal model of childhood trauma and HIV risk, several preliminary analyses were conducted to verify the individual constructs of the model. These involved PCAs of each model construct, internal consistency calculations for each construct using coefficient alpha, and cross-sectional analyses of the proposed model. Analyses were conducted with the SAS (1989) and EQS (1995) computer programs.

☐ Initial Factor Structure

Data from 760 women were obtained during 1993-1994 at the first time point. These participants were followed for 1 year, with a second assessment at 6 months and the third and final one 6 months after that. The average age of participants at the first time point was 31 years. Reflecting the ethnic and racial characteristics of the community from which they were recruited, 83% of participants identified themselves as White; 9% as African American; 3% as Hispanic American; 1% as Native American; less than 1% as Asian American; and 3% as "other." For a more complete description of this sample's demographics, see Table 6.1.

PCAs with oblique Promax rotation were conducted as a preliminary evaluation of the integrity of the scales to be used in the structural equation model analyses. A random subsample of approximately 15% ($N = 119$) of the 760 subjects from whom data had been collected at the first

TABLE 6.1   Sample demographics at Time 1 *(N=760)*

	Mean	Standard Deviation
Mean age (years)	M=31.12	SD=9.98
Mean # children	M=.88	SD=1.26
Mean # pregnancies	M=1.62	SD=1.62

	Frequency	Percentage
Ethnicity		
White	630	83%
African American	70	9%
Native American	10	1%
Asian American	4	< 1%
Hispanic American	22	3%
Other	24	3%
Education		
Less than 8th grade	5	1%
Grade 8–12	40	5%
High school graduate	56	7%
Some college	387	51%
College graduate	141	19%
Graduate coursework	131	17%
Occupation		
None	235	31%
Clerical/manual	113	15%
Service/sales	163	21%
Business/technical	59	8%
Professional	142	19%
Other	48	6%
Income		
Less than $10,000	351	46%
$10,000—$19,999	190	25%
$20,000—$34,999	174	23%
$35,000—$50,000	33	4%
Over $50,000	12	2%
Marital status		
Single, never married	441	58%
Married	99	13%
Separated or divorced	197	26%
Widowed	23	3%
Live with sex partner		
No	436	57%
Sometimes (at least several days a month)	107	14%
Yes, all the time	217	29%

TABLE 6.1   (continued)

	Frequency	Percentage
Religion		
Catholic	353	46%
Protestant	138	18%
Jewish	34	5%
Muslim	3	< 1%
Eastern	11	1%
Other	119	16%
None	102	13%

time point was used for these preliminary analyses. Scale integrity was assessed by scree plots, percent of variance accounted for, and patterns of factor loadings, including an evaluation of complex items as well as the absolute value of the loadings. Items which loaded on more than one factor or which loaded poorly (less than .35) were deleted from scales in further analyses. Internal consistencies for all scales are presented in Table 6.2.

Item parcels, which form more stable indicators of latent constructs than individual items, were formed from single factor scales by averaging one positively and one reverse-scored negatively worded item. Scales that were handled in this manner include: Positive Family-of-Origin Environment (yielding three indicators assessing perceptions of family as understanding, helpful, and happy); Sexual Self-Acceptance (three indicators assessing sexual meaning, sexual control, and sexual esteem); Sexually Assertive Communication Regarding HIV Risk (three indicators measuring assertiveness regarding STD/HIV status, partner's partners, and partner and injection drugs); Sexual Assertiveness to Refuse Unwanted Sex (three indicators assessing refusal regarding oral sex, refuse even if pressured, and refuse regarding foreplay); and Sexual Assertiveness for Condom Use (three indicators measuring assertiveness even if partner doesn't want to use condoms, even if partner insists on not using condoms, and even if partner doesn't like condoms).

Item parcels from multiple factor scales were formed by averaging the items which comprise each factor and using these averages as indicators of the latent construct. Scales that were handled in this manner include Childhood Sexual Abuse (three item parcels representing three types of sexual victimization before age 14: unwanted exhibition, touching, and sexual penetration); Adult Sexual Victimization (two item parcels representing experiences of sexual coercion and experiences of sexual victimization involving physical force; a third indicator was a single item

TABLE 6.2   Coefficient α internal consistencies for scales used in structural equation model(N=760)

Scale	α
Childhood Sexual Abuse (7 Items)	α=.94
Family-of-Origin Environment (6 Items)	α=.88
Adult Sexual Abuse (11 Items)	α=.89
Relationship Violence (12 Items)	α=.90
Sexual Self-Acceptance (6 Items)	α=.84
Anticipated Negative Partner Reaction (3 Items)	α=.77
Sexual Assertiveness for HIV Risk Communication (6 Items)	α=.89
Sexual Assertiveness Regarding Refusal of Unwanted Sex (6 Items)	α=.74
Sexual Assertiveness Regarding Condom Use (6 Items)	α=.82
Unprotected Sex (3 Composite Items)	α=.63
Perception of Risk (3 Composite Items)	α=.68
Partner Risk (2 Composite Items)	α=.51

regarding experiences of unwanted sexual intercourse during adolescence); Relationship Violence (three item parcels representing typical approach to settling arguments, experience of threats of physical abuse, and experience of physical violence within a sexual relationship); Unprotected Sexual Experience (three indicators summed across partners for the prior 6 months: unprotected vaginal, oral, and anal sex); and Perception of Risk (three indicators: how sure the woman is that her sexual partners have not exposed her to HIV, perception of risk, and risk-preventive behaviors used).

Anticipated Negative Partner Reaction was found to be a single-factor scale, three items of which were retained for subsequent analyses. Item content focused on the degree to which a negative partner reaction would be anticipated if a women refused oral sex, refused to touch her partner, and refused sex without a condom.

Partner risk was assessed with two indicators: one was an average of reported risk factors assessed across partners; the second was the number of sexual partners reported over a woman's lifetime.

Due to assumptions regarding linearity and because of the extreme nonnormality of eight of the item parcels, log transformations were used for measures of unprotected vaginal, oral, and anal sex; lifetime number of sexual partners; reported partner risk factors; sexual victimization in adolescence; experience of relationship violence; and childhood sexual abuse that included penetration. Means and standard deviations for all revised item parcels are presented in Table 6.3.

Once item parcels were formed from the various scales proposed, they were used in a single PCA that was calculated in order to evaluate the relationships among the 12 scales and to determine whether the expected number of factors would emerge from this larger analysis. This analysis was once again conducted on the randomly selected subsample of approximately 15% of the total sample ($N = 119$). Using scree plots and percent of explained variance to evaluate the various solutions, a 10-correlated-factor solution emerged as the most plausible, with 72% of total variance accounted for. Factor loadings and intercorrelations are presented in Tables 6.4 and 6.5. Although two pairs of scales were not distinguishable in this solution (indicators of adult and childhood sexual abuse loaded together on the same factor; and indicators of unprotected sex and partner risk loaded together on the same factor), a relatively clear factor pattern was revealed, with other scales emerging as single factors in this solution. This virtually simple structure pattern of loadings suggests that these factors are largely distinct from one another and that meaningful patterns of relationships among them may be revealed with the use of structural equation analysis.

☐   Cross-Sectional Analysis

In this phase of exploratory cross-sectional analysis, a random sample of approximately one third ($N = 267$) of Time 1 participants was used. A larger subsample than that used for the preliminary PCAs was necessary due to the heavy computational demands of structural equation modeling and in order to ensure that stable parameter estimates could be calculated. The hypothesized pattern of relationships is presented in Figure 6.1 and consists of two latent predictors (childhood sexual abuse and family-of-origin environment), seven proposed latent mediators (adult sexual victimization; relationship violence; sexual self-acceptance; anticipation of a partner's negative reaction to HIV-assertive behaviors; sexual assertiveness to communicate with partners regarding their HIV risk status; to refuse unwanted sex; and to insist on condom use), and three latent dependent constructs assessing HIV risk behaviors and attitudes (unprotected sex, perceptions of risk, and reported partner risk factors). The

TABLE 6.3   Means and standard deviations for revised scales (*N*=760)

Factor Indicator	Mean	Standard deviation
Childhood Sexual Abuse		
Exhibition	1.77	.96
Touching	1.71	.94
Penetration	1.21	.41
Family-of-Origin Environment		
Understanding	3.18	1.00
Helpful ˙	3.01	.99
Happy	3.02	1.07
Adult Sexual Abuse		
Coercion	2.38	.84
Force	1.79	.92
Adolescent	1.25	.42
Relationship Violence		
Arguments	2.50	.72
Throwing	2.07	1.03
Hitting	1.34	.39
Sexual Self-Acceptance		
Meaning	3.74	.92
Control	4.23	.81
Esteem	3.99	.90
Anticipated Negative Partner Reaction, if refuse		
Oral Sex	1.42	.61
Touching	1.47	.62
Unprotected Sex	1.49	.74
Sexual Assertiveness for HIV Risk Communication, re		
STD/HIV status	4.41	.96
Partners	4.22	1.03
Injection drugs	4.37	1.07
Sexual Assertiveness for Refusal of Unwanted Sex, re		
Oral sex	3.94	1.04
Pressure	3.99	.94
Foreplay	3.75	1.03
Sexual Assertiveness for Condom Use, even if		
Unwanted	3.01	1.25
Insisting	3.75	1.19
Doesn't like	3.34	1.25
Unprotected Sex		
Vaginal[a]	32.37	54.84
Oral[b]	18.92	36.52
Anal[c]	00.57	02.22

TABLE 6.3   (continued)

Factor Indicator	Mean	Standard deviation
Perception of Risk		
How sure	02.55	0.87
Perceived risk	02.47	0.97
Prev. behavior	04.71	0.62
Partner Risk Factors		
#Life partners[d]	32.18	355.42
Partner status	01.43	1.15

[a]Median = 12; 80% reported ≥ 50; 20% reported 51–500.
[b]Median = 6; 80% reported ≥ 25; 20% reported 26–406.
[c]Median = 0; 85% reported 0; 15% report 1–27.
[d]Median = 9; 90% reported ≥ 30; 10% report 31–1000.

total number of measured indicators for the 12 latent constructs was 35. Analyses were conducted using structural equation modeling with maximum likelihood estimation within the EQS (Bentler, 1995) computer package.

Indices used to assess overall fit included the χ^2, which should be low relative to degrees of freedom; the CFI (Bentler, 1990) which ranges from 0–1 with values closer to 1 indicating good fit; and the AASR, which is a measure of deviation between the proposed relationships and the data, and where values close to 0 are preferred. Good overall fit for the proposed cross-sectional analysis was revealed, with χ^2 (494) = 814.3, CFI = .93, and AASR = .04. In addition to good overall fit, from 28% to 47% of the variance in HIV-risk-dependent constructs could be explained by the set of predictors (childhood sexual abuse, family-of-origin environment) and mediators (sexual and physical victimization in adult relationships; sexual self-acceptance; anticipation of a negative partner reaction; and sexual assertiveness regarding communication, condom use, and refusal). Individual Z-tests for the parameter estimates revealed that all factor loadings were significant at $p < .05$ or better. Beta weights of significant standardized regression paths and R^2 for each dependent construct are presented in Figure 6.1.

Based on this preliminary analysis, the influence of the independent constructs of childhood sexual abuse and family environment on the dependent constructs of HIV risk behaviors and attitudes appears to be primarily an indirect one, potentially mediated through one or more of the proposed mediating constructs. Only one significant direct path from these constructs to the dependent factors was revealed in this analysis.

TABLE 6.4 Factor loadings greater than .35 from PCA with oblique rotation for all indicators from structural equation model analyses (N=119)

Indicator	Factor 1	Factor 2	Factor 3	Factor 4	Factor 5	Factor 6	Factor 7	Factor 8	Factor 9	Factor 10
Childhood Sexual Abuse										
Exhibition	.843									
Touching	.842									
Penetration	.784									
Family-of-Origin Environment										
Understanding		.767								
Helpful		.869								
Happy		.870								
Adult Sexual Abuse										
Coercion	.443							.439		
Force	.697									
Adolescent	.625									
Relationship Violence										
Arguments		−.358				.473				
Throwing						.800				
Hitting						.800				
Sexual Self-Acceptance										
Meaning					.780					
Control					.825					
Esteem					.816					
Anticipated Negative Partner Reaction, if refuse										
Oral sex				.813						
Touching				.768						
Unprotected sex				.820						
Sexual Assertiveness for HIV Risk Communication, regarding										
STD/HIV status							.840			
Partners							.841			
Injection drugs							.816			

TABLE 6.4   (continued)

Indicator	Factor 1	Factor 2	Factor 3	Factor 4	Factor 5	Factor 6	Factor 7	Factor 8	Factor 9	Factor 10
Sexual Assertiveness for Refusal of Unwanted Sex, regarding										
Oral sex										.814
Pressure										.648
Foreplay			.493							.450
Sexual Assertiveness for Condom Use, even if										
Unwanted			.874							
Insisting			.774							
Doesn't like			.842							
Unprotected Sex										
Vaginal			−.354					.579		
Oral								.848		
Anal								.608		
Perception of Risk										
How sure									.833	
Perceived risk									−.776	
Prev. behavior									.473	
Partner Risk Factors										
#Life partners	.403									
Partner status						.754		.384		

Factor 1 = Childhood Sexual Abuse / Adult Sexual Abuse
Factor 2 = Family-of-Origin Environment
Factor 3 = Sexual Assertiveness for Condom Use
Factor 4 = Anticipated Negative Partner Reaction
Factor 5 = Sexual Self-Acceptance
Factor 6 = Adult Relationship Violence
Factor 7 = Sexual Assertiveness Regarding HIV Risk Communication
Factor 8 = Unprotected Sex / Partner Risk Factors
Factor 9 = Perception of HIV Risk
Factor 10 = Sexual Assertiveness for Refusal of Unwanted Sex

TABLE 6.5   Interfactor correlations from principle component analysis (N=119)

Factor	Factor 1	Factor 2	Factor 3	Factor 4	Factor 5	Factor 6	Factor 7	Factor 8	Factor 9	Factor 10
Factor 1	1.00									
Factor 2	-.08	1.00								
Factor 3	.13	-.20	1.00							
Factor 4	.05	-.23	-.07	1.00						
Factor 5	-.25	.09	.14	-.24	1.00					
Factor 6	.22	-.19	-.20	.15	-.24	1.00				
Factor 7	-.03	-.06	.22	-.19	.22	-.05	1.00			
Factor 8	.08	.09	-.10	-.20	-.05	.25	.03	1.00		
Factor 9	-.03	.09	.11	-.06	.09	-.09	.02	.01	1.00	
Factor 10	.08	.08	.09	-.30	.07	-.04	.21	.18	.09	1.00

Factor 1 = Childhood Sexual Abuse / Adult Sexual Abuse
Factor 2 = Family-of-Origin Environment
Factor 3 = Sexual Assertiveness for Condom Use
Factor 4 = Anticipated Negative Partner Reaction
Factor 5 = Sexual Self-Acceptance
Factor 6 = Adult Relationship Violence
Factor 7 = Sexual Assertiveness Regarding HIV Risk Communication
Factor 8 = Unprotected Sex / Partner Risk Factors
Factor 9 = Perception of HIV Risk
Factor 10 = Sexual Assertiveness for Refusal of Unwanted Sex

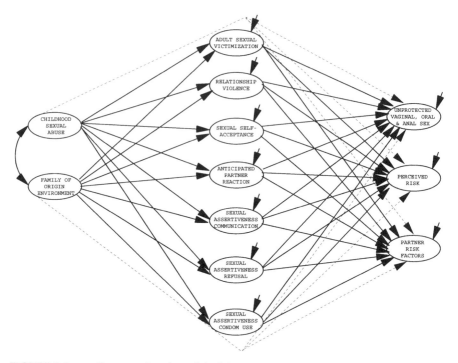

FIGURE 6.1.   Cross-sectional model of time 1 constructs.

Experiences of childhood sexual abuse are nevertheless significant direct predictors of three of the proposed mediating constructs, including reports of more adult sexual victimization and relationship violence, as well as anticipation of negative reactions from partners for HIV assertiveness. Similarly, reporting a positive family-of-origin environment is significantly predictive of three of the proposed mediating constructs, including more sexual self-acceptance, as well as less reported adult sexual victimization and relationship violence. Neither independent construct significantly predicts sexual assertiveness regarding condom use, refusal of unwanted sex, or HIV risk communication.

Significant predictors of the dependent construct of unprotected sexual behaviors are: greater experience of adult sexual victimization, more sexual self-acceptance, and less reported ability to insist on condom use. The only significant predictor in this analysis of the second dependent construct, reported perception of HIV risk, was more sexual self-acceptance.

Significant predictors of the final dependent construct, reported partner risk, are more adult sexual victimization, fewer expectations of negative reactions from partners to condom use, and less ability to refuse unwanted sex. A small, but significant, direct path between childhood sexual abuse and this latter dependent construct was also revealed.

In these preliminary analyses, relationship violence and sexual assertiveness regarding HIV risk communication were not predictive of HIV risk behaviors and attitudes.

The good overall fit and the high percentage of variance in the dependent constructs accounted for in this preliminary cross-sectional analysis suggest that an evaluation of the plausibility of longitudinal relationships is justified. Longitudinal analyses are evaluated in Chapter 7.

7

CHAPTER

Longitudinal Model Analyses

Longitudinal structural equation modeling was conducted to examine the plausibility of a three-stage model that links childhood sexual abuse and family-of-origin environment to subsequent HIV risk through the mediation of several factors occurring between these two constructs. In contrast to cross-sectional modeling, longitudinal analyses allow for tests of temporal relationships showing potential causal links. Ideally, data on all constructs are modeled at each time point, providing a test of a fully cross-lagged longitudinal model. In our model, there are over 30 measures, meaning that almost 100 measured variables would need to be modeled in a fully cross-lagged model over three time points. Even with our fairly large longitudinal sample size ($N = 519$), there would not be enough information in the data to estimate all of the necessary parameters for such a model. Thus, we chose to include constructs and their measures only for those time points in which they are hypothesized. Childhood trauma, as measured by childhood sexual abuse and family-of-origin environment, was hypothesized as an independent (retrospective) predictor to the three outcomes of unprotected sex, perceived risk for HIV, and partner risk for HIV. Seven mediating constructs were posited: adult sexual victimization, relationship violence, anticipated partner reaction, sexual self-acceptance, and sexual assertiveness for each of communication, refusal, and condom use. Results from our longitudinal data are expected to provide rich information regarding how constructs are related over time, which in turn can provide potential clues for how interventions may be developed to reduce risk.

In all of the longitudinal and subsequent analyses, data were used from the 519 participants from whom longitudinal data (collected at all three time points) had been received at the time of this writing. Estimates of the attrition rates reveal that approximately 83% of participants at Time 1 returned data at Time 2, and approximately 70% of this sample is available for longitudinal analyses.

As presented in Chapter 4, the average age of the 519 participants was 31 years at Time 1. Approximately 84% of these participants reported being White; 9% African American; 2% Hispanic American; 1.2% Native American; .5% Asian American; and 3.3% "other." Demographic information from this longitudinal sample is presented in Table 7.1.

☐ Longitudinal Structural Equation Model

In the longitudinal model, the two independent constructs, retrospective reports of family-of-origin environment and childhood sexual abuse, were assessed at Time 1; the seven proposed mediators were assessed at Time 2, 6 months later; and the three HIV risk behavior and attitude constructs were assessed at Time 3, 1 year after initial assessment.

Summary indices indicate that the proposed longitudinal relationships offer an excellent representation of the data: $\chi^2(494) = 892.2$, AASR = .036, and CFI = .95, with 35% of the variance in unprotected sex, 20% of the variance in perception of HIV risk, and 51% of the variance in reported partner risk factors explained by the other constructs. Z-tests show that all loadings are significant at $p < .05$ or better. Correlations among the constructs are presented in Table 7.2. Note the significant negative relationship ($r = -.31$) between the two independent constructs of childhood sexual abuse and positive family-of-origin environment. All correlations among the mediator disturbances (prediction errors) were significant, as were two of the three correlations among the outcome disturbances.

Figure 7.1 identifies significant relationships, as well as R^2 values for each dependent construct. Within the Time 1 assessment, childhood sexual abuse is negatively associated with positive perceptions of family-of-origin environment, as expected.

An examination of links between childhood sexual victimization reported at Time 1 and potential mediators measured at Time 2 reveals that earlier abuse is significantly associated with more adult sexual victimization and less assertiveness to refuse unwanted sex as an adult.

Further examination of the links between Time 1 and Time 2 reveals that positive perceptions of a family-of-origin environment is significantly

7197$$$$$7   CUT HERE   10-06-98 09:47:13

TABLE 7.1. Demographic information for longitudinal sample (N=519)

	Mean	Standard Deviation
Mean age (years)	M=31.47	SD=10.23
Mean # children	M=.87	SD=1.23
Mean # pregnancies	M=1.58	SD=1.80

	Frequency	Percentage
Ethnicity		
White	434	84%
African American	50	9%
Native American	5	1%
Asian American	2	1%
Hispanic American	11	2%
Other	17	3%
Education		
Less than 8th grade	4	1%
Grade 8–12	26	5%
High school graduate	36	7%
Some college	265	51%
College graduate	99	19%
Graduate coursework	89	17%
Occupation		
None	158	31%
Clerical/manual	72	14%
Service/sales	111	21%
Business/technical	43	8%
Professional	98	19%
Other	37	7%
Income		
Less than $10,000	227	44%
$10,000–$19,999	135	26%
$20,000–$34,999	124	24%
$35,000–$50,000	26	5%
Over $50,000	7	1%
Marital status		
Single, never married	313	60%
Married	60	11%
Separated or divorced	133	26%
Widowed	13	3%
Live with sex partner		
No	311	60%
Sometimes (at least several days a month)	82	16%
Yes, all the time	126	24%

TABLE 7.1.   (continued)

	Frequency	Percentage
Religion		
Catholic	240	46%
Protestant	88	17%
Jewish	25	5%
Muslim	2	< 1%
Eastern	7	1%
Other	88	17%
None	69	13%

associated with five mediators. Women who reported more positive family environments showed a pattern of less adult sexual victimization, fewer reports of relationship violence, more sexual self-acceptance, less anticipation of a negative reaction from a partner following refusing sexual requests, and more assertiveness to ask sexual partners about their HIV risk factors.

Six of the seven hypothesized mediators show significant associations with one or more of the early childhood factors of sexual abuse and family-of-origin environment. In this analysis, the only mediator in which there was no link from Time 1 to Time 2 was assertiveness regarding condom use. Additional analyses, presented shortly, further explore the importance of retaining this construct of condom use assertiveness in our predictive model of childhood sexual abuse and HIV risk.

Turning to the findings for each of the three HIV risk constructs measured at Time 3, we find that there were significant relationships with four of the mediators. Unprotected sex was linked with reporting in the previous 6 months: more adult sexual victimization, more sexual self-acceptance, more assertiveness to ask partners about their HIV risk factors, and less assertiveness regarding condom use. A small, though significant, direct path between childhood sexual abuse (Time 1) and unprotected sex (Time 3) suggested that more reports of childhood victimization may be associated with less unprotected sex as an adult. In order to interpret this unexpected finding, we returned to the data to examine the zero-order correlations between the three variables that make up the childhood sexual abuse construct and the three variables that comprise the unprotected sex construct. These correlations ranged from −.09 to .07, with an average correlation of −.01. We concluded that there is in fact little to no relationship between these constructs, and that the statistical significance of the path was an artifact of sample size.

Perception of HIV risk was the second HIV risk outcome assessed at Time 3. We find that greater perception of risk was significantly predicted

TABLE 7.2. Intercorrelations among factors in structural equation analysis for full model, all paths specified

Factors	CSA	FOE	ASA	RV	APNR	SSA	SA-CU	SA-R	SA-C
Time 1 correlations									
Childhood sexual abuse (CSA)	—								
Family-of-origin environment (FOE)	-.43***	—							
Time 2 correlations (Factor disturbance)									
Adult sexual abuse (ASA)			—						
Relationship violence (RV)			.272***						
Anticipated partner negative reaction (APNR)			.077***	-.085***	—				
Sexual self-acceptance (SSA)			-.092***	-.092**	-.166***	—			
Sexual assertiveness—communication (SA-C)			-.071***	-.074*	-.096***	.211***	—		
Sexual assertiveness—refusal (SA-R)			-.079***	-.083**	-.113***	.199***	.188***	—	
Sexual assertiveness—condom use (SA-CU)			-.072**	-.089*	-.092***	.114**	.199***	.292***	—

Factors	Unprotected sex	Perception of risk	Partner risk factors
Time 3 Correlations (Factor disturbance)			
Unprotected sex	—		
Perception of risk	-.105 n.s.	—	
Partner risk factors	.159*	-.119***	—

Significance level p< * .05; ** .01; *** .001

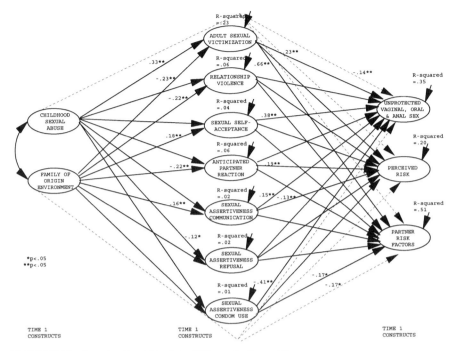

FIGURE 7.1 Longitudinal Model of Times 1, 2, and 3.

by a Time 2 reporting of less assertiveness to ask about a partner's HIV risk factors, and by being more likely to anticipate a negative reaction from a partner regarding HIV assertiveness.

Findings for the third HIV risk outcome reveal that having more reported partner risk factors was significantly predicted by reports in the previous 6 months of more adult sexual victimization and less assertiveness regarding condom use; a direct relationship showing a more positive family-of-origin environment retrospectively at Time 1 was inversely associated with later partner risk at Time 3.

Finally, from Figure 7.1, it is evident that all of the mediators except for sexual assertiveness for condom use have significant links with at least one of the hypothesized independent constructs of childhood sexual abuse and family-of-origin environment. Further, six of the seven hypothesized mediators (all but relationship violence) show significant associations with one or more of the three HIV risk outcomes. Only two small, though significant, direct links were found between Time 1 and Time 3 constructs: (a) a negative association between childhood sexual abuse and later unprotected sex; and (b) a negative relationship between positive family-of-origin environment and later partner risk.

☐ Interpretation and Discussion

These findings from longitudinal analyses highlight that the relationship between childhood sexual abuse, family environment, and adult HIV risk is largely mediated by several adult abuse and attitudinal constructs, suggesting several potential points of intervention to reduce adult HIV risk. Our hypothesized model identifies at least six key mediators: adult sexual abuse, relationship violence, anticipated partner negative reaction, sexual self-acceptance, sexual assertiveness for communication, and sexual assertiveness for refusal. Each of these can be described as concomitants of interpersonal powerlessness, emphasizing the central nature of this theme in understanding the link between childhood trauma and HIV risk.

Women who have experienced childhood sexual abuse are more apt to have negative perceptions of their family-of-origin, and in turn are more likely to have feelings of powerlessness within interpersonal interactions. Our data suggest that these feelings of powerlessness are being manifested in adulthood in relationship problems such as abuse and in less assertiveness, leading to behaviors within sexual relationships that could put a woman at greater risk for HIV. Specifically, women who were abused as children and who had negative perceptions of their family growing up were more likely to anticipate or actually experience adult sexual and/or physical abuse, and were less likely to feel sexually assertive enough to either request condom use or communicate with a partner about their sexual history. These experiences were, in turn, related to engaging in more unprotected sex, greater perceptions of HIV risk, and choosing partners who had greater risk for HIV.

Although our data were retrospective and thus cannot yield definitive evidence, the longitudinal nature of the data, along with high levels of explained variance, provide some evidence on the direction of prediction from childhood abuse to adult HIV risk. Indeed, more than 50% of the variance in partner risk factors and more than a third of the variance in unprotected sex could be largely explained by knowing that a women had experienced adult sexual abuse and by knowing that she was not sexually assertive about using condoms. Similarly, a fifth of the variance in perceived risk for HIV was largely explained by a woman having greater anticipation of a negative reaction from her partner and from feeling sexually unassertive about communicating with a partner about sexual experiences. These results suggest that women, particularly those who are sexually abused, could benefit from skills training to enhance feelings of empowerment and assertiveness within sexual relationships.

Two of the associations in our data were in the opposite direction of hypotheses, showing that more sexual self-acceptance and sexual assertiveness communication were associated with greater frequency of unprotected sex. One explanation for these findings is that women who feel positive about their sexuality and who feel confident and assertive about their ability to communicate with their partner may have less need to use protection when engaging in sex, particularly if they are involved in a long-term monogamous relationship. Thus, condom use may be less important in relationships in which there is little perceived risk for HIV transmission. Future research should examine this issue further by collecting data on the actual HIV risk status of women's sexual partners.

In summary, the longitudinal analyses suggest that our hypothesized mediational model of childhood trauma and HIV risk is plausible with these data. Reports of childhood sexual abuse and a negative family environment are associated with several mediating factors, most notably adult sexual victimization, which in turn showed significant links with one or more HIV risk factors. Although causation cannot be established with our data, results are suggestive that negative childhood experiences can have lasting effects on the behaviors and attitudes of adult women, with considerable evidence that previously abused women are at greater risk for HIV by higher incidence of unprotected sex and sex with partners who are suspected to be at high HIV risk.

In the next chapter, we examine our longitudinal model more closely to determine the importance of each of the mediators.

8

CHAPTER

Analysis of Model Mediators

Relationships between independent and dependent constructs are often mediated by other relevant constructs (see Baron & Kenny, 1986; Biddle & Marlin, 1987). These mediating constructs often provide information on the intervening mechanisms by which people move from one state (e.g., childhood sexual abuse and a poor family environment) to another (e.g., HIV-risky behavior). Although previous research has found a small link between childhood sexual abuse and subsequent HIV risk (e.g., Johnsen & Harlow, 1996; Zierler et al., 1991), other research suggests that explanations for these associations lie in the mediating mechanisms that explain the link between these two constructs. Only with a more complete understanding of the mediators involved in the relationship between sexual abuse and poor family environment and HIV-risky behavior can appropriate and effective interventions be developed.

In Chapter 7 we demonstrated that the set of seven mediators we hypothesized to help explain the relationship between the independent (sexual abuse and family environment) and dependent (HIV-risky behavior) constructs were significant in the longitudinal framework.

To be complete, using longitudinal structural modeling, the following questions are addressed in this chapter: are all of these mediators important to our model, or could some of them be eliminated without a great loss of information; and, which mediators are the most salient (that is, most predictive of HIV-risky behavior)? To assess the role of the mediators between both childhood sexual abuse and family environment and the outcome of HIV-Risk, a number of structural equation models were assessed and compared.

Sexual assertiveness to refuse unwanted sex and to insist on condom use were correlated, however. To avoid potential problems with collinearity in the mediational analyses, we chose to drop one of these. Thus, sexual assertiveness for refusal was not included in the remainder of the analyses for methodological reasons, though we recognize that it is an important theoretical concept in our model.

☐ Nested Analyses

First, a series of nested models were analyzed to assess the role of each mediator separately. In each of these models, the specific path of one of the mediators was set to zero, and the strength of the model from the remaining paths was evaluated. Then, each of these nested models was compared to a full model in which all hypothesized paths were included and none were set to zero. A χ^2 difference statistic was used to evaluate these nested analyses, which involved subtracting the χ^2 value as well as the corresponding degrees of freedom of the nested version from the same values in the full model version.

When the χ^2 difference statistic reveals that the nested analysis is significantly different from the full analysis, we can conclude that there is a significant decrement in fit when the paths that were set equal to zero are eliminated. This suggests that the mediators whose paths were excluded in the nested analysis are important to the model, and that retaining them would significantly improve overall fit (see Hoyle & Panter, 1995, for a discussion of this analysis). The following analyses were conducted to verify the importance of each set of relationships to our model of childhood sexual abuse and HIV risk.

Analysis 1, depicted in Figure 7.1, is the full longitudinal model tested in the previous chapter. In this analysis, there is a full set of paths from the two Time 1 constructs of childhood sexual abuse and family-of-origin environment to each of the Time 2 mediators, which in turn have a full set of paths to each of the three HIV risk outcomes assessed at Time 3. Also included is the set of direct paths from the Time 1 to Time 3 constructs (see dashed lines in Figure 7.1). This full model, labeled as Analysis 1 here, was already shown to provide a good representation of the data in Chapter 7. The current set of analyses more carefully examined specific aspects of the full model in order to verify the verisimilitude of the hypothesized mediational model.

Analysis 2, shown in Figure 8.1, sets direct paths from Time 1 to Time 3 constructs equal to zero. Thus, in Analysis 2, only mediated effects of childhood sexual abuse and family-of-origin environment are estimated.

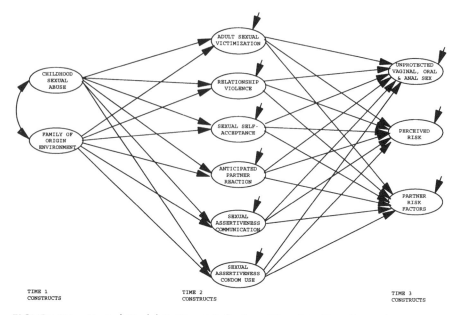

FIGURE 8.1. Nested Model 2: Direct Paths from Time 1 to Time 3 equal zero.

Comparing this to the fuller model of Analysis 1 reveals whether the specification of a direct relationship between the Time 1 constructs of childhood sexual abuse and family-of-origin environment improves overall fit. If the X^2 difference statistic between this nested analysis and the full analysis is significant, it suggests that the direct paths from childhood sexual abuse and family-of-origin environment to the three HIV risk constructs are important to include. If the X^2 difference statistic is not significant, a more parsimonious analysis would eliminate these direct paths and thus would suggest that the relationship between these Time 1 constructs and the risk constructs is strictly a mediated one.

Analysis 3, depicted in Figure 8.2, sets the paths from Time 1 to Time 2 constructs equal to zero. Thus, in Analysis 3, direct paths from all Time 1 and 2 constructs to the three Time 3 dependent constructs are estimated as in a multiple regression model, and the potential for any mediating roles is eliminated. Comparing this analysis to Analysis 1 reveals whether it is important to include indirect associations to HIV risk, through the mediation of our Time 2 constructs concerned with interpersonal power (lessness), or whether the relationships between the risk constructs and the Time 1 and 2 constructs are direct only.

Analysis 4, pictured in Figure 8.3 with paths from Time 2 to Time 3 constructs set equal to zero, tests whether the data can be explained with the mediating and dependent constructs predicted only by childhood

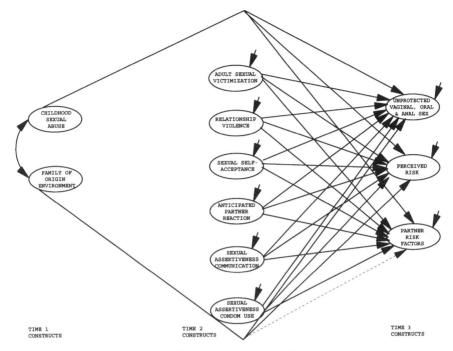

FIGURE 8.2.   Nested Model 3: Paths from Time 1 to Time 2 equal zero.

sexual abuse and family-of-origin environment, eliminating any predictive role for the Time 2 mediating constructs. Comparing this analysis to Analysis 1 reveals whether the proposed mediators have a significant role in the prediction of risk behaviors or if they only serve as dependent constructs predicted by the childhood sexual abuse and family-of-origin environment.

Analysis 5, shown in Figure 8.4, has paths from Time 1 to Time 2 and from Time 2 to Time 3 constructs set equal to zero. Thus, in Analysis 5, the proposed mediators are eliminated completely, with only the direct relationship between childhood sexual abuse/family-of-origin functioning and the three HIV risk constructs estimated. Comparing this to Analysis 1 provides a further test of the veracity of our proposed mediational model. If the elimination of all paths to and from the proposed mediators does not result in a significant X^2 difference statistic, then we can conclude that they have no role in the prediction of risk behaviors in this sample.

Conversely, if there is a significant difference between Analyses 5 and 1, we have then established that this set of mediators plays an important role in mediating the process between childhood sexual abuse and HIV risk.

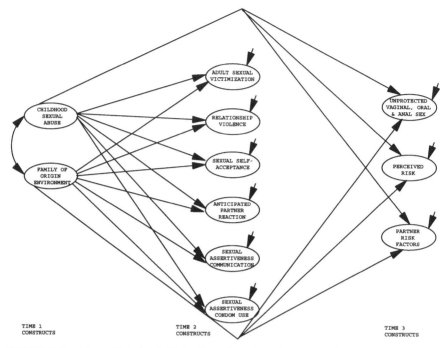

FIGURE 8.3. Nested Model 4: Paths from time 2 to time 3 equal zero.

Analysis 6, depicted in Figure 8.5, sets the paths from Time 1 constructs to Time 2 and 3 constructs equal to zero. Thus, in Analysis 6, the predictive roles of childhood sexual abuse and family-of-origin environment are eliminated, with the set of proposed mediators acting as the only independent predictors of the HIV risk constructs. Comparing this to Analysis 1 reveals whether childhood sexual abuse and family-of-origin environment have any role in the prediction of risk or whether the proposed mediators function as independent predictors of risk.

Summary statistics for Analyses 1–6, including X^2 difference statistics, are presented in Table 8.1. It can be seen that all X^2 difference statistics except the first were significant at $p < .001$. From these comparisons, it can be seen that the specification of all paths, direct as well as mediated, significantly improved overall fit. Only in the first nested comparison, the mediated analysis with direct paths from the Time 1 constructs to the dependent Time 3 HIV risk constructs set equal to zero, did the X^2 difference statistic approach nonsignificance, suggesting that these direct paths may not be essential to include. These findings offer more evidence that the link between both childhood sexual abuse and family environment and HIV risk is mediated by several factors, rather than having a direct association.

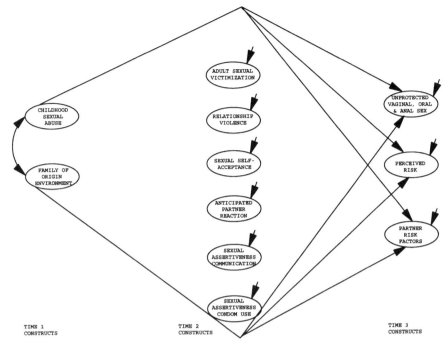

FIGURE 8.4.   Nested Model 5: Paths from Time 1 to Time 2 equal zero; paths from Time 2 to Time 3 Equal zero.

☐ Comparisons of Nested and Full Analyses

Next, the individual roles of the proposed mediators were examined within this set of longitudinal relationships. For each of the six mediating constructs, an analysis was evaluated in which all paths leading to and coming from the specified construct were set equal to zero. Six analyses (Analyses 7–12 in Table 8.2) were evaluated and compared to the full longitudinal model (Analysis 1 above). Both the X^2 difference statistic and the percentage of variance accounted for in each of the three dependent constructs were used to evaluate the proposed mediators. Summary statistics and R^2 for each construct are found in Table 8.2.

From this information, it can be seen that the elimination of each mediating construct produced a significant X^2 difference statistic, suggesting that including each construct significantly improves overall fit. In addition to improved overall fit, the percent of variance accounted for in the dependent constructs is also improved by the inclusion of all but one

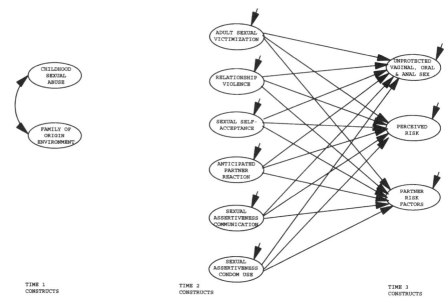

FIGURE 8.5. Nested Model 6: Paths from Time 1 to Times 2 and 3 equal zero.

(i.e., relationship violence) of the proposed mediators; in some analyses the improvement in R^2 is striking when the mediators are included.

The inclusion of adult sexual victimization as a mediator of the relationship between childhood sexual victimization and HIV risk behavior was particularly important to the proposed set of relationships. Without this mediator, the model lost 3% of the explained variance in unprotected sex; 1% of the explained variance in perception of HIV risk; and 16% of the explained variance in partner risk factors.

The exception is the mediating effect of the relationship violence construct; the R^2 in each dependent construct was the same in the full analysis as it was in the analysis from which the construct of relationship violence is eliminated. Overall fit was improved when this construct was included, due to the predictive relationship between positive family-of-origin environment and relationship violence. Because of the conceptual importance of this construct and because of its significant relationship with this independent construct, it was decided to retain it along with the five other mediating constructs in the final analysis. As previously noted, a seventh mediating variable, sexual assertiveness for refusal, is also retained in the final analysis.

Without the mediating effect of sexual self-acceptance, 8% of the explained variance in unprotected sex and 1% of the explained variance in partner risk were lost.

TABLE 8.1.   Summary statistics from longitudinal analysis and nested comparisons (without refusal sexual assertiveness)

Model*	AASR	CFI	X²(*df*)	X²(*df*) difference*	Significance level
Analysis 1	.037	.95	782.2(409)	—	—
Analysis 2	.039	.95	798.4(415)	16.2(6)	$p<.02$
Analysis 3	.063	.94	903.7(421)	121.5(12)	$p<.001$
Analysis 4	.053	.93	992.1(427)	209.9(18)	$p<.001$
Analysis 5	.080	.91	1115.8(439)	333.6(30)	$p<.001$
Analysis 6	.065	.94	922.3(427)	140.1(18)	$p<.001$

Analysis 1 = all paths specified.
Analysis 2 = direct paths from Time 1 to Time 3 constructs set equal to zero; all others estimated.
Analysis 3 = paths from Time 1 to Time 2 constructs set equal to zero; all others estimated.
Analysis 4 = paths from Time 2 to Time 3 constructs set equal to zero; all others estimated.
Analysis 5 = paths from Time 1 to Time 2 and from Time 2 to Time 3 constructs set equal to zero; all others estimated.
Analysis 6 = paths from Time 1 to Time 2 and 3 constructs set equal to zero; all others estimated.
*X² difference statistic is used to compare each nested model (Analyses 1–6) to Analysis 1; a significant X² difference suggests that deleting the indicated paths significantly reduces fit and consequently that the paths should be retained.

Without the mediating effect of anticipated partner reaction, the model lost 1% of the explained variance in unprotected sex; 2% of the explained variance in perception of HIV risk; and 1% of the explained variance in partner risk.

Without the mediating effect of sexual assertiveness regarding HIV risk communication, 1% of the explained variance in unprotected sex and 1% of the explained variance in perception of HIV risk were lost.

Without the mediating effect of sexual assertiveness regarding condom use, 19% of the explained variance in unprotected sex and 3% of the explained variance in partner risk factors were lost.

☐ Interpretation and Discussion

Results from structural equation analyses revealed that as a whole, the mediators are essential to explain the relationships between both childhood

TABLE 8.2. Summary statistics and analysis of the roles of mediating constructs

Model*	AASR	CFI	$X^2(df)$	$X^2(df)$ difference	Significant level	R^2 (Unprot. sex)	R^2 (Perc. of risk)	R^2 (Partner risk)
Analysis 1	.037	.95	782.2 (409)	—	—	.35	.20	.51
Analysis 7	.063	.91	1118.7(419)	336.4(10)	$P<.001$	.32	.19	.35
Analysis 8	.055	.93	994.9(419)	212.7(10)	$P<.001$	.35	.20	.51
Analysis 9	.058	.93	959.0(419)	176.8(10)	$P<.001$	.34	.18	.50
Analysis 10	.059	.93	987.1(419)	204.8(10)	$P<.001$	.27	.20	.50
Analysis 11	.053	.94	903.8(419)	121.5(10)	$P<.001$	.34	.19	.51
Analysis 12	.048	.94	900.1(419)	117.8(10)	$P<.001$	.16	.20	.48

Analysis 1=all paths specified; Analysis 7=paths to and from adult sexual victimization set =0; Analysis 8=paths to and from relationship violence set =0; Analysis 9=paths to and from anticipated negative partner reaction set =0; Analysis 10=paths to and from sexual self-acceptance set =0; Analysis 11=paths to and from sexual assertiveness for HIV risk communication set =0; and Analysis 12=paths to and from sexual assertiveness for condom use set =0.

sexual abuse and family environment and the three HIV risk outcomes. Without the set of six mediators, the model is a poor representation of the data. Further, the analysis that included only mediational paths (see Analysis 2 in Table 8.1), without any direct paths from Time 1 to Time 3 constructs, was virtually indistinguishable from the full model (see Analysis 1 in Table 8.1) that included all paths. Thus, our analyses offer evidence that the mediators are important for understanding the link between childhood sexual abuse and HIV risk in women.

Analyses of specific aspects of the mediator relationships (see Analyses 7–12 in Table 8.2) revealed that some mediators worked better than others. Omitting sexual assertiveness for condom use and adult sexual victimization as mediators resulted in dramatic drops in explained variance, particularly for unprotected sex and partner risk factors, respectively. These two mediators appear to play central mediating roles, highlighting once again the theme of powerlessness in the lives of women who experience childhood sexual abuse, leaving them more vulnerable for adult abuse, little assertiveness to insist on condom use, and hence greater frequency of unprotected sex as adults.

Three other factors, less central than condom assertiveness and adult sexual victimization, were still important mediators: sexual self-acceptance, anticipated negative reaction, and sexual assertiveness for HIV risk communication. These mediators help explain additional unique variance in the three outcomes, particularly for unprotected sex and perception of risk. This suggests that women who had childhoods marked by sexual abuse or negative family environments are less apt to accept their sexuality or less able to be assertive about discussing sexual histories. They are also more apt to anticipate negative reactions from their partners, in response to sexual requests. As discussed briefly in Chapter 7 and revisited in our conclusions, these mediators each speak to a woman's powerlessness around sexual relationships which may translate into greater actual and perceived risk for HIV transmission.

Relationship violence was the only Time 2 factor that did not operate as a mediator. When paths to and from this factor were removed from the model (see Analysis 8 in Table 8.2), the proportions of explained variance for each of the three HIV risk outcomes remained unchanged. Still, greater relationship violence seemed to occur in families of women who had negative family environments growing up, suggesting that this factor is important conceptually in the set of factors concerned with interpersonal powerlessness, and thus was retained in our model.

The longitudinal model of childhood trauma and HIV risk, along with the six mediators, was next evaluated in the two different subsamples which comprise the full sample. This is described in Chapter 9.

Cross-Sample Comparisons

☐ Two Subsamples: Continuing Education and Community Women

Our sample of 519 women was obtained from two major recruitment efforts within the state. The first subsample, the "continuing education sample," was obtained by recruiting participants from the urban campus of a local university-based CE program. Although these women did not live on campus, most did not live in the urban area immediately surrounding the college. Many worked or had small children, and took courses part-time. They were older and more likely to have been in more and in longer-term relationships than typical college students.

This sample nevertheless may be subject to many of the often-noted limitations of college student samples, namely, that participants are likely to be relatively high functioning as compared to the general population. Furthermore, the act of returning to school is for many an empowering experience, and it may serve in itself as an intervention with respect to one's sense of powerlessness.

Other participants, whom we have labeled the "community sample," were recruited from direct contacts, primarily in the urban community: from literacy programs, from an ongoing study of individuals at high risk of exposure to HIV, from HIV testing facilities, and from advertisements in newspapers primarily serving a minority population.

There were 217 women in the continuing education sample and 302 women in the community sample. Demographic information from the two samples is presented in Table 9.1. χ^2 analyses revealed that there were significantly more minority women in the community sample than in the continuing education sample and that women in the continuing education sample were more likely to have education beyond high school than women in the community sample. Women in the community sample were significantly older than women in the continuing education sample and reported having more children. No significant differences were revealed between samples in the distributions for type of employment or income; similarly, no differences were revealed between the groups in marital status or in whether they currently had or were living with a sex partner.

Mean Differences

Although these samples are not probability ones from which inferences to their respective populations may be drawn, differences between the samples on the entire set of indicators used in these analyses were evaluated using MANOVA with follow-up ANOVAs. The two groups differed significantly on the best linear combination of this set of indicators, with Wilks's $\Lambda = .844$; $F(32,486) = 2.75$, $p < .0001$. Follow-up analyses indicated that with sample as a grouping variable, the groups differed significantly on a number of the variables in question. Because of the multiple analyses being conducted, a significance level of $p < .01$ or better was chosen to evaluate significant group differences in these follow-up analyses.

Women in the continuing education sample reported significantly more certainty that their sexual partners had not exposed them to HIV, less perception of risk of exposure to HIV, fewer sexual partners, fewer HIV risk factors among their sexual partners, more assertiveness regarding condom use, less sexual coercion in adult relationships, less relationship violence (threats or actual violence), more positive sexual self-acceptance, less childhood sexual victimization (exhibitionism and touching), and finally, more positive family-of-origin environment than women in the community sample. No significant differences were noted in the other variables used in the analyses.

Cross-Sample Structural Equation Modeling Analyses

Multiple sample comparisons of the longitudinal model described in Chapter 7 were performed using the EQS computer package. Multiple

TABLE 9.1. Demographic information and comparison of continuing education (*N*=217) and community (*N*=302) subsamples

	Continuing education		Community sample
Mean age (years)	30.28 (*SD*=10.77)	*	32.33 (*SD*=9.87)
Mean # children	.69 (*SD*=1.20)	**	1.00 (*SD*=1.24)
Mean # pregnancies	1.26 (*SD*=1.61)	***	1.80 (*SD*= 1.89)
Ethnicity		↑	
White	201		237
African American	6		40
Native American	3		3
Asian American	1		1
Hispanic American	0		10
Other	6		11
Education		↑↑	
Less than 8th grade	0		3
Grade 8–12	0		26
High school graduate	0		38
Some college	132		133
College graduate	49		49
Graduate coursework	36		53
Occupation		N.S.	
None	58		99
Clerical/manual	37		36
Service/sales	44		67
Business/technical	21		22
Professional	38		62
Other	19		16
Income		N.S.	
Less than $10,000	103		128
$10,000–$19,999	50		86
$20,000–$34,999	53		69
$35,000–$50,000	8		15
Over $50,000	3		4
Marital status		N.S.	
Single, never married	138		164
Married	25		38
Separated or divorced	52		89
Widowed	2		11
Live with sex partner		N.S.	
No	129		174
Sometimes (at least several days a month)	39		40
Yes, all the time	49		88

TABLE 9.1.   (continued)

	Continuing education	Community sample
Religion	↑	
Catholic	110	135
Protestant	44	48
Jewish	13	11
Muslim	0	2
Eastern	4	4
Other	20	63
None	26	39

*ANOVA significantly different at $p<.05$.
**ANOVA significantly different at $p<.01$.
***ANOVA significantly different at $p<.001$.
↑ X^2 test significantly different at $p<.05$.
↑↑ X^2 test significantly different at $p<.001$.

group comparisons address the question: Does a particular set of relationships appear plausible in two different subsamples? The imposition of a series of ever more restrictive constraints enables the researcher to assess in turn whether factor patterns, patterns of correlations among independent and dependent factors, and regressions weights between factors are similar across groups. If the set of relationships appears plausible in both groups with these restrictions imposed, then there is strong evidence that these patterns are, in fact, comparable across groups.

Analysis 1 for these multiple samples is the least restrictive, simultaneously assessing overall fit in both groups without any equality constraints imposed across samples. This is labeled as a "congeneric analysis." Overall fit was good, suggesting that with this least restrictive analysis, the relationship among the latent factors is similar across the two groups: $\chi^2(818) = 1212.2$ and CFI = .95. The AASR for the continuing education sample was .045; for the community sample, AASR = .039. Because overall fit was good within this least restrictive analysis, a series of equality restrictions was imposed to test the limits of the cross-group similarities. Summary statistics for this and subsequent analyses, including multiple sample comparisons, may be found in Table 9.2.

Analysis 2, the first multiple sample analysis with cross-group equality constraints imposed, had factor loadings that were constrained to be equal across both samples. This set of constraints is conceptually an important one because it addresses whether the measurement structure linking the variables to their respective constructs is similar across the two groups. Once again, overall fit was good, with $\chi^2(839) = 1244.5$ and CFI = .95,

TABLE 9.2.   Cross-group comparisons with constraints imposed; Sample 1= continuing education (N=217); Sample 2= community sample (N=302)

Model	AASR1 (N=213)	AASR2 (N=297)	CFI	$X^2(df)$	$X^2(df)$ difference	Significance level
Analysis 1	.045	.040	.95	1212.2 (818)	—	—
Analysis 2	.048	.043	.95	1244.5 (839)	32.3 (21)	N.S.
Analysis 3	.043	.051	.92	1429.3 (850)	217.1 (32)	$p<.001$
Analysis 4	.055	.047	.94	1270.8 (845)	58.6 (27)	$p<.001$
Analysis 5	.054	.045	.95	1258.9 (854)	46.7 (36)	N.S.
Analysis 6	.068	.054	.94	1358.4 (902)	146.2 (84)	$p<.001$
Analysis 7	.058	.049	.95	1297.6 (891)	85.5 (73)	N.S.

Analysis 1= Congeneric model with no parameter constraints across samples.
Analysis 2= Loading constrained to be equal across samples.
Analysis 3= Errors constrained to be equal across samples.
Analysis 4= Variances and covariances constrained to be equal across samples.
Analysis 5= Regression paths constrained to be equal across samples.
Analysis 6= Loadings, variances, and covariances, and regression paths constrained to be equal across samples.
Analysis 7= Final model with implausible constraints released.

further suggesting that the proposed set of relationships holds across the two different subsamples. The AASR for the continuing education sample was .048; for the community sample, AASR = .043.

Comparing this analysis to the congeneric one using a χ^2 difference statistic, it can be seen that the imposition of this set of constraints yields a nonsignificant difference in fit, suggesting that as a set, these constraints are plausible and furthermore, that the parsimonious set of parameter estimates (i.e., one set of factor loadings for the two groups) in these analyses is preferred over the fuller congeneric model, tested initially, that allowed two sets of loadings.

Further support for this conclusion comes from the statistical test of the plausibility of the individual constraints, the Lagrange Multiplier test (Chou & Bentler, 1990); if the release of a particular constraint would reduce the overall χ^2 summary statistic by a significant amount (in other words, if the release of the constraint would improve model fit by a significant amount), then that constraint is considered an implausible one. In this analysis, the Lagrange Multiplier test reached significance at $p < .05$ for only one of the 21 imposed equality constraints. By chance, with this level of significance, we would expect one significant result even when no differences in fact exist. It was concluded that it is reasonable to constrain the factor loadings to be equal across the two groups.

Although considered by some statisticians to be overly restrictive (e.g., Byrne, 1994), for completeness, it was decided in this project to constrain error variances across samples in order to determine if they differed in the two groups. This was labeled as Analysis 3, with overall fit that was acceptable: $\chi^2(850) = 1429.3$ and CFI = .92. AASR within the continuing education sample was .043; within the community sample, AASR = .051. The highly significant χ^2 difference between this and the congeneric analysis suggests, however, that the imposition of these constraints, as a set, is not plausible in these samples. The Lagrange Multiplier test identified 8 of the 32 constraints imposed as being implausible at $p < .001$. It was therefore concluded that, as a set, the error variances could not be considered identical across groups.

In Analysis 4 of the multiple sample analysis, factor variances and covariances and unexplained variances in dependent constructs and covariances among these were constrained to be equal across the two samples. Also important conceptually, the imposition of this set of equality restrictions addresses whether variances and patterns of relationships among the factors and their disturbances are similar across the two groups. Overall fit with variances and covariances constrained was good, with $\chi^2(845) = 1270.8$ and CFI = .94. The AASR within the continuing education sample was .054; within the community sample, AASR = .047. Once again, however, the significant χ^2 difference between this and the congeneric analysis suggests that, as a set, the imposition of these constraints across samples is implausible.

The Lagrange Multiplier test identified four constraints that, if released, would significantly improve fit at $p < .01$. These were the variance of the disturbance factor, or amount of unexplained variance, for the relationship violence construct; the disturbance factor for sexual assertiveness regarding HIV risk communication; the disturbance factor for sexual self-acceptance; and the covariance between adult sexual abuse and relationship violence. The release of these equality constraints in a final multiple sample analysis will yield independent estimates of these parameters which may then be compared across groups.

In Analysis 5 of the multiple sample analysis, the regression weights between factors were constrained to be equal across both samples. This set of constraints is important conceptually because it allows a comparison of the patterns of relationships among the factors across time and evaluates whether these are statistically similar in the two different samples.

Overall fit was good, with $\chi^2(854)$ = 1258.9 and CFI = .95. The AASR for the continuing education sample was .054; within the community sample, AASR = .045.

Although the χ^2 difference statistic suggested that this and the congeneric analyses were not significantly different at p < .05, the Lagrange Multiplier test identified five constrained regression paths that, if released, would significantly improve fit. These were the direct paths from childhood sexual abuse to both sexual assertiveness constructs, the direct path from family-of-origin functioning to the construct of perceived risk, and the mediated paths toward the partner risk construct from anticipated partner reaction and sexual assertiveness regarding HIV risk communication. By releasing these constraints in a final analysis, independent estimates of these parameters could be compared across samples.

In Analysis 6 with very strict constraints imposed, the most restrictive multiple sample analysis was tested; it consisted of a single analysis with all factor loadings, all factor variances and covariances and variances and covariances of disturbances, and all regression weights constrained to be equal across the two samples. Indices of overall fit suggest that this most restrictive analysis is a reasonable description of the data, with $\chi^2(902)$ = 1358.4 and CFI = .94. The somewhat larger average absolute standardized residuals observed in this analysis (AASR = .068 in the continuing education sample; AASR = .054 in the community sample) suggest, however, that this restrictive pattern is straining to fit these data. The highly significant χ^2 difference between this restrictive analysis and the congeneric one offers further evidence that the imposition of the entire set of constraints does not produce a plausible representation of the data in these two samples.

For this reason, Analysis 7, a final multiple sample analysis, was analyzed with the four implausible equality constraints from the set of variances and covariances among the factors and the five implausible equality constraints from the set of factor regressions released. Overall fit in this analysis was good, with $\chi^2(891)$ = 1297.6 and CFI = .95. The AASR for the continuing education sample was .058; within the community sample, AASR = .049. Explained variance in each dependent construct within each sample was high, with 35% of the variance in unprotected sex explained in each sample; 19% of the variance in perception of risk in the continuing education sample and 23% in the community sample was explained. For reported partner risk factors, 84% of the variance was accounted for in the continuing education sample, while 39% was accounted for within the community sample. The χ^2 difference statistic revealed a nonsignificant difference between this and the congeneric analysis, suggesting that the fit of this more restrictive and parsimonious Analysis 7 cannot be distinguished from that of the fuller congeneric

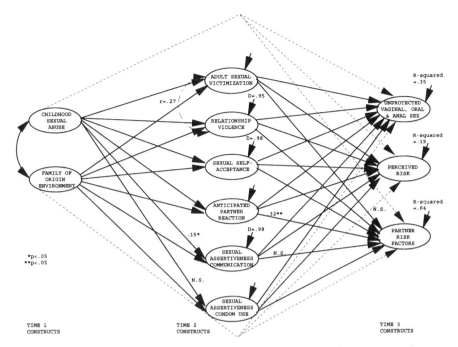

FIGURE 9.1.   Independent parameter estimates in continuing education sample.

analysis, in which there were no constraints across the two samples. Thus a model that imposes equal factor loadings across groups and nearly all of the variances, covariances, and regressions constrained to be equal across groups offers a reasonable representation of the data.

The independent parameter estimates resulting from the release of these constraints reveal the nature of the differences between the two samples. These independent parameter estimates are presented in Figures 9.1 and 9.2.

Releasing the specified variances and covariances reveals that this analysis accounted for slightly more variance within the continuing education sample as compared to the community sample for two dependent factors: relationship violence and assertiveness regarding HIV risk communication. No difference between the groups in the percentage of variance in sexual self-acceptance was revealed in this analysis. A slightly greater correlation between adult sexual victimization and relationship violence was also revealed within the community sample as compared to that within the continuing education sample.

Releasing the specified regressions between factors reveals a slightly different pattern of relationships within the two samples. The regression path from childhood sexual abuse to assertiveness regarding HIV risk

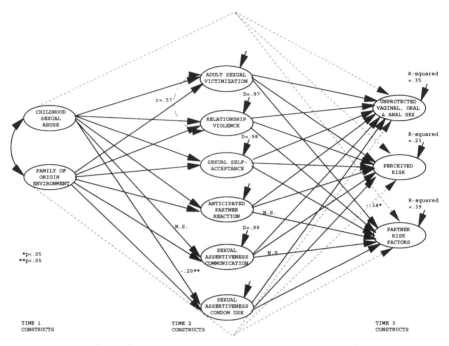

FIGURE 9.2.   Independent parameter estimates in community sample.

communication is a significant positive one in the continuing education sample, and nonsignificant in the community sample. In the continuing education sample, then, experiences of childhood sexual abuse are significantly predictive of assertiveness regarding HIV risk communication. In contrast, the regression path from childhood sexual abuse to assertiveness regarding condom use is a significant negative one in the community sample and nonsignificant in the continuing education sample. In other words, childhood sexual abuse is significantly predictive of less assertiveness regarding condom use in the community sample, but statistically unrelated in the continuing education sample. The direct path between family-of-origin environment and perception of HIV risk is a significant negative one within the community sample and nonsignificant within the continuing education sample. In the community sample, then, reporting a more positive family-of-origin environment is significantly predictive of less perception of risk. The regression path from anticipation of a negative partner reaction to HIV prevention is a significant positive predictor of reported partner risk in the continuing education sample, but is nonsignificant in the community sample. In other words, among women in the continuing education sample, anticipating a negative reaction from a partner to HIV prevention is predictive of engaging in sex with riskier partners. The regression path from assertiveness regarding HIV risk communication to reported partner risk was nonsignificant in both samples.

☐ Interpretation and Discussion

In this chapter, our longitudinal model of childhood trauma and HIV risk was analyzed and compared in two distinct subgroups representing women recruited from an Adult Continuing Education facility and women recruited from the wider community. Initial descriptive comparisons showed that compared to the women from continuing education, women from the wider community tended to be slightly older, have more children, have more pregnancies, include more minorities, have less education, and have slightly different religious backgrounds. Thus, the makeup of the community women from our sample appears more similar to that of a heterogeneous urban population than of a more homogeneous, less urban New England population.

Comparisons of our model across the two subsamples revealed strong consistency in the basic (congeneric) model structure and factor loadings. Using the same set of factors and paths with identical factor loadings provided a reasonable fit to the data in both groups. Other analyses demonstrated that although some differences were present, using a single set of regression weights across the two samples was not statistically different from a separate set for each sample. Thus our results suggest that model findings are largely similar across the two diverse groups, despite differences in demographics. This indicates that though frequencies and means for descriptive characteristics may differ between these adult college and wider community samples, the pattern of relationships in our proposed model appears to be fairly robust and consistent across the two groups. Though our findings cannot necessarily generalize to more diverse populations from differing geographical areas, they do suggest that correlational results from college samples may also hold within the larger community. This is encouraging to consider, since much research is conducted within a college population.

Still, it is important to point out that significant model differences did occur between the two groups. For women from the community, there are stronger links between sexual abuse, relationship violence, and lowered sexual assertiveness for condoms than for women from continuing education. This may indicate a more protected and more empowering environment in the continuing education sample as opposed to that found in the wider community.

The protective role of a positive family environment, however, was stronger in the community sample. Community women were less apt to perceive themselves at risk for HIV when also reporting a positive family environment while growing up. This finding suggests that positive family interactions should be encouraged in an intervention aimed at reducing HIV risk.

The next chapter examines different ways of grouping women, according to their psychosocial functioning. By investigating possible differences among women, based on different categorization schemes, whether from differing levels of abuse, living environments, or psychological attitudes, we can begin to understand what factors appear to link childhood trauma to subsequent HIV risk in women.

Psychosocial Functioning Clusters

This chapter investigates factors that might be associated with better resilience among women. Since our data includes several variables tapping psychosocial functioning, we investigated whether women could be statistically clustered into different psychosocial functioning groups, and whether these groups differed on our set of abuse, attitude, HIV risk, and demographic variables. Ultimately, an understanding of these factors could be applied to interventions to help improve a sense of well-being among women, particularly those who have experienced childhood trauma.

The construct of psychosocial functioning has been defined in earlier chapters. This construct is intended to capture essential elements of well-being: purpose and meaning in life, self-esteem, and hopefulness/hopelessness about one's life. Harlow (1990) and her colleagues have developed and refined a set of measures addressing psychosocial functioning regarding purpose and meaning in life. A sense of meaninglessness and a lack of purpose in life have been found to be related to drug use and suicidal behavior (Harlow, Newcomb, & Bentler, 1986) and to poorer physical and psychological well-being (e.g., Reker, Peacock, & Wong, 1987). In a community sample of 739 young adults, Harlow and Newcomb (1990) found that purpose and meaning in life were highly positively related to good peer, family, and intimate relationships, perceived opportunity, and work and health satisfaction, and negatively related to powerlessness.

Stress and coping in high-risk African American women were assessed by Nyamathi, Wayment, and Dunkel-Schetter (1993). Their results indicated that self-esteem and threat appraisal were the strongest predictors of emotional distress, and that emotional distress was highly associated with HIV risk behavior. Self-esteem was associated with risk behavior through the mediator of active coping, which was negatively associated with risk behavior.

Even among children, abuse survivors have been observed to have lower self-reported self-esteem and more anxiety and depression (e.g., Gomes-Schwartz, Horowitz, & Cardarelli, 1990). However, up to 50% of abused children show no serious emotional symptoms (e.g., Caffaro-Rouget, Lang, & Van Santen, 1989). In understanding differential responding, it is helpful to recall Finkelhor's (1988) four traumagenic outcomes discussed in Chapter 2: traumatic sexualization, powerlessness, stigmatization, and betrayal. Any of these could negatively impact the adult's psychosocial functioning.

Consistent with our longitudinal focus, we examined data separated by a 1-year time frame rather than keeping all data in a single cross-section of time. To do this, we investigated whether women could be clustered, or classified, into statistically cohesive types based on their levels of psychosocial functioning at Time 1, and then evaluated whether these psychosocial types were associated with predictable patterns of subsequent experiences, attitudes, behaviors, and characteristics assessed at Time 3. It was expected that several clusters of women would be identified that varied as to their level and type of psychosocial functioning. Specifically, women with low psychosocial functioning—women who experienced distress, as well as a poor sense of esteem, competence and power in their general and sexual interactions—were expected to have a higher incidence of poor family-of-origin environment, adult sexual victimization, relationship violence, unprotected sex, anticipated negative reactions from partners, perceived risk of HIV, and partner risk; as well as less sexual assertiveness, sexual self-acceptance, and socioeconomic resources.

To investigate this, several sets of analyses were conducted. First, the larger sample of women was separated into two random subsamples that were stratified by type of abuse. That is, each subsample would have approximately the same number of women who had never been abused, experienced unwanted "exhibition," experienced unwanted "touching," or experienced unwanted "penetration." The purpose of having two subsets was to provide both calibration and validation samples for subsequent factor and cluster analyses, providing an opportunity to explore patterns in one dataset, and then validate findings in the second subsample. This allowed for greater reliability and validity of our findings. Second, a set of psychosocial scales was factor analyzed in the first subsample, and verified in the second subsample, to determine whether several composites could be identified that could be used to separate women into meaningfully distinct psychosocial clusters. Third, data from each of the two subsamples were cluster analyzed using the psychosocial composites determined from preliminary factor analyses. Several cluster solutions were examined, including three-, four-, and five-cluster groupings. Cluster solutions were evaluated for reliability across the two subsamples, and the most reliable solution was retained. Fourth, a series of MANOVAs was conducted, using the resulting clusters as the levels of the independent variable, psychosocial cluster. Dependent variables were the sets of variables in each of 11 major construct areas of: (1) childhood sexual abuse, (2) family environment, (3) adult sexual victimization, (4) relationship violence, (5) anticipated negative reaction, (6) sexual self-acceptance, (7) sexual assertiveness (for communication, refusal, and condom use), (8) unprotected sex, (9) perceived HIV risk, (10) partner risk, and (11) demographics. The clusters of women were expected to differ in meaningful ways on the set of 11 constructs. Compared to women with higher functioning, women with poorer psychosocial functioning were expected to: (1) have had greater childhood sexual abuse; (2) have had poorer perceptions of their family environment; have greater (3) adult sexual victimization, and (4) relationship violence; (5) have greater anticipated negative reactions from partners in response to sexual requests; (6) have less sexual self-acceptance; (7) have less sexual assertiveness (for communication, refusal, and condom use); have more (8) unprotected sex, (9) perceived HIV risk; and (10) partner risk, and (11) have fewer socioeconomic resources.

Finally, results are discussed in terms of the initial research question of identifying patterns of behavior, attitudes, and experiences that were a part of these women's lives. The discussion includes a presentation of four hypothetical case studies, one for each of the four clusters of women. The case study examples could be viewed as clinical composites and are an attempt to epitomize the findings from our cluster analyses with characteristics and experiences ascribed to each of the four hypothetical women. The intent is to take some potentially abstract analyses and make the findings more salient and understandable. In the concluding paragraphs, we suggest ways in which the findings could inform future interventions aimed at improving the psychosocial quality of life for women who have been sexually abused.

☐ Stratified Random Subsamples

Data from the full set of 519 women were stratified into four patterns of childhood sexual abuse with frequencies given in parentheses: ''no abuse" ($N = 212$), "unwanted exhibition abuse only" ($N = 54$), "unwanted touching and possibly also exhibition" ($N = 156$), and "unwanted penetration with possible exhibition and touching" ($N = 97$). Each of these four stratified subsets was then randomly split into two groups of approximately equal sizes. Finally, by combining the random subsets from each of the four categories of abuse, two subsamples of 258 and 261 women, respectively, were formed for use in subsequent analyses.

☐ Preliminary Factor Analyses

Psychosocial items from several scales were identified for use in preliminary factor analyses: the four items from the Brief Esteem Scale (Harlow et al., 1993); the six items from each of the Subjective Competence and Distress subscales of the Demoralization Scale (Harlow, 1990); the five items from the General Powerlessness Scale (Newcomb & Harlow, 1986); and these same 17 items from the latter 3 scales that were specific to sexual attitudes and behavior (i.e., sexual subjective competence; sexual distress; sexual powerlessness). These 38 items were analyzed on the first subsample with a principal components (PCA) extraction procedure, followed by oblique Promax rotations using the SAS PROC FACTOR subroutine (SAS, 1989). Based on the five eigenvalues greater than 1, the scree plot, and theoretical considerations, results showed that the five expected factors were present, explaining 58% of the variance in the 38 items. The factors largely fell into the five readily interpretable sets of: I. self-esteem, II. subjective competence; III. distress, IV. powerlessness, and V. psychosexual functioning.

To maintain parsimony and consistency with the four-item Self-Esteem Scale, it was decided to retain the four best items from Factors II through IV and to retain the corresponding 12 items on the Psychosexual Functioning Scale (Factor V). Table 10.1 shows the patterns of loadings and factor correlations. Factor I had high loadings on the four Self-Esteem Scale items. On Factor II, items 3, 5, 7, and 9 from the Demoralization Scale were retained to assess subjective competence. For Factor III, Demoralization Scale items 4, 6, 8, and 12 were retained to measure distress. Factor IV included items 2–4 from the Powerlessness Scale, as well as item 11 from the Demoralization Scale due to similarity in content and factor loadings with the other items on this factor. Factor V assessed Psychosexual functioning with items 3–9 and 11–12 from the Sexual Demoralization Scale, and items 2–4 from the Sexual Powerlessness Scale.

The retained subset of 28 items was reanalyzed with PCA to verify their structure in the second subsample. This resulted, as expected, in five

TABLE 10.1.   Factor loadings and intercorrelations for 38 psychosocial items on 5 factors

Items	Factor I Self Esteem	Factor II Subjective Competence	Factor III Distress	Factor IV Powerlessness	Factor V Psychosexual Functioning
I like me as a person.	.74	—	—	—	—
I'd like to change...	−.86	—	—	—	—
I like the way I am.	.83	—	—	—	—
I wish I was different...	−.83	—	—	—	—
I know what to do..	—	.59	—	—	—
I feel confused about life.	—	−.38	.40	—	—
I can cope ...	—	.85	—	—	—
My life is too complex.	—	—	.78	—	—
I can get things done...	—	.64	—	—	—
The world is threatening...	—	—	.44	—	—
I can make things better.	—	.65	—	—	—
I just get by...	—	—	.59	—	—
I can fix a problem.	—	.72	—	—	—
I let myself down.	—	—	—	—	—
I make my own decisions.	—	—	—	−.36	—
I feel there's no way out.	—	—	.57	—	—
I am not in control ...	—	—	.44	.32	—
I succeed because of me...	—	—	—	−.54	—
Others run my life.	—	—	.47	.34	—
I can change my life.	—	—	−.39	−.63	—
Things just happen to me.	—	—	.71	—	—
I know what to do ... sex.	—	—	—	—	.68
I feel confused about sex.	—	—	—	—	−.77
I can cope with ... sex.	—	—	—	—	.70
My sex life is too complex.	—	—	—	—	−.72
I can manage my sex life.	—	—	—	—	.60
...sex is threatening ...	—	—	—	—	−.51
I can make sex ... better.	—	.35	—	—	.62
I just get by with ...sex.	—	—	—	—	−.73
I can fix a sexual problem.	—	.32	—	—	.68
I let myself down in sex.	—	—	—	—	−.69

TABLE 10.1.   (continued)

	Psychosocial functioning				
Items	Factor I Self Esteem	Factor II Subjective Competence	Factor III Distress	Factor IV Powerlessness	Factor V Psychosexual Functioning
I make decisions ...sex.	—	—	—	−.34	**.65**
...no way out of sex ...	—	—	—	—	**−.77**
... not in control of sex ...	—	—	—	—	.60
I have a say in my sex life.	—	—	—	−.45	**−.66**
Others run my sex life.	—	—	—	.33	**.73**
I can change my sex life.	—	—	—	−.40	**−.60**
Things happen in my sex life.	—	—	—	—	.63

Factor intercorrelations	I	II	III	IV	V
Factor I	1.00				
Factor II	.44	1.00			
Factor III	−.49	−.42	1.00		
Factor IV	−.19	−.12	.01	1.00	
Factor V	.44	.39	−.29	−.24	1.00

Note:—indicates a loading < .30. Marker items are in boldface print. Deleted items are italicized (due to either complex, low loading, wrong factor, and/or not retained).

correlated, but distinct, factors explaining 63% of the variance in the 28 retained items. Loadings were high on the relevant factors, with only a few complex loadings of nonrelevant items loading on more than 1 factor. Coefficient alphas on the revised five factors revealed moderate to high internal consistency: self-esteem (.90), subjective competence (.81), distress (.82), powerlessness (.73), and psychosexual functioning (.92). Factor loadings and correlations for this final solution are given in Table 10.2. Unit-weighted composite means (on a 1–5 scale) were formed for each of the five factors, such that high mean scores reflected greater self-esteem, subjective competence, distress, powerlessness, and psychosexual functioning, respectively. These five composites were then used to help differentiate women into psychosocial types through subsequent cluster analyses.

☐ Cluster Analyses

In each of the two subsamples (labeled A and B), the five clustering variables (self-esteem, subjective competence, distress, powerlessness,

TABLE 10.2.   Factor loadings and intercorrelations for 28 retained psychosocial items on 5 factors.

| Items | Psychosocial functioning | | | | |
	Factor I Self esteem	Factor II Subjective Competence	Factor III Distress	Factor IV Powerlessness	Factor V Psychosexual functioning
I like me as a person.	.67	—	—	—	—
I'd like to change...	−.87	—	—	—	—
I like the way I am.	.87	—	—	—	—
I wish I was different...	−.85	—	—	—	—
I can cope ...	—	.79	—	—	—
My life is too complex.	—	—	.70	—	—
I can get things done...	—	.73	—	—	—
The world is threatening...	—	—	.64	—	—
I can make things better.	—	.57	—	.30	—
I just get by...	—	—	.56	—	—
I can fix a problem.	—	.63	—	.35	—
I feel there's no way out.	—	—	.57	—	—
I make my own decisions.	—	—	—	−.62	—
I succeed because of me...	—	—	—	−.62	—
Others run my life.	—	—	—	.56	—
I can change my life.	—	—	—	−.75	—
I can cope with ... sex.	—	—	—	—	.74
My sex life is too complex.	—	—	.30	—	−.51
I can manage my sex life.	—	—	—	—	.53
...sex is threatening...	—	—	.51	—	−.46
I can make sex... better.	—	—	—	—	.68
I just get by with ...sex.	—	—	.40	—	−.57
I can fix a sexual problem.	—	—	—	—	.73
...no way out of sex...	—	—	—	—	−.68
I make decisions...sex.	—	—	—	—	.82
I have a say in my sex life.	—	—	—	—	.82
Others run my sex life.	—	—	—	—	−.73
I can change my sex life.	—	—	—	—	.77

TABLE 10.2.   (continued)

Items	Factor I Self esteem	Factor II Subjective Competence	Factor III Distress	Factor IV Powerlessness	Factor V Psychosexual functioning
			Psychosocial functioning		
Factor intercorrelations	**I**	**II**	**III**	**IV**	**V**
Factor I	1.00				
Factor II	.32	1.00			
Factor III	−.43	−.44	1.00		
Factor IV	−.46	−.32	−.26	1.00	
Factor V	.42	.35	−.39	−.34	1.00

Note:—indicates a loading <.30. Marker items are in boldface print.

and psychosexual functioning) were entered into the cluster analysis. Ward's method of clustering, which has been shown to be effective in extracting clusters (Aldenderfer & Blashfield, 1984; Kuiper & Fisher, 1975), was used to organize the data into clusters of women with similar profiles on the five psychosocial composites.

Scores for the five clustering variables were standardized as Z-scores, with a mean of 0 and a standard deviation of 1. Since it was not clear how many different psychosocial groups would be identified, several different cluster solutions were examined in each subsample. Using Ward's (1963) linkage method (SAS, 1989), analyses were conducted to obtain three-, four-, and five-cluster solutions. Three methods were used to decide on the number of clusters to retain. First, cubic clustering criterion values were compared across solutions. Though very little guidance is provided on deciding the correct number of clusters to retain, research has shown that these values tend to show local peaks at the correct number of clusters (Sarle, 1983). Second, cluster means for the four clustering variables were correlated across the two subsamples for the three-, four-, and five-cluster solutions, separately. Solutions which yield a high correlation would indicate consistency in cluster composition across subsamples, and hence would indicate a generalizable cluster solution (Harlow, Rose, Morokoff, & Quina, 1993). Third, the pattern of means and marker variables (i.e., variables that were highly endorsed for a cluster) was examined for the different solutions. A solution that was clearly interpretable within the theoretical framework was preferred.

Table 10.3 presents the cluster patterns for the three-, four-, and five-cluster solutions. Using the three criteria, a four-cluster solution was retained as the most consistent, generalizable, and interpretable across both subsamples.

TABLE 10.3. Psychosocial cluster patterns for three-, four-, and five-cluster solutions in samples A and B

Cluster Variables	Three-Cluster Solution A	Three-Cluster Solution B	Four-Cluster Solution A	Four-Cluster Solution B	Five-Cluster Solution A	Five-Cluster Solution B
1 Self esteem	4.69	4.07	4.69	4.32	4.69	4.32
Subj. competence	4.50	4.21	4.50	4.70	4.50	4.70
Distress	1.58	1.80	1.58	1.43	1.58	1.43
Powerlessness	1.35	1.50	1.35	1.20	1.35	1.20
Psychosexual funct.	4.73	4.50	4.73	4.80	4.73	4.80
2 Self esteem	3.84	3.33	3.84	3.99	4.05	3.99
Subj. competence	4.00	3.78	4.00	4.05	3.96	4.05
Distress	2.05	2.56	2.05	1.92	1.89	1.92
Powerlessness	1.63	2.01	1.63	1.60	1.68	1.60
Psychosexual funct.	4.24	3.78	4.24	4.41	3.57	4.41
3 Self esteem	3.01	2.32	3.10	3.33	3.78	3.55
Subj. competence	3.48	3.22	3.57	3.78	4.01	3.74
Distress	2.91	3.54	2.71	2.56	2.10	2.64
Powerlessness	2.34	2.61	2.21	2.01	1.61	2.00
Psychosexual funct.	3.75	3.50	3.90	3.78	4.42	4.18
4 Self esteem			2.52	2.32	3.10	3.02
Subj. competence			2.98	3.22	3.57	3.85
Distress			4.00	3.54	2.71	2.45
Powerlessness			3.06	2.61	2.20	2.01
Psychosexual funct.			2.93	3.50	3.90	3.24
5 Self esteem					4.00	3.54
Subj. competence					2.98	3.22
Distress					4.00	3.54
Powerlessness					2.94	3.39
Psychosexual funct.					2.93	3.50
Cubic Clustering Criterion	−7.5	−9.67	−7.07	−8.72	−8.43	−7.19
Cross-Sample r	.92		.96		.92	

Pooling across the two subsamples, the following clusters emerged, with labels and percentages of women given in parentheses for each cluster. Cluster 1 women (high functioning: 16%) had the highest levels of all five psychosocial composites; Cluster 2 women (good functioning: 43%) reported the next highest levels of all five psychosocial composites and was the largest cluster; Cluster 3 women (fair functioning: 31%) had lower levels of esteem, competence, and psychosexual functioning, as well as higher distress and powerlessness than women from the first two groups; women in Cluster 4 (poor functioning: 10%) were characterized by the lowest levels of esteem, competence, and psychosexual functioning, as well as the highest levels of distress and powerlessness.

☐ MANOVAs and Follow-Up ANOVAs and Tukey Tests

The four psychosocial clusters of women, pooled across the two subsamples, were further examined using 11 separate one-way MANOVAs with cluster type as the independent variable with four levels and the set of 11 relevant behaviors, attitudes, and experiences as dependent variables. Significant differences were found for 10 of the 11 sets of variables (see Table 10.4), with no significant differences among clusters demonstrated for unprotected sex. Proportions of variance in the dependent variables that were explained by the grouping variable of psychosocial cluster ranged from 2% and nonsignificant (for unprotected sex) to 14% and significant (for sexual self-acceptance). Over all 11 sets, including the nonsignificant finding for unprotected sex, there was an average of 8% shared variance between cluster membership and each of the 11 sets of variables, indicating a small, but significant, multivariate effect size.

Results for follow-up ANOVAs and Tukey analyses are also presented in Table 10.4 for the 11 sets of variables, with actual means provided in Table 10.5. For 9 of the 11 sets of variables, the means followed a consistent pattern, with values associated with the least problems and the highest positive attitudes being highest in the high functioning Cluster 1 women, followed by the well (good) functioning Cluster 2 women, followed by the fair functioning Cluster 3 women, and lastly by the poor-functioning Cluster 4 women. For one of the partner risk variables, number of partners, the highest functioning Cluster 1 women reported the lowest number of partners, as expected, though the middle two groups had more partners than the poor-functioning Cluster 4 women, possibly reflecting less sexual involvement for this latter group. Further, the pattern of means for unprotected vaginal and oral sex, though nonsignificant across groups, suggested a counterintuitive trend of greater frequency when moving from poorer to higher psychosocial functioning.

☐ Generated Case Studies for the Four Psychosocial Clusters

Four hypothetical case studies were generated to help describe the four psychosocial clusters that resulted from our analyses. For each example, we tried to incorporate and highlight the significant demographics, behaviors, interpersonal experiences, and psychosocial attitudes of a woman who might typify each of the clusters. Though these were not taken from actual women, they could be viewed as clinical composites, analogous to

TABLE 10.4. MANOVAs, ANOVAs, and Tukey tests for four psychosocial clusters on 11 factors

Factors Variables	F	df	p	η^2 R^2	Cluster Signif.
Childhood sexual abuse	3.42	(9,1249)	***	.06	
Unwanted exhibition	5.47	(3,515)	.001	.03	3>2,1
Unwanted touching	5.96	(3,515)	***	.03	4,3>1,2
Unwanted penetration	3.36	(3,515)	.019	.02	3 >2
Family environment	12.15	(6,1028)	***	.13	
Positive perceptions	22.87	(3,515)	***	.12	1>2>3>4
Negative perceptions	20.32	(3,515)	***	.11	4>3>2>1
Adult sexual victimization	7.18	(9,1249)	***	.12	
Adult coercion	18.84	(3,515)	***	.10	4>3>2>1
Adult force	9.04	(3,515)	***	.05	4>3,2,1; 3>1
Adolescent intercourse	8.20	(3,515)	***	.05	4>2,1
Relationship violence	6.21	(9,1249)	***	.10	
Argument violence	15.02	(3,515)	***	.08	4>3,2,1; 3>1
Throwing violence	6.20	(3,515)	***	.04	4>2,1
Hitting violence	3.04	(3,515)	.028	.02	4>1
Sexual self-acceptance	18.31	(6,1028)	***	.18	
Positive attitudes	35.70	(3,515)	***	.17	1>2>3>4
Negative attitudes	22.50	(3,515)	***	.12	4,3>2,1
Anticipated negative reaction	6.46	(9,1249)	***	.10	
If refuse to do oral sex	11.99	(3,515)	***	.07	4>3>2,1
If refuse to touch partner	17.04	(3,515)	***	.09	4,3>2,1
If refuse sex w/o condom	6.40	(3,515)	***	.04	4,3>2,1
Sexual assertiveness	9.22	(9,1249)	***	.14	
Communication	19.53	(3,515)	***	.10	1>2>3>4
Refusal	17.82	(3,515)	***	.09	1>2>3>4
Condom use	5.00	(3,515)	.002	.03	1>2,3,4
Unprotected sex	.50	(9,1249)	.870 NS	.01	
Vaginal	1.09	(3,515)	351 NS	.01	NS
Oral	0.55	(3,515)	.651 NS	.00	NS
Anal	0.35	(3,515)	.786 NS	.00	NS
Perceived HIV risk	8.46	(9,1249)	***	.13	
How sure of safety	12.13	(3,515)	***	.07	1,2>3>4
Perceived risk	10.46	(3,515)	***	.06	4>2,1; 3>1
Preventive behavior	17.93	(3,515)	***	.09	1,2>3>4
Partner risk	1.96	(6,1028)	.07 NS	.02	
Partner status	.64	(3,515)	.59 NS	.00	NS
Number of partners	3.10	(3,515)	.026	.02	3>1

TABLE 10.4.   (continued)

Factors Variables	F	df	p	η^2 R^2	Cluster Signif.
Demographics	2.96	(18,1443)	***	.10	
Age	1.28	(3,515)	.28 NS	.01	NS
Education	7.47	(3,515)	***	.04	1,2>3>4
Income	2.82	(3,515)	.038	.02	NS[a]
Religiosity	1.31	(3,515)	.27 NS	.01	NS
Number of pregnancies	1.38	(3,515)	.25 NS	.01	NS
Health problems	6.48	(3,515)	***	.04	4,3>2,1

Note: ***$p<.001$, unless otherwise noted; NS= nonsignificant; η^2 = Pillai's trace for MANOVAs; R^2 = proportion explained variance for ANOVAs; cluster signif. = Tukey test results showing cluster means to left of arrow significantly larger than means to right (psychosocial functioning clusters: 1 = high; 2 = good; 3 = fair; 4 = poor). [a] ANOVA was significant, though Tukey analysis was not for income.

those used in Chapter 5 when describing the different levels of sexual abuse.

Hypothetical Case Study for Cluster 1: High Functioning

Anna is a 32-year-old woman. She works as an elementary school teacher and is working toward her master's degree in education. Anna has many positive memories of her childhood. Her parents were caring and believed in talking things out when a problem arose. Both parents worked (her mother and father were both high school teachers) and she fondly remembers times when she was allowed to go to her parents' school for graduations and special convocations. Anna's favorite memories from childhood are holidays when she would get together with grandparents, aunts, uncles, and cousins.

Anna had friends during high school but did not date very much. She lived at home during college but dated and became involved in a sexual relationship when she began dating the man who she would later marry. She was very cautious and did not become sexually active until after they became engaged. Anna feels confident in her own ability to control her sexual experience and does not expect a negative reaction from her husband if she tells him she would rather not engage in a specific activity,

TABLE 10.5. Cluster means for the five psychosocial clustering variables and the 11 sets of experiences, behaviors, attitudes, and demographics

Experiences, Behaviors, Attitudes, & Demographics	Psychosocial functioning clusters			
	High	Good	Fair	Poor
	Cluster 1 $N = 83$ 16%	Cluster 2 $N = 225$ 43%	Cluster 3 $N = 161$ 31%	Cluster 4 $N = 50$ 10%
Self esteem	4.54	3.88	3.23	2.37
Subj. competence	4.58	4.02	3.69	3.16
Distress	1.52	1.99	2.63	3.66
Powerlessness	1.29	1.62	2.10	2.73
Psychosexual functioning	4.76	4.32	3.84	3.35
Childhood abuse				
Exhibition abuse	1.54	1.71	2.01	1.92
Touching abuse	1.51	1.56	1.84	2.00
Penetration abuse	1.27	1.24	1.48	1.43
Family-of-origin perceptions				
Positive perceptions	3.92	3.46	3.21	2.70
Negative perceptions	2.76	3.15	3.49	4.01
Adult sexual victimization				
Adult coercion	1.96	2.32	2.58	2.97
Adult force	1.54	1.71	1.87	2.32
Adolescent abuse	1.19	1.25	1.43	1.72
Relationship violence				
Argument violence	2.22	2.38	2.49	2.97
Throwing violence	1.76	1.84	2.07	2.34
Hitting violence	1.30	1.38	1.45	1.64
Sexual self-acceptance				
Positive attitudes	4.34	3.93	3.38	2.94
Negative attitudes	1.56	1.85	2.21	2.53
Anticipated negative reaction				
If refuse oral sex	1.20	1.20	1.38	1.62
If refuse touching	1.18	1.26	1.52	1.70
If refuse sex w/o condom	1.25	1.30	1.52	1.58
Sexual assertiveness				
Communication	4.86	4.57	4.28	3.88
Refusal	4.49	4.20	3.93	3.75
Condom use	3.90	3.57	3.45	3.32
Unprotected sex (NS)				
Vaginal (NS)	27.67	24.65	20.84	18.90
Oral (NS)	15.18	13.46	11.30	12.62
Anal (NS)	00.56	00.43	00.34	00.57

TABLE 10.5.   (continued)

Experiences, Behaviors, Attitudes, & Demographics	Psychosocial functioning clusters			
	High	Good	Fair	Poor
	Cluster 1 N = 83 16%	Cluster 2 N = 225 43%	Cluster 3 N = 161 31%	Cluster 4 N = 50 10%
Perceived HIV risk				
How sure (of safety)	2.45	2.29	2.06	1.72
Perceived risk	1.86	2.14	2.35	2.73
Preventive behavior	4.97	4.88	4.72	4.40
Partner risk (NS)				
Partner status (NS)	1.28	1.25	1.31	1.41
Number of partners	10.19	17.92	18.84	13.52
Demographics				
Age (NS)	32.05	33.12	31.06	32.02
Education	4.76	4.57	4.40	3.96
Income	2.18	2.09	1.88	1.84
Religiosity (NS)	2.66	2.96	2.91	2.82
# pregnancies (NS)	1.30	1.68	1.55	1.90
Health problems	1.89	2.02	2.47	2.57

Note: NS indicates no overall significant differences across clusters; otherwise $p <$ .05 or better.

which she does if she is not in the mood. She also feels free to talk to her husband about sexual issues or problems she is having. Anna trusts her husband and does not use condoms during intercourse.

Anna is satisfied with her marriage and feels that she and her husband have a good way of working out problems. Both are committed to talking out problems rather than letting problems get to the point where they would be yelling or screaming at each other.

Hypothetical Case Study for Cluster 2: Good Functioning

Christine is a 27-year-old woman. She graduated from college several years ago and is now working as a sales manager at a department store. Her father was an attorney and her mother was a nurse. She remembers her family as being supportive to her for the most part, although she had some significant conflicts with her mother during adolescence. This was a time in which her father was involved in working toward partnership and had to spend most evenings at the office. Christine felt her mother was highly restrictive of her social activities, never allowing her to go out in the evenings with friends during the week. Christine perceived her mother to be excessively conservative. Although she did not see her father often, she felt she was disappointing him by not getting better grades in school.

When Christine went away to college she enjoyed her freedom and quickly got involved with a several boys she met at school. She entered into sexual relationships, but found that she was not always able to refuse sexual activities that she didn't want. She did not maintain very good study habits and soon was involved in some academic trouble. In addition, she became pregnant and decided to have an abortion. At this point she decided to go to counseling, which turned out to be very positive in helping Christine to refocus her energies on staying in school.

At present Christine is involved with a young man she met at her job. She still experiences some of the same difficulty in saying no if she is not in the mood for sexual activity, but on the whole she feels accepting of her own sexuality and she is hoping that this may turn out to be a serious relationship. She also is pleased with her progress at work and has a good sense that she is in control of her life.

Hypothetical Case Study for Cluster 3: Fair Functioning

Debbie is a 29-year-old woman who is a licensed home health worker and does additional work cleaning houses. She has an associate's degree from the local community college and is taking additional courses. As a child the atmosphere at home was frequently tense. Debbie's father was physically abusive toward her mother and she witnessed him assault her mother on numerous occasions, usually after drinking. Debbie's father would also physically discipline her and her siblings. As a result she lived in some fear of her father and would walk around on eggshells to try to accommodate him and keep him from getting angry. Her parents divorced when she was 12 years old. After the divorce, she lived with her mother but her two older brothers went to live with her father. Though Debbie has trouble with these painful memories, she is also aware of some positive memories.

After her father moved out Debbie began running around with a "bad crowd." She had sex for the first time soon thereafter and began experimenting with marijuana. One night she slept over at a friend's house and woke up to find a strange boy having sex with her. She did not conceptualize this experience as a rape, however. She became pregnant at age 15 and lived with her mother, who took care of her baby. Debbie was able to finish high school and go on to community college. In the meantime she became involved with a man with whom she had another baby. She and her partner had frequent arguments, sometimes involving shouting and name-calling, but he was not physically abusive. Nevertheless the relationship did not last and they separated 4 years later.

At present, Debbie feels demoralized. She is experiencing health problems and she has a lot of concerns about her children. While she feels competent at work, she has many doubts about her ability to get things done and make good decisions.

Hypothetical Case Study for Cluster 4: Poor Functioning

Claire is a 35-year-old mother of two teenage children who works at a convenience store. She graduated from high school and has taken a few courses at the local community college but was never able to seriously work toward a degree. When she was growing up she lived most of the time with her mother but occasionally would live with her aunt when her mother was in the hospital for alcohol detoxification. Her mother had a recurrent problem with alcohol abuse. Claire's father left the family when she was 5. After that, Claire saw him only occasionally, and her mother had several boyfriends over the years. One of these boyfriends had engaged in unwanted touching with her when she was 7. Claire recalls much time in which there was no one to care for her, because her mother was out drinking. When her mother came home, she was often physically abusive. When Claire was 14, her mother's boyfriend, who she did not get along with, moved in with them. As a result, Claire ran away from home. Although Claire gets along with her mother now, she was not supported and protected as a child.

When she was 19, Claire married the father of her then 2 year old. This was a stormy relationship characterized by alcohol abuse and frequent arguments. During arguments, Claire and her husband would throw things at each other and he would sometimes hit or assault her. He would also coerce her into having sex when she did not wish to. Claire was working as a cocktail waitress at the time, and her husband would frequently become abusive when she arrived home from work late at night. Because of his violent temper, Claire was afraid of refusing his sexual demands. She anticipated a very negative reaction if she refused specific sexual requests and consequently would accommodate her husband.

After a while Claire's husband left her and later she became involved with another man, who is the father of her second child. This relationship did not last either, however, and Claire has a very low opinion of her ability to maintain a relationship. She has little confidence in her ability to solve life problems. Her current boyfriend also has a very controlling style, but is a recovering alcoholic and is able to provide for Claire and her children. Claire does not like herself very much as a person and feels a lot of doubt about whether she can make the kind of changes in her life that she would like to make.

☐ Childhood Sexual Abuse and Psychosocial Functioning

Within this project, we have worked with two categorization schemes: (a) the four categories of childhood sexual abuse discussed in Chapter 5 (none, exhibition abuse, touching abuse, and penetration abuse); and (b) four categories of psychosocial functioning described in this chapter (high, good, fair, and poor). Each of these classifications offers a useful way of understanding the experiences, behaviors, and attitudes of these women, providing insights into helpful ways to intervene. To clarify the nature of these categories even further, it was useful to examine the relationship between these two sets of groups.

A χ^2 test of independence was conducted to investigate the association between the four childhood sexual abuse categories and the four psychosocial clusters. If the χ^2 ended up being nonsignificant, we could conclude that there was not enough evidence to show any association between these two sets of groups. In contrast, a significant χ^2 would demonstrate a clear relationship between abuse and psychosocial functioning, which would be potentially useful information in designing effective interventions.

As expected, the χ^2 test revealed that there was a small, though statistically significant, relationship between type of childhood sexual abuse and type of psychosocial functioning [$\chi^2(9) = 18.32$, $p = .032$, phi coefficient $= .19$]. Approximately three quarters of the women, across categories, were classified as "fair" or "good" on the composite psychosocial functioning scale. However, the pattern of frequencies revealed differences for the categories of "high" and "low" psychosocial functioning across the categories of abuse. Results were exactly the same for no and exhibition-only abuse groups, and likewise were the same for the touch and penetration groups. Women who had reported either no incidence or only exhibition abuse were more likely to have high adult psychosocial functioning (20%) than women with touching or penetration abuse (12%). Conversely, women with touching or penetration abuse were found disproportionately in the lower levels of psychosocial functioning

(12%), compared to the women with exhibition-only or no abuse (7%). Thus, while a small proportion of abused women were able to maintain a high positive psychosocial functioning, an equivalent number (12%) fell into the lowest functioning group, who are likely to feel less capable or empowered psychosocially. This could translate into less satisfying interactions with others, as well as more feelings of stress and demoralization within themselves.

☐ Interpretation and Discussion

Results from two random subsamples of women from New England provided consistent evidence for four clusters of psychosocial functioning, with the majority (74%) of the women falling into the middle two clusters that reported moderate functioning, and smaller groups of women in either extreme reporting high (16%) and poor (10%) levels of psychosocial functioning, respectively. The four clusters of women were further differentiated by demonstrating predictable patterns on 10 of 11 sets of relevant experiences, attitudes, behaviors, and demographics. Frequency of unprotected sexual behavior (vaginal, oral, and anal) was the only set to show nonsignificant findings.

Relative to the other women in our samples, women in Cluster 1 (high functioning) reported less childhood sexual abuse, more positive perceptions of their family-of-origin, less adult sexual abuse and relationship violence, more sexual self-acceptance, less anticipated negative reactions from their partners, greater sexual assertiveness, less perceived risk and partner risk, and better education, income and health. This extends previous research that shows relationships between childhood sexual abuse and adult risky sexual behavior (e.g., Johnsen & Harlow, 1996; Zierler et al., 1991). Though the direction of causation cannot be established with these data, strong associations are evident between psychosocial functioning and abuse, whether anticipated, physical, or sexual. Women who anticipate or experience abuse are less apt to have psychosocial, family, partner, or psychoeconomic supports and resources, leaving them very vulnerable and powerless. The quality of life for abused women is further compromised by reportedly greater health problems, partners with higher HIV risk, and greater perceived HIV risk than women who do not report abuse.

These results indicate that there are differences in the way that women behave, experience, think, and feel, related to their levels of psychosocial functioning. Previous research in other areas of health promotion (e.g., McKusick, Hoff, Stall & Coates, 1991; Prochaska, Norcross & DiClimente,

1994; Prochaska, Redding, Harlow, Rossi, & Velicer, 1994; Velicer et al., 1993) has found that interventions tailored to the specific needs of the individual are the most effective. It is hoped that current results can provide information that would help in preparing more effective tailored interventions for sexually abused women, gearing them towards their specific level of psychosocial functioning. Interventions are needed that offer skills training to enhance levels of self-esteem, subjective competence, psychosexual functioning, and sexual assertiveness, while also reducing feelings of distress and powerlessness. Women would then be better able to negotiate interpersonal situations with greater confidence, thereby reducing further incidence of either abuse or HIV risk.

The consistency of findings across our two subsamples of New England women provides some degree of reliability as to the nature and size of the clusters in this population. Still, we recognize that our findings may not generalize to all women. We did not use a random sample, we focused specifically on adult women in a limited geographical area (New England), and we had relatively little diversity with respect to ethnicity, education, income, and religion. Cultural issues should be considered when planning interventions, since previous research (e.g., Amaro, 1988; Jemmott & Jemmott, 1991) has identified specific HIV prevention issues relevant to different ethnic groups. Incorporating information on actual incidence of HIV would also be helpful to assess more accurately the actual risk levels of the different clusters. Future studies should be conducted in more diverse populations of adolescent girls and women if we want to broaden our understanding of, and effectively prevent, childhood trauma and HIV risk in women.

11

CHAPTER

Discussion

This investigation offers an evaluation of a theoretical model linking traumatic childhood experiences with HIV risk behaviors. In addition, it provides a categorization of childhood sexual abuse experience, an analysis of how model variables differ depending on level of childhood sexual abuse, and an analysis of how model variables discriminate among psychosocial functioning clusters. Together, these analyses offer new information on how childhood sexual abuse and family-of-origin environment predict, through a set of mediators, HIV risk behaviors, how different levels of sexual abuse are associated with model variables, and how the variables in the model discriminate among four clusters varying in psychosocial functioning.

☐ Overview of the Multivariate Model

Our research offers an integrated, cohesive model of the relationship between childhood trauma and adult risky sexual behavior that addresses the roles of sexual abuse and family environment as independent predictors. The model incorporates a large number of variables that had previously only been studied with a univariate approach. It was a goal of this work to clearly examine whether traumatic childhood factors directly predict risky adult sexual behavior, or whether such a relationship is mediated by other factors. Our previous research suggested the possibility of a mediated relationship and this hypothesis was put to a test. Further-more, our research extends previous research by incorporating a longitu-dinal design with three data collection time points, each 6 months apart. The longitudinal model provided the opportunity to assess the pattern of relationships among variables across time.

The variables we wished to explore as mediators emerged in previous research, in which we examined the interpersonal aspect of sexual experi-ence. This set of variables included constructs of sexual victimization, sexual assertiveness, and anticipated negative reaction of a partner to sexual requests. Each of these variables focus on an interaction between the participant and a sexual partner. In addition, we were interested in the role of sexual self-acceptance. In previous research we examined the relationship of these variables to risky sexual behaviors in adults. This research demonstrated that many of these variables were predictors of risky adult behavior (Harlow et al., 1993).

In our previous research, we further explored differences between col-lege women with childhood sexual abuse histories and nonabused college women. College women with abuse histories reported more adult sexual victimization, less assertiveness in refusing unwanted sex, less assert-iveness for AIDS prevention, anticipation of a more negative partner reac-tion to sexual requests, stronger perceptions of HIV risk, and less sexual self-acceptance than nonabused women (Johnsen & Harlow, 1996).

The combined results of the two studies just discussed suggest the possi-bility that the interpersonal aspects of sexual experience and sexual self-acceptance might serve as mediators between childhood sexual abuse and adult risky sexual behavior. Therefore, in the present study, we sought to evaluate a mediational model that would test the extent to which variables including adult victimization, sexual assertiveness, anticipated negative partner reaction, and sexual self-acceptance function as media-tors between childhood sexual abuse history and adult risky sexual be-haviors. We sought to further extend our findings by evaluating this model in a community sample of women.

In addition to examining childhood sexual abuse as a predictor variable, we also included family-of-origin environment. Several lines of research have found a link between early family environment and later adult sexual functioning. It has also been shown that families of women with sexual abuse histories were higher in conflict, and lower in cohesion, expressiveness, and active reaction than families of women without sex-ual abuse histories (Lanktree et al., 1991). Case study evidence further suggests that the inability of a family to offer support, trust, and openness to a victimized child can lead to adult problems including the experience of coercive sex (Witchel, 1991). Therefore, this variable was added as an independent predictor, broadening the focus to childhood trauma that included both childhood sexual abuse and family-of-origin environment.

☐ Predictor Variables: Measurement and Participant Characteristics

Childhood Sexual Abuse

As discussed in Chapter 5, we recommend a four-level categorization of childhood sexual abuse. The four categories that emerged from a PCA of our data, in ascending order of trauma, were "no sexual abuse," "exhibition abuse," "touch abuse," and "attempted/completed penetration abuse." Utilization of four categories was superior to a dichotomous categorization with respect to both reliability across time and greater capacity to differentiate among demographic and other variables.

High levels of victimization were reported by women in this study. Women were categorized by the most severe type of abuse reported. Only 41% of women reported no sexual abuse and 10% of women were categorized in the exhibition abuse group. However, 30% were categorized in the touch abuse group and 19% were categorized in the penetration abuse group. Among African American women (the only group besides White for whom there was a sufficient sample size for analysis), the percentages of exhibition abuse and touch abuse were roughly the same as for the total sample. However the percentage of women in the no abuse group was lower (30%) and the percentage of women in the penetration abuse group was higher (28%).

For the sample as a whole, 59% of women reported some level of childhood sexual abuse. Among White women, 56% reported childhood abuse, and among African American women, 70% reported abuse. Our figures are quite similar to those reported by Wyatt et al. (1993). In this study, 45% of women reported at least one sexual abuse incident, where sexual abuse was restricted to incidents involving body contact (either touch or penetration). In our sample, 48% of women fell into these abuse groups, with an additional 10% in the exhibition abuse group (not measured in the Wyatt et al. study). That these figures are substantially higher than those reported in many studies may be accounted for by the fact that the present sample was selected in part on the basis of multiple sexual partners (a correlate of childhood sexual abuse) and also by the fact that we included exhibition abuse.

Among the four categories, women who had experienced penetration abuse were significantly different from all three other abuse groups on several dependent measures. They reported less education, more pregnancies, more children, less religious orientation, lower sexual self-acceptance, more negative family-of-origin environments, more adolescent and adult sexual victimization, more relationship violence, a greater perceived risk of HIV exposure, and more partner risk factors. For most of these variables, women from the three nonpenetration categories of abuse did not differ significantly among each other. These data confirm and extend the findings of Wyatt et al. (1993), indicating that sexual penetration, or an attempt to penetrate, is the key characteristic of childhood sexual abuses that is associated with adult difficulties.

It should be noted that type of abuse was confounded with frequency of abuse. We found that women who experienced penetration as children reported more frequent instances of all three types of sexual abuse than women in the other abuse categories. It is thus clear that the sexual trauma endured by the penetration abuse group was more severe on multiple dimensions than the sexual abuse experienced by the other groups of women. For this reason, we feel it is important to distinguish among all four categories of abuse.

Family-of-Origin Environment

In this research we also sought to measure an evaluative dimension of perceived family-of-origin functioning. In order to do so we developed a six-item scale assessing the extent to which a family was perceived as understanding, helpful, or happy. Item content was balanced with a three-item measure of positive family functioning and a three-item measure of negative family functioning. People who score high on the positive dimension report having felt understood by their family, that their choices were respected, and that they were happy with their family life. People who score high on the negative dimension report not having felt understood, having experienced a lot of upset, and not being able to stand their situation at home.

☐ The Relationship Between Childhood Sexual Abuse and Family-of-Origin Environment

Women who report childhood sexual abuse frequently report a negative family environment. This conclusion is drawn from a strong significant negative correlation between childhood sexual abuse experiences and family-of-origin environment.

It is relevant to examine the relationship to family-of-origin environment individually for each category of childhood sexual abuse. The women in the most severe abuse category, penetration abuse, reported the most negative (and least positive) perceptions of family environment of women in any abuse category; conversely, women who experienced no sexual abuse reported the most positive (and least negative) perceptions of family environment. Women in intermediate abuse categories (exhibition abuse and touch abuse) were also intermediate in their family perceptions. These data indicate a linear relationship between family-of-origin environment and type of childhood sexual abuse, with decreases in perceived quality of family environment associated with increasingly more traumatic forms of abuse.

This is a relationship that one would intuitively expect if the abuser is a family member. In interpreting this relationship, however, it is important to understand that the perpetrator of the abuse need not be a family member. Yet women who experienced each type of abuse tended to rate their family environments as more negative than women who had not experienced these forms of abuse as children. One reason for this could be that children may have perceived their families as being responsible for conditions which allowed the abuse to occur. Although we cannot determine from our data the extent to which children's abuse resulted from a lack of protection by family members, it would seem reasonable to assume that this was the case some of the time. In such a scenario, a child might be left unattended with a relative (e.g., an uncle, cousin, or grandfather) who parents might have had reason to know was not completely trustworthy. In such cases, children often are afraid to report abusive experiences to parents, or if they do report them, are often told that the solution is for them to modify their own behavior. In other cases children's reports of abuse are not believed. Any such occurrence could result in children believing that their family environment was a negative one.

Furthermore, experience teaches that where one boundary is violated, others are frequently also violated. For example, evidence suggests that parents of men who were sexually abused as children drank alcohol to excess (Bartholow et al., 1994). Data on the co-occurence of sexual and physical abuse indicates that incest is associated with an elevated incidence of physical abuse (Wind & Silvern, 1992). It is not possible to make a direct comparison between these other studies and our findings because they did not categorize abuse with respect to the categories employed here (e.g., penetration). Furthermore, we did not assess childhood physical abuse. However, it is a possibility that our category of penetration abuse, the most extreme form of abuse in our schema, was also associated with increased physical abuse.

Consider the family of Jennifer, whose case was presented in Chapter 5. Jennifer was touched inappropriately by her grandfather, and yet did not feel she could disclose this experience to her mother. Jennifer was frequently blamed and subsequently physically punished by her mother and imagined that if she disclosed this incident to her mother she would have again been held responsible. Because Jennifer's parents had problems with substance abuse, it is likely that Jennifer did not experience the constancy of responsible care that helps children feel secure and valued. In this extended family, several boundary violations can be identified. One is the violation of the grandfather meeting his sexual needs through his granddaughter. A second is the imposition of a substance abuse problem by the parents on their children. A third was the psychologically abusive atmosphere present in the household. A fourth was physical abuse that Jennifer experienced. It should not be a surprise to mental health professionals that where severe sexual abuse exists or is tolerated, other violations of children's rights will also be present. It thus makes sense that it need not be the sexual abuse alone that leads adults to retrospectively evaluate their childhood family environments as negative, but also other abusive or neglectful aspects of the family. Although such aspects were not measured in this study, it would be fruitful in future research to pursue an inquiry into the co-occurence of abusive behaviors in families.

☐ Childhood Sexual Abuse and Risky Sexual Behaviors

Does the experience of childhood sexual abuse create an increased likelihood that women will not protect themselves sexually with partners? Through evaluation of this model we sought to determine whether childhood sexual abuse experience would predict current risky sexual behavior. Although our model focuses on a mediational relationship, it was important to also examine the direct path from childhood sexual abuse to risky sexual behavior.

Although our data do show evidence of a direct relationship between childhood sexual abuse and risky sexual behavior, the relationship was weak and, counter to expectations, a negative one. When we tested a model without direct paths, it was barely discernible from the full model with these paths included (see Analysis 2 results in Chapter 8). As a result, we explored the possibility that the direct relationship could be spurious. The matrix of correlations among the three individual variables making up risky sexual behavior and the four variables comprising childhood sexual abuse was examined. All relationships were close to zero, with some tending in a slightly positive direction and others going in a slightly negative direction. We concluded that this direct relationship was spurious. If our interpretation is correct, this means that the experience of childhood sexual abuse does not provide us with direct information about how well a woman will protect herself in sexual relationships, either by use of condoms or through choice of safer partners. Instead, this relationship can best be demonstrated through the mediation of several relevant variables.

Childhood Sexual Abuse Indirectly Predicts Risky Sexual Behavior Through the Mediator of Adult Victimization

Our primary focus was to discover whether the experience of childhood sexual abuse has an indirect effect on risky sexual behaviors. One proposed mediating variable was adult sexual victimization. In our model, childhood sexual abuse is conceptualized as an independent variable and adult sexual victimization is conceptualized as a mediating variable. Results showed that adult sexual victimization mediates the effects of childhood sexual abuse to risky sexual behavior: (a) childhood sexual abuse had a significant path to adult sexual victimization, and (b) adult sexual victimization was positively related to engaging in risky sexual behavior, including both unprotected sex and partner risk. Thus, women who have experienced childhood sexual abuse have an increased likelihood of reporting adult sexual victimization. Those women who experience adult sexual victimization have an increased likelihood of reporting risky sexual behavior. To understand the implication of these relationships we must explore the findings further.

We will first look at the relationship between childhood sexual abuse and adult sexual victimization and then examine the relationship of adult sexual victimization to components of HIV risk. The relationship of childhood sexual abuse to adult sexual victimization was very strong, explaining 23% of the variance in adult sexual abuse. The relationship was found in both the Time 1 structural equation model and the longitudinal model relating Time 1 predictors to Time 2 mediators. Women with a history of childhood sexual victimization were 5 times more likely to report sexual victimization in adulthood than women without such a history.

To understand this finding more fully, we can look separately at the categories of sexual abuse. Results showed that women who experienced the most severe type of childhood sexual abuse, penetration, reported experiencing more adult sexual victimization. Women who experienced less traumatic forms of childhood sexual abuse, exhibition and touch abuse, did not report higher levels of adult sexual victimization. Thus, our data suggest that it is specifically women who endured childhood rape who are at increased risk for adult sexual victimization.

We furthermore examined whether the victim's relationship to the perpetrator was related to further revictimization. We found that, overall, women with a childhood sexual abuse history reported more adolescent and adult victimization than women who reported no abuse, regardless of whether the perpetrator was a family or nonfamily member. However, women who were victims of penetration by a family member tended to report higher levels of adolescent victimization than women similarly victimized by a nonfamily member. For example, women who were victims of inappropriate touch reported the same levels of adolescent victimization regardless of whether the perpetrator was a family member or not, and levels were not higher than among women without sexual abuse histories. Among those who experienced exhibitionism only, those victimized by family members actually reported less adolescent victimization than those victimized by nonfamily members.

The implications of these data are that women who have childhood abuse experiences, especially those with more frequent and severe childhood abuse experiences, are vulnerable to revictimization as an adolescent and/or as an adult. Among those with severe abuse (i.e., penetration), especially those women who were abused by family members are even more vulnerable to later revictimization. This pattern has been previously reported in a number of studies. For example, Wyatt et al. (1993) describe this phenomenon as the cycle of revictimization. In a structural modeling analysis of developmental patterns in women related to childhood sexual abuse, Wyatt et al. report greater risk of victimization throughout the life course for women who were severely sexually abused in childhood, either by a family member or a nonfamily member. Similar findings were reported by Urquiza and Goodlin-Jones (1994), who examined the relative likelihood of adult revictimization in women of different ethnicities with childhood sexual abuse histories. Overall, they reported that women with a childhood sexual abuse history were 3 times more likely to experience rape as adults than women without a childhood abuse history. This ratio differed depending on ethnicity, however, with the highest ratio reported for African American women and the lowest for Asian women. A connection between childhood sexual abuse history and adult victimization has also been reported in other studies (e.g. Briere & Runtz, 1988; Koss & Dinero, 1989). Wind and Silvern (1992) only found an increased likelihood of adult sexual assault among women who were victims of both physical and sexual abuse. As previously discussed, although we did not measure physical abuse, it is possible that our group of women who experienced penetration abuse also experienced physical abuse.

In the case example introduced in Chapter 5, Jill was raped by her stepfather at age 8. Later, as an adolescent she was forced to have sex by her boyfriend, who was 7 years older than she. As a young adult, she was raped again. These life experiences conform to the pattern that emerged in our data. Following her rape as a child, Jill was vulnerable to revictimization as an adolescent and as an adult. Consistent with our data, Jill was in the highest risk group because, as a victim of penetration abuse, she had been abused by a family member. Later in this chapter we will discuss a possible explanatory mechanism for this relationship based on reduced agency for sexual decisions resulting in decreased sexual assertiveness in women with childhood sexual abuse histories.

Moving to the right-hand side of the model, adult sexual victimization is associated with increased HIV risk, both with respect to increased unprotected sex and choice of riskier partners. Adult sexual victimization thus proved to mediate the relationship between childhood sexual abuse and unprotected sex and risky partners. This means that the experience of childhood sexual abuse (especially more severe abuse) creates a vulnerability for sexual revictimization. If that revictimization occurs, the likelihood of the woman participating in unprotected sex is increased, as is the likelihood that she will report that her partner(s) are more risky. These findings support results from a previous investigation on a population of college women (Harlow et al., 1993) in which a relationship was found between adult victimization and choice of risky partners. A longitudinal investigation based on a stratified random sample of 602 youths attending clinic programs was conducted by Cunningham et al. (1994). Youths were interviewed at three time periods; the first and third interviews were 5 years apart. The design allowed evaluation of aspects of childhood experience as predictors of HIV risk in both adolescence and young adulthood. HIV risk in this study represented the total of some risk behaviors including sex without contraception, IDU, engaging in or using prostitution, male homosexual and bisexual activity, and partner risk. Because of the different nature of the dependent variables, results in this study are not directly comparable to ours. Nevertheless, there is overlap in findings. Cunningham et al. found that childhood sexual abuse did not directly predict adolescent or adult HIV risk behaviors. Importantly, other aspects of childhood experience were found to be predictors, including physical abuse, rape, and multiple abuse. As previously indicated, we did not measure childhood physical abuse. Evidence suggests that future research should include both physical and sexual abuse variables.

In Jill's case, she is uncertain of whether she is at risk for HIV infection through sexual contact with her current boyfriend. She suspects that he may have sexual relations with other women and she is concerned that he may have used injection drugs in the past. Nevertheless, her boyfriend does not use a condom all the time when having sex with her.

It is possible that the experience of rape increases the likelihood of engaging in risky sexual behavior. Anecdotally, women have described feeling damaged by the rape experience and therefore no longer caring about protecting themselves sexually. Some women describe feeling like they are now damaged goods and can never be made whole. Such an attitude could lead to carelessness about sexual protection. However, this hypothesis remains to be empirically supported. It is furthermore possible that the interaction between childhood sexual abuse and adult rape, perhaps in the context of an uncaring family environment, best accounts for failure to protect oneself sexually. Future analysis should examine whether it is primarily rape victims with a sexual abuse history and/or poor family environment who do not subsequently protect themselves sexually. The adoption of the perspective of "damaged goods" could occur to a greater extent in women with sexual abuse or poor family environment histories.

Other Mediators of Childhood Sexual Abuse and Risky Sexual Behavior

In our model we proposed a number of variables focused on aspects of interpersonal experience as possible mediators between childhood sexual abuse and adult risky sexual behavior. In addition to adult sexual revictimization these included relationship violence, anticipated negative partner reaction to sexual requests, sexual self-acceptance, and sexual assertiveness. None of these variables were directly predicted by childhood sexual abuse history.

☐ Family Environment and Risky Sexual Partners

A direct relationship was found between family-of-origin environment and choice of risky partners, indicating that the more positive the family environment, the less likely women were to select risky partners. As discussed in Chapter 8, a model that excluded this direct path could not be distinguished from a model that included it. We think a better explanation for the relationship can be provided by including the mediator of adult victimization, as discussed below.

Family Environment Indirectly Predicts Risky Sexual Behavior Through the Mediator of Adult Victimization

In addition, we looked at the extent to which adult victimization mediated the relationship of family-of-origin environment to risky sexual behavior. Family environment was conceptualized here as an independent variable, with adult sexual victimization again conceptualized as a mediating variable. We discovered that adult sexual victimization mediates the relationship of family environment to risky sexual behavior, just as was the case for childhood sexual abuse.

We found that a woman who perceived her family-of-origin environment more positively was less likely to have experienced adolescent or adult sexual victimization. This is a very reliable relationship that was found in both the Time 1 and the longitudinal models. A positive family environment thus appears to serve a protective role with respect to adolescent and adult sexual victimization. It may be that when women have a positive family experience, they have good role models for relationships and are better able to recognize and avoid partners and situations that may be abusive. It is also possible, although not evaluated here, that self-perception of a negative family environment is associated with experience of psychological abuse, physical abuse, or both.

It is worth further conceptualizing some of the possible effects of a negative family environment. It is important to acknowledge that self-worth is learned through interactions with family members. This developmental concept was proposed by Rogers (1961), who theorized that positive self-regard was environmentally determined. We can further develop this conceptualization relevant to sexual self-protection. Appropriate self-care and protection is learned in part through how parents and other family members care for and protect children. Ignoring children's pain and traumatic experience may teach the child that how she feels is not important, and therefore that it is not important to engage in self-protection. When girls are simultaneously sexually abused and not protected by parents, the message they learn may be that it is important to have sex in order to please men and protecting themselves is not important.

In addition, though not studied in our model, childhood victimization has been found to be associated with increased likelihood of drug and alcohol use (Briere & Runtz, 1988; Stein, Golding, Siegel, Burnam, & Sorenson, 1988; Zierler et al., 1991). Evidence indicates that childhood victimization contributes to greater use of alcohol and drugs among adolescents and adults. Among rape victims, childhood history was associated with significantly greater lifetime drug use prior to the rape experience (Resnick & Kilpatrick, 1996). Furthermore, substance use and risky sexual behavior (i.e., multiple partners, one-night stands, having sex soon after meeting a partner) both predicted severity of adult victimization (Testa, 1996). Children who have been severely victimized may use drugs or alcohol as a coping strategy. However, these data suggest that this strategy, in combination with other nonprotective sexual behaviors, puts them at risk for further victimization.

It also may be that women who grow up in a positive family environment do not experience urgency with respect to a need to leave home or form other significant relationships. The adolescent who runs away from home or seeks to fill emotional needs outside the family at a young age is probably at greater risk for sexual exploitation. The case example of Jill again illustrates this experience. Jill was raped by her stepfather while her mother was away from home. When Jill told her mother of this experience, her mother did not believe her. Her assessment of her family environment as a child was a very negative one: She did not feel her choices were supported, she did not feel understood, and she couldn't stand her home situation. She was very eager to find emotional support, and as a teenager became involved with a man 7 years older than she who was abusive to her. Because her home situation was so negative, she may have been strongly motivated to find someone seemingly mature, who could provide a different home for her. Unfortunately, adults who enter into sexual relationships with teenagers typically do so in an exploitive rather than protective manner.

☐ Sexual Assertiveness

Sexual assertiveness was studied here in order to understand more fully how childhood and adult experience effect the individual's agency to protect herself sexually and to assert her sexual interests.

Childhood Sexual Abuse and Sexual Assertiveness for Refusal of Unwanted Sex

A relationship between childhood sexual abuse and less sexual assertiveness for refusal of unwanted sexual activity was found. This relationship suggests a possible mechanism for the relationship of childhood sexual abuse to adult sexual victimization. The experience of childhood sexual abuse involves an adult's expectation or demand of sexual behavior from the child. This suggests that the sexual behavior is coerced on different levels, in part because of the power differential between adult and child which produces an implicit threat, in part because overt threats may have been made, and in part because the child may be instructed by her parents that she must obey adults.

Sexual coercion of a child has several consequences with respect to the child's conceptualization of her ability to refuse sexual activity. One consequence is fear of refusal, which occurs especially when overt or covert threats are made. Another consequence is that a child may become convinced that refusal of sexual activity is not an option. Another consequence is that children will not learn skills for how to refuse sexual activity. With this set of experiences, it may be predicted that an impairment of ability to refuse sexual activity will continue in adulthood, leaving women feeling too vulnerable to refuse sexual activity even in supposedly consensual sexual contexts. In fact, a small but significant negative correlation was found between sexual assertiveness for refusal and adult sexual victimization. One would not expect to explain a large amount of variance in adult sexual victimization from the individual's characteristics (e.g. level of assertiveness), but rather from situational characteristics including characteristics of the offender.

A covert message of the sexual abuse is that the victim is valued for her sexuality. This may be very significant if the abuser has a relationship with a victim. Often, any time or attention the victim receives from the abuser has a sexual focus. A victim may receive a strong and consistent message that if she is to receive the time and attention of men it will be as a result of what she can offer them sexually. It is possible that this scenario may be made worse if the child is not valued in her family. In other words, if a child does not have alternative sources of self-worth and, in extreme cases, is valued only as a sexual object, a vulnerability is created for further abuse. The combination of worth focused on sexuality and fear of the negative consequences of refusing sex creates a circumstance in which even into adulthood, many childhood sexual abuse survivors are unable to decline unwanted sex appropriately, as indicated by the significant inverse relationship between sexual assertiveness for refusal and childhood sexual abuse. The use of drugs or alcohol may further weaken attempts to protect herself.

Jill's case further exemplifies this pattern. As a child she had never fully learned her own self-worth and the subsequent need to engage in protective behavior. Her mother left her in the care of a man who her daughter had warned her was engaging in inappropriate behaviors. A certain message behind this action was that Jill was not worth protecting.

The fact that Jill's mother did not do everything she could to protect Jill in no way diminishes the responsibility of Jill's stepfather for assaulting her. However, it did send a message concerning self-worth to Jill. It is plausible to hypothesize that Jill internalized this view of self into her own behaviors as an adult, and that she did not adequately protect herself. Jill increased her risk by accepting a ride home from a man she met in a bar. She might, for example, have felt that it would have been self-centered to decline a ride home from someone just in order to keep herself safe. Furthermore, having been valued primarily as a sexual entity by her stepfather, she may have felt she needed to accommodate this man in order to interest him, putting herself in a vulnerable situation. Even if she disliked her stepfather, he may still have been her model for men's interests. Making these choices in the context of alcohol consumption further impaired her ability to reach a good decision.

The relationship of adult sexual victimization to choice of risky partners requires further explanation. This relationship may be explained in part by the correlation between childhood sexual abuse and low self-esteem and subjective sense of competence (Briere & Runtz, 1988). Such a negative self-concept may lead women to be less selective in choosing a partner. One may conceptualize partner choice from various perspectives. For example, from a psychodynamic perspective, unconscious aspects of conflict may be identified within a partner, leading to attraction. From a behavioral perspective, a woman may consciously feel that a partner with more problems will be more interested in her as a partner. From a lifestyle perspective, if one is using alcohol or other drugs, one may choose a partner who shares similar interests.

Sexual Assertiveness for Condom Use

It is clear that women who have difficulty refusing unwanted sex may also have difficulty refusing sex without a condom or insisting on condom use, as suggested by the small positive correlation between sexual assertiveness for refusal and sexual assertiveness for condom use. It further makes sense that women who are not assertive with respect to condom use may have more unprotected sex. This relationship was supported by a significant negative regression path from sexual assertiveness for condom use to unprotected sex. This indicated that women who reported more assertiveness for condom use also reported less unprotected sex.

A significant regression path was also found from sexual assertiveness for condom use to partner risk factors. This negative relationship showed that more sexual assertiveness for condom use was related to reported choice of partners with fewer risk factors. This relationship could be explained through the construct of health-protective behaviors. Women who are concerned about protecting themselves might have an interest in being assertive about condom use and also be interested in making sure that their sexual partners are not risky. It should be noted that in this study, neither of the predictor variables, childhood sexual abuse or family-of-origin environment, predicted sexual assertiveness for condom use. Since this variable is strongly (negatively) correlated with unprotected sex, it is possible that other variables such as adult victimization similarly mediate the relationship of predictor variables to this variable.

Sexual Assertiveness for Communication: A Mediator of the Relationship of Family Environment to Risky Sex

We unexpectedly found that a positive family environment was indirectly related to more unprotected sex and less perceived risk through the path of sexual communication assertiveness. As would be expected, a positive family environment was positively related to sexual communication assertiveness. This assertiveness, however, was positively related to unprotected sex. It appears that an ability to question a partner about their sexual history leads to a false sense of security concerning their risk level, which was perceived as low. We describe this as a "false" sense of security because other data indicates that men frequently do not provide accurate information to their female partners concerning sexual risk variables (Mays & Cochran, 1993).

☐ Family-of-Origin Environment and Relationship Violence

It is possible that relationship violence would play a more central role in other populations of women. Our sample was geographically located in a largely suburban and middle-class New England community, where the rates of HIV transmission are not as severe as in major epicenters and the rates of current relationship violence were relatively low (although a number of women had left earlier violent relationships). We expect that in larger urban areas, where the rates of HIV infection are higher (and hence partners from that population are statistically more dangerous as transmitters of the virus) and the number of resources to help the victim escape are lower, the experience of relationship violence may be different. The ultimate consequence, HIV infection, is more serious when one feels unable to refuse unwanted sex with a partner whose other partners have a high probability of being infected.

Furthermore, women who are currently in a relationship that is violent may respond differently from women who have been able to leave such a relationship and are now engaged with nonviolent partners. Our research approach did not enable us follow up on this important question; in fact, the use of surveys mailed to the home may have reduced the number of women in currently abusive relationships who felt safe to fill it out. It remains for future research in other populations from different geographical environments to verify the relevance of the relationship violence factor.

☐ Sexual Self-Acceptance: A False Sense of Security

An unexpected finding was that a positive family environment was also indirectly related to more unprotected sex through the mediator of sexual self-acceptance. A positive family environment was associated with greater sexual self-acceptance, as would be expected. However, sexual self-acceptance was in turn associated with more unprotected sex. This same pair of relationships was found in the Time 1 data as well, supporting the reliability of these relationships. The relationship of sexual self-acceptance to increased unprotected sex appears to be a paradoxical one in which a sense of sexual well-being imparts a sense of false security which leads to engaging in unprotected sex. This is similar to a very reliable finding that positive psychosocial attitudes are related to riskier sexual practices (Harlow et al., 1993). It is important to note, however, that sexual self-acceptance was not associated with greater partner risk or greater perceived risk. The likely meaning of these relationships is that women with a positive sense of their own sexuality engage in unprotected sex, but do so with partners they do not believe to be risky. Although this behavior puts them at some risk (for example, one can never know, even in a long-term marriage, whether one's partner is monogamous), it is not as risky as having unprotected sex with a partner who has known risk characteristics.

☐ Family-of-Origin Environment Indirectly Predicts Perceived Risk Through the Mediator of Anticipated Negative Partner Reaction

A positive family-of-origin environment was related to a decreased expectation for a negative partner reaction to sexual requests. This means that women who had positive childhood experiences tended to have relationships with men who they felt would react positively to their sexual requests. Decreased expectation for a negative partner reaction (or, alternatively phrased, increased expectation for a positive partner reaction) was in turn associated with decreased perceived risk for HIV. Women who expected a positive reaction to a sexual request from a partner rated their perceived risk as relatively low. Anticipation of a negative partner reaction thus mediated the relationship between family environment and perceived HIV risk. These associations may reflect the child's experience of expecting that their initiatives will be met with a negative response. This negative expectation appeared to be associated with an accurate perception of increased risk. Thus, when women expect a negative response to requests for condom use, they realize that they are not as safe as they might otherwise be.

☐ A Review of the Cross-Sample Comparisons

In Chapter 9, the overall sample was subdivided into two major groupings: women who were recruited from a commuter campus (continuing education), who represented a more homogeneous statewide sample, and women recruited from more urban-based sites (community), including media, agencies, and mailings. The community group was on the average older, with more children, and was more ethnically diverse than the continuing education sample. They also had experienced more violence and less positive family environments, they measured higher on risk from unprotected sex and from risky partners, and they perceived themselves to be at greater risk for HIV. Sexual assertiveness for condom use and sexual self-acceptance were lower in the community group.

In spite of these differences, the model showed considerable robustness for the majority of the paths, when the relationships within each subsample were compared to the overall pattern and to each other. Thus we can have confidence that for the range of women we assessed, the findings are valid.

On the other hand, perhaps because the concentrations of abuse were higher among the community subsample, the model revealed significantly stronger links between childhood sexual abuse, relationship violence, and sexual assertiveness for condom use, and a stronger protective role for a positive family-of-origin environment, for the community women.

☐ Overview of Cluster Analysis

Our research offers a unique analysis in which women were classified into statistically cohesive types based on psychosocial functioning. Cluster analysis allowed an investigation of a typology of psychosocial functioning among the four levels of sexual abuse, ranging from no abuse to penetration abuse. If distinct psychosocial clusters emerged that could be differentiated on our model variables, we could begin to understand more about the interaction between psychosocial functioning, childhood experiences, HIV risk, and interpersonal mediators. These findings could then provide information that would aid in developing interventions to increase quality of life for women by decreasing interpersonal powerlessness and HIV risk.

The cluster analysis was conducted separately in two randomly divided samples that had been stratified on the childhood sexual abuse variable. This resulted in a reliable four-cluster solution. We characterized these clusters as representing high functioning, good functioning, fair functioning, and poor functioning. We then conducted multivariate analyses to determine how the model variables differed across clusters of women with these varying levels of psychosocial functioning.

Five psychosocial functioning scales were identified to differentiate among the clusters: self-esteem, subjective competence, distress, powerlessness, and psychosexual functioning. The four resulting clusters clearly differentiated women into categories reflecting a descending order of psychosocial functioning on each of these scales. For example, high-functioning women were characterized by high self-esteem and subjective competence, low distress and powerlessness, and high levels of psychosexual functioning, whereas low-functioning women were characterized by the converse for each scale.

Characteristics of Psychosocial Functioning Clusters

In order to validate these clusters, we submitted them to further multivariate analysis. The 11 main sets of model variables were examined across each of the four clusters. Ten of the eleven sets of variables showed expected significant differences across the four clusters of women.

Perhaps most importantly for our analysis, the two childhood model variables, childhood sexual abuse and family environment, were clearly associated in the expected direction, with psychosocial functioning clusters. Women with high psychosocial functioning reported very positive perceptions of their family environment, whereas women in the poor psychosocial functioning cluster reported very negative perceptions of family-of-origin environment. Further, childhood sexual abuse showed predictable patterns of occurrence, with higher abuse in the fair and poor psychosocial functioning clusters and lower abuse in the high and good clusters.

A linear increase in adult sexual victimization means occurred across the psychosocial functioning clusters, with high victimization reported by low-functioning women. This finding parallels the relationships found between childhood abuse and psychosocial functioning, highlighting the pervasive association between these variables.

Model mediators showed consistent associations with psychosocial functioning. Women with low psychosocial functioning were characterized by greater relationship violence, greater anticipated negative partner response to sexual requests, less sexual self-acceptance, and less sexual assertiveness for communication. Higher perception of HIV risk was also associated with poorer psychosocial functioning, as was a greater number of sexual partners and the risk status of partners. A clear pattern emerges in which higher risk behaviors and more adverse life experience are associated with poorer psychosocial functioning, whereas more self-protective behaviors and less trauma are associated with higher psychosocial functioning.

☐ Family Experience and Sexual Abuse: Interconnections With HIV Risk

It is important to understand the interconnections among variables studied here in order to conceptualize interventions in working with women at risk for HIV. Suggestions for interventions based on our results are discussed in Chapter 12. Our data demonstrate a relationship between adult sexual victimization and risky sexual behavior. The nature of this relationship remains to be clarified. However, previous research has established other correlates of both experiences. For example, both rape and unprotected sexual activity are predicted by a higher number of sexual partners (which is itself an HIV risk factor, although not one examined in this study). For example, Fromuth (1986) found that the number of sexual partners was the best predictor of sexual victimization in both adolescence and young adulthood. Other researchers have also reported a relationship between number of consensual sexual partners and the experience of rape (Koss & Gidycz, 1985; Mandoki & Burkhart, 1989). A picture emerges that women who have frequent sexual activity (Wyatt,

1992) and more partners are more susceptible to rape. In our previous research we have found a connection between sexual experience and unprotected sex (women with more sexual experience reported more unprotected sex; Harlow et al., 1993).

To this pattern, our data adds information concerning perceived family environment. Those women who report a more negative family environment, independent of sexual abuse history, have a greater likelihood of reporting rape as an adult. It remains to be established what the major determinants of a perceived negative family environment are and how childhood sexual abuse and family environment interact to increase the likelihood of rape. Promising areas for further study include looking at the relationship of sexual behavior to family environment, as well as childhood sexual abuse history, and their interaction with alcohol or other drug use in establishing the individual's agency for good sexual decision making and self-protection.

12
CHAPTER

Implications

In this chapter we seek to identify what we see as the most important contributions of this research. In addition, we identify limitations, along with suggestions for future research. Finally, we address the implications of our findings for interventions.

☐ Contributions of This Study

This research provides a link between two research literatures, the childhood sexual abuse and trauma literature and the HIV prevention literature, and contributes in different ways to each.

With respect to our understanding of childhood sexual abuse and trauma, we feel our results make an important contribution through:

1. Development of a classification schema for childhood sexual abuse. Our schema allows for categorizing women into four groups: no abuse history, history of exhibition abuse, history of touch abuse, and history of penetration abuse. Each category can then be crossed with relationship to the abuser. In previous research, exhibition abuse is frequently not measured. Failure to include this type of abuse in theoretical conceptualizations leads to a less complete understanding of the nature of psychosocial and sexual consequences of sexual abuse.
2. Support for the relationship between childhood sexual abuse and adult sexual victimization that has been previously identified in the literature.

3. Exploration of the importance of family-of-origin environment in its relationship to childhood abuse and its role as a copredictor of adult sexual victimization. It is an important finding that women's perceptions of their family environments is an independent predictor of adult sexual and physical victimization from childhood sexual abuse. It remains to be determined how perceived family environment relates to a broader constellation of childhood abuse variables including physical abuse, emotional abuse, and neglect.

4. Identification of a link between childhood sexual abuse and HIV risk behaviors including unprotected vaginal, oral, and anal sex as well as partner risk factors through the mediator of adult victimization. Although previous research has established that childhood sexual abuse victims often have more sexual partners, the relationship to sexual behaviors that create a risk for disease has not been adequately explored.

5. Identification of a relationship between history of childhood sexual abuse and reduced sexual assertiveness for refusing unwanted sex. Knowledge of this relationship aids us in understanding how women abuse survivors have decreased agency for sexual decision making.

6. Determination of the relationship of childhood sexual abuse to clusters of women based on psychosocial functioning. Although previous literature has established behaviors and psychological characteristics that are correlates of abuse history, a cluster analysis has not been previously undertaken demonstrating how a set of variables including abuse cluster together.

With respect to the HIV risk literature, we feel our findings make some additional contributions:

1. Identification of a set of theoretically based predictors of HIV risk behavior. We have previously proposed a multidimensional model of HIV risk (MMOHR) and tested it in several samples of women (Harlow et al., 1993). This model taps behavioral, interpersonal, and psychosocial variables that have relevance to HIV risk behaviors. Many of these variables reflect the fact that HIV protection occurs in an interpersonal context. In the present study, these variables served as mediators between childhood sexual abuse and family-of-origin environment. As in previous research, this variable set was effective in predicting a substantial portion of variance in HIV risk variables.

2. Utilization of multiple indicators of HIV risk behavior. In this study we utilized three separate sets of dependent variables: unprotected sex, perceived HIV risk, and partner risk factors.

3. Clarification of the role of childhood sexual abuse in predicting HIV risk behavior. We know that individuals with a childhood sexual abuse history are at an increased likelihood to be HIV seropositive. The link between childhood sexual abuse and specific behaviors that put an individual at risk has been unclear, however. Our results clarify the mediational nature of this relationship.

4. Identification of the role of family-of-origin environment as a direct predictor of choice of a risky partner and an indirect predictor of unprotected sex. Again, the determinants of perceived family environment have yet to be determined and may emerge as highly related to other forms of abuse.

Several aspects of our methodology should also be identified as contributions to the literature. These include:

1. Use of structural modeling to test a hypothesized set of relationships. This method requires multiple indicators of each model construct, allowing an evaluation of relationships among variables that take into account the relationships among the indicators.
2. Use of longitudinal data sampling. Data for this study were collected at three time points, each 6 months apart. In conducting the cluster analysis, we were able to relate clusters of women based on their initial psychosocial functioning scores to self-reports of model variables made 1 year later. This provides a very conservative test of relationships. The fact that such strong associations were found between psychosocial variables and other model variables attests to the confidence in which we can hold these findings. Again, in the structural model, we were able to look at childhood sexual abuse and family history variables measured at Time 1, utilizing mediators from Time 2 data and HIV risk behaviors at Time 3. These were compared to the same relationships found when all variables were measured at Time 1. We can have very great confidence in those findings that remain consistent across both models.
3. Scales were developed and worded for a community sample. This involved extensive pilot testing of instruments in focus groups to ensure that women would not be offended by the wording of questions in this survey, which required disclosure of highly sensitive information. In addition, we sought to word all instruments at a 6th-grade reading level.

☐ Limitations of This Research and Directions for Future Research

There are a number of limitations of the present research project. Our sample is restricted in a number of ways. First, it is not a random sample, preventing us from drawing conclusions about the representativeness of sample means. In addition, the sample did not represent an extremely high-risk group. Although women met criteria for HIV risk, their behaviors did not put them in a class in which one would expect highly elevated percentages of HIV infection. For example, we did not extensively tap populations of mentally ill (e.g., Taylor, Amodei, & Mangos, 1996), homeless, drug-addicted (e.g., Bagnall & Plant, 1991; Booth, Koester, Brewster,

Weibel, & Fritz, 1991), incarcerated women (e.g., Bond & Semaan, 1996), or prostitutes (Weisberg, 1984). Furthermore, our sample was 84% White. Future research should explore the relationships established here in other populations (e.g., Wingood & DiClemente, 1997). It is especially important to determine the links between childhood sexual abuse and adult revictimization and HIV risk behaviors, as well as other variables studied here, in higher risk groups.

This study examines only a subset of potential mediators of the relationship between childhood sexual abuse and HIV risk behaviors. Other factors than those assessed here may prove to be equally relevant to the important processes of both risk prediction and intervention to reduce risk behaviors. For example, assessing depression in future studies may provide some insight into the different behavioral and psychosocial outcomes of those with a history of childhood sexual abuse. Similarly, as was discussed in Chapter 10, psychosocial functioning is an important factor to consider in risk prediction and subsequent interventions. Some women with abuse histories have quite positive psychosocial functioning together with the ability to protect their health in sexual relationships. Our research team recommends that future research be directed toward identifying how such women develop their effective coping strategies which have enabled them to come to terms with their sexual victimization. These are the women who have been able to move beyond some of the lasting negative sequelae of abuse. Such resilient women have much to teach us about how to develop effective interventions to promote the sexual health of women with a victimization history. Assessing such factors as stress and coping style could begin to provide some of this information in future studies.

As our thinking about heterosexual HIV risk taking has evolved over the past 5 years, we have clarified our conceptualization of interpersonal power and the impact of gender on the process of negotiation of and desire to use safer sexual practices. In future research, we recommend developing and using measures which directly elicit women's perceptions of power within relationships. Although sexual decision making is an obvious area to assess, we include other interpersonal domains in this recommendation, such as decision making regarding financial resources, childrearing and housework, job and/or career choices and opportunities, and recreational/leisure time and expenditures. We believe that these arenas shape and influence the context in which negotiations for safer sex take place and are thus relevant to any understanding of sexual risk behaviors.

From our current vantage point we would like to test some additional variables in a model. As more data on the co-occurrence and consequences of different forms of abuse emerge, it becomes clear that the three central types of childhood abuse should be evaluated together. These include childhood sexual abuse, childhood physical abuse, and childhood emotional abuse and neglect. Measurement and inclusion of all three in models, including an examination of relationships to combined abuse, can provide us with important information not available when these types of abuse are studied separately. We are also interested in some additional mediating variables that were not examined in the present model. For example, drug and alcohol use has been demonstrated to correlate with the experience of rape. It would be of great interest to test a model in which drug or alcohol use mediates between childhood abuse and adult sexual victimization. Other predictors of adult sexual victimization that would be of great interest to test include frequency of sexual activity and number of sexual partners. As we attempt to determine what differentiates women with abuse histories who become revictimized from women who do not, it seems relevant to assess feelings of self-worth and other coping strategies. Structural variables such as educational level and SES may shed important light on issues of revictimization and HIV risk behaviors. Finally, it would be useful to test separate models among women from different ethnicities so that targeted interventions could be conceptualized.

An important future step is to look at interactions among predictor and mediator variables in our current or future models. It is of great interest, for example, to know whether the sexually revictimized woman is more likely to engage in risky sexual behaviors than the woman who experiences a first sexual victimization as an adult. The question asks whether there is an interaction between childhood sexual abuse and adult sexual victimization in predicting risky sexual outcome variables. It is also crucial to look at interactions among different types of abuse in predicting revictimization and risky sexual behaviors. Some investigators have begun to do this, such as Cunningham et al. (1994) in their study of abuse predictors of adolescent and adult risky behavior. They found that the experience of childhood sexual abuse intensified the effect of being physically beaten and raped on HIV risk behavior in adolescence.

☐ Implications for Intervention

The results of our research make clear that no one experience locks a woman into a pattern of risky sexual behavior. Negative childhood experiences, with respect to either sexual victimization or a negative family environment, are not directly associated with risky behavior, but have only an indirect influence. Both are mediated by adult sexual victimization. Additional variables that mediated the effects of negative family environment included sexual self-acceptance, anticipation of a negative partner reaction to sexual requests, and sexual assertiveness.

It is also clear, however, that childhood abuse has severe consequences, greatly increasing a woman's risk of adult sexual assault. In our study, women who had been sexually victimized as children were 5 times more likely to be sexually assaulted as adults than women who had not been so victimized. There was also a strong association with being physically abused by a partner, although this variable was not significant in our model. A clear implication of this research, then, is the need for community programs that decrease the likelihood of children's abuse. This can include the possibility of early interventions among families under stress. Because our and other's data underline the extensive co-occurence of different types of abuse in families, social service agents should be alert to the possibility of child abuse in homes where alcohol or other drug problems exist. As we begin to understand more concretely how a childhood sexual abuse history translates into increased susceptibility to adult rape, interventions may be developed for children and adolescents who have been victimized that may help disrupt the cycle of victimization. Certainly this should include working with families to ensure constancy of responsible care for children.

Further intervention and research would benefit from an examination of the women who report some type of childhood sexual victimization, yet in adulthood do not appear to be at increased risk of exposure to HIV through their sexual behavior. Some factors are operating among these women to enable them to maintain lower risk behaviors. Perhaps by examining structural variables (such as social class, income, education, etc.), coping strategies, or opportunities for nonabusive relationships, we may learn important information on resilience factors that can be used to design programs for children.

Research indicates that programs to decrease risky sexual behavior that focus on learning sexual assertiveness and sexual empowerment can be effective (e.g. Kelly et al., 1994; Moore, Harrison, & Doll, 1994; St. Lawrence et al., 1997). Nevertheless, nonsignificant results for such interventions have also been reported, and even in the most successful programs, most women are still at risk for HIV infection. A crucial question for intervention research is to determine whether there is a benefit to directly intervening on sequelae of childhood sexual abuse and other forms of maltreatment, or whether it is most efficient for interventions to target the interpersonal variables that served as mediators in this study. Very few high-quality studies of the effectiveness of treatment of childhood sexual abuse have been reported, and no large-scale study examining HIV risk behaviors as outcome variables for such an intervention have been reported.

An important finding in our study is that the adult experience of rape is associated with both increased unprotected sex and choice of riskier sexual partners. We have already suggested the need to determine more thoroughly in future research how this interrelates with childhood abuse history. The number of women who have been raped as adults is high, with especially high figures among subpopulations. Many women have never received psychological services for this trauma. Our knowledge of the connection between rape and risky sexual behavior should lead to interventions for HIV risk reduction based on the empirical literature for interventions following rape. Women who are sexually traumatized will not be as effective as nontraumatized women in accurately perceiving sexual risks, requesting sexual history data from partners, and negotiating effectively with partners concerning safer sexual behaviors.

An important goal for all levels of interventions discussed is an increase in sexual assertiveness for refusing unwanted sex. In our data this was negatively correlated with childhood sexual abuse history. Designing interventions or creating circumstances which allow sexual assertiveness to increase in women is a difficult task, however (Morokoff et al., 1997). It appears that an initial step in this process is for women to identify that they lack assertiveness. This may be difficult to acknowledge, especially among adolescents. In one study, sexual assertiveness actually declined following a sexual assertiveness training program (Deiter, 1993), apparently because women became more accurate in identifying their own difficulties in being assertive over the course of the program. It may be that the one-shot intervention over a few-week period will not be effective in altering attitudes that are so fundamental to women's sexual functioning. Interventions may need to be accessible to women in convenient settings (e.g., health care clinics) where they may participate regularly over time.

Assertiveness for condom use was directly related to both frequency of unprotected sex and choice of riskier partners. This is an expected finding. Most interventions to increase safer sex behaviors for women already focus on training women to be more assertive in asking a partner to use condoms. This appears to be a necessary component of programs but does not seem to be sufficient. In other words, progression from sexual risk taking to sexual safety requires a comprehensive lifestyle change in which women begin to value themselves, act toward meeting personal goals, and do not tolerate relationships in which they do not feel respected. This is a tall order, and one that cannot be achieved quickly or easily.

A disturbing relationship observed in the data is the significant positive relationship between communication assertiveness regarding communicating about a partner's HIV risk factors and engaging in unprotected sex. Research (e.g., Mays & Cochran, 1993) does suggest that sexual partners both lie in order to misrepresent their riskiness to their partners and expect to be lied to about past behaviors. Some women who ask their partners about their current and past HIV risk behaviors may be relying too much on their partners' honesty and may be engaging in sexual behaviors that are not as safe as they are led to believe. Interventions could be useful in helping women to learn not to rely completely on a partner's report of his or her past risk behaviors.

Interventions can similarly be useful in helping women to make accurate assessments of sexual risk. Women with positive family environments who accept themselves tended to engage in more unprotected sex. As previously discussed, these women may trust their partners and believe themselves to not be at risk. If, in fact, the social networks of such women do not include many persons with HIV or AIDS, their actual risk level may be relatively low. However, if their sexual networks include persons with HIV or AIDS, they are very much at risk. Of course it is dangerous to play the odds, and any unprotected sex provides some risk exposure.

Du Guerny and Sjoberg (1993) address the complex topic of gender relations and the HIV/AIDS epidemic, suggesting that social inequities between men and women, with women in positions of less social and economic power, will "fuel the spread" of HIV/AIDS. Amaro (1995) echoes these concerns and urges researchers and social planners to consider the "realities of women's lives" when predicting and intervening upon risky sexual behavior.

Violence against women is one important manifestation of women's relative lack of power in heterosexual relationships in our society. Such inequities have already become part of the lives of women who have experienced such violence; they must also be considered and acknowledged in any intervention with individuals or groups. Du Guerny and Sjoberg (1993) consequently support the development of woman-controlled methods of protection, such as virucides, as alternatives to or in conjunction with programs which encourage condom use. The clear importance of victimization history and other relationship factors to the prediction of HIV risk in women in this sample is demonstrated. In order to use such information effectively and responsibly for health promotion and prevention of HIV and other sexually transmitted diseases among women, we must take women's roles in our society into account and recognize that even among women, gender expectations vary widely among different socioeconomic and ethnic groups. To expect women to be assertive in sexual situations runs counter to many of our society's gender expectations. Compound such expectations with histories of victimization and we have a group of women for whom intervention is critical, yet potentially most difficult to implement effectively. Work to overcome the vulnerability resulting from a history of victimization is essential to women's health promotion.

APPENDIX

Childhood Sexual Abuse

As children, many women were in sexual situations with someone older than them. A sexual situation could mean someone showing their genitals to you. It could mean someone touching you in a sexual way. It could also mean someone putting his penis in your mouth, vagina, or rectum. Think back to when you were a child up to age 14, and answer the next questions. Please circle your answer. If these questions are upsetting and you want to talk, please use the phone numbers in the letter that we sent with the survey. Thank you for your help.

A=No
B=Once
C=A few times
D=Many times

Before you were 14 years old:
1. Did anyone older ever show their genitals to you?
2. Did you ever see anyone older touch their genitals in front of you?
3. Did anyone older ever touch your breasts or genitals?
4. Did anyone older ever try to make you touch their genitals?
5. Did anyone older ever rub their genitals against your body?
6. Did anyone older ever **try** to put his penis in your mouth, vagina, or rectum?
7. Did anyone older ever **put** his penis in your mouth, vagina, or rectum?
8. For #1 to 7, please tell who those people were. Check all that apply.
_____ I did not have any of these experiences before I was 14 years old.
_____ A person I didn't know at all
_____ A person I didn't know well
_____ A friend or relative not in my close family

———— A brother or sister
———— My father, mother, or stepparent
———— Someone else

Adolescent Sexual Abuse

When you were 14–18 years old, were you ever forced to have sex with anyone?
1=No
2=Yes, once
3=Yes, a few times
4=Yes, many times

Family-of-Origin Environment

The next set of questions asks about your family life when you were growing up. Please say how much they describe your family life when you were growing up. Remember that there are places you can call that are listed in the letter we sent with the survey if you want to talk to someone about your feelings. Please circle your answer.

A=Never
B=Rarely
C=Sometimes
D=Often
E=Very often

When I was growing up:
1. I felt like the people who brought me up did not understand me.
2. I made choices that my family liked.
3. The people who brought me up helped make my life better.
4. There were times when I couldn't stand my situation at home.
5. People in my family were upset a lot of the time.
6. I was pretty happy with my family life.

Adult Sexual Victimization

Please think about whether these things have ever happened to you. We understand that these may be difficult questions to answer, but please try to answer them as honestly as you can. Circle your best answer. If these questions make you uncomfortable and you want to talk to someone, please look at the phone numbers in the letter we sent with the survey. Thank you for your help.

A=Definitely yes
B=Probably yes
C=Probably no
D=Definitely no

1. . . . had a man mistake how far you wanted to go with sex.
2. . . . been with a man who got so turned on that you couldn't stop him, even though you didn't want to have sex.
3. . . . had sex with a man even though you didn't want to because he might break up with you.
4. . . . had sex with a man when you didn't want to because you thought he might argue or put pressure on you.
5. . . . found out that a man talked you into sex by saying things he didn't mean.
6. . . . had a man use force (twist your arm, hold you down, etc.) to make you kiss or feel him when you didn't want to.
7. . . . had a man **try** to have sex with you when you didn't want to by saying he would use force, but then sex didn't happen.
8. . . . had a man **use** force to make you have sex when you didn't want to, but then sex didn't happen.
9. . . . had sex with a man when you did not want to because you thought he would use force (twist your arm, hold you down, etc.).
10. . . . had vaginal sex (penis in your vagina) with a man when you didn't want to because he used force.
11. . . . had anal or oral sex (penis in your rectum or mouth) with a man when you didn't want to because he used threats or force.
12. . . . ever been raped.

Relationship Violence

1. When you argue with your partner, what do you usually do?

A=Give in
B=Try to settle things
C=Ignore my partner or leave
D=Yell at my partner
E=I become violent

2. When you argue with your partner, what does **your partner** usually do?

A=Gives in
B=Tries to settle things
C=Ignores me or leaves
D=Yells at me
E=Becomes violent

How often in your life has a sex partner done these things to you? Circle your best answer. Please answer these questions as honestly as you can. If you want to talk about your feelings, please use the phone numbers listed in the letter that we sent with the survey. Remember that no one will know that these answers came from you. There are no ''right'' or ''wrong'' answers.

A=Never
B=Rarely
C=Sometimes
D=Often
E=Very often

3. Threatened to hit you or throw something at you?
4. Threw, smashed, hit, or kicked something?
5. Pushed, shoved, or grabbed you?
6. Slapped you?
7. Kicked, bit, or hit you with a fist, or with something else?
8. Beat you up?
9. Forced you to have sex or do sexual things?
10. Threatened or attacked you with a knife or gun?

Anticipated Partner Reaction

Think about the person you usually have sex with or someone you used to have sex with. Answer the next questions thinking about what that person would do. If you have never been in this situation, imagine how your partner might act if you were. Then answer the question. Circle your best answer. Please remember that there are no ''right'' or ''wrong'' answers to this survey. Also remember that no one will know that these answers came from you.

A=Go along happily
B=Go along but not be happy
C=Not go along
D=Not go along and be upset with me for even asking

1. If I tell my partner how I want to be touched during sex, **my partner would:**
2. If I start sexual touching with my partner, **my partner would:**
3. If I ask my partner to use a condom or latex barrier during sex, **my partner would:**

Think about the person you usually have sex with or someone you used to have sex with. Answer the next questions thinking about what that person would do. If you have never been in this situation, imagine how your partner might act if you were. Then answer the question. Circle your best answer. Please remember that there are no "right" or "wrong" answers to this survey. Also remember that no one will know that these answers came from you.

A=Accept my decision
B=Accept my decision but be upset
C=Insist that I do it anyway
D=Force me to do it anyway

4. If I refuse to do oral sex (your mouth on your partner's genitals) when my partner wants me to, **my partner would:**
5. If I refuse to touch my partner the way my partner wants me to, **my partner would:**
6. If I refuse to have sex with my partner without a condom or latex barrier, **my partner would:**

Sexual Self-Acceptance

For the next questions, think about the past 6 months. How often have you felt this way? Please circle your answer.

A=Never
B=Rarely
C=Sometimes
D=Most of the time
E=Always

1. Sex is a positive part of my life.
2. I do not like some parts of my sex life.
3. I have control of my sex life.
4. I feel powerless in sex situations.
5. I like the way my sex life is going.
6. I have little or no say about my sex life.

Sexual Assertiveness

Think about a person you usually have sex with or someone you used to have sex with regularly. Answer the next questions with that person in mind. Think about what you *would* do even if you have not done some of these things. Circle your best answer.

A=Never
B=Sometimes
C=About half of the time
D=Usually
E=Always

1. I ask my partner to touch my genitals if I want to.
2. I would ask if I want to know if my partner ever had an HIV test.
3. I refuse to put my mouth on my partner's genitals if I don't want to, even if my partner insists.
4. I have sex without a condom or latex barrier if my partner doesn't like them, even if I want to use one. (R)
5. I begin sex with my partner if I want to.
6. I would ask my partner about the AIDS risk of his or her past partners, if I want to know.
7. I put my mouth on my partner's genitals if my partner wants me to, even if I don't want to. (R)
8. I tell my partner what I do not like in sex.
9. I make sure my partner and I use a condom or latex barrier when we have sex.
10. I ask my partner to touch me in a way I like.
11. I give in and kiss if my partner pressures me, even if I already said no. (R)
12. I wait for my partner to be the one to touch my breasts. (R)
13. I tell my partner to keep doing something that I like in sex.
14. I let my partner kiss my genitals if my partner wants to, even if I don't want to. (R)
15. I say something if my partner does not please me in sex.
16. I wait for my partner to be the one to touch my genitals. (R)
17. Women should wait for men to start things like breast touching. (R)
18. I let my partner know if I want to have my genitals kissed.
19. I would ask if I want to know if my partner ever had a sexually transmitted disease (STD).
20. I insist on using a condom or latex barrier if I want to, even if my partner doesn't like them.
21. If I want to know, I would ask my male partner if he ever had sex with a man.
22. I would ask if I want to know if my partner ever had sex with someone who shoots drugs with a needle.

23. I have sex without using a condom or latex barrier if my partner insists, even if I don't want to. (R)
24. I would ask if I want to know if my partner ever used needles to take drugs.
25. If I said no, I won't let my partner kiss my genitals even if my partner pressures me.
26. I have sex without using a condom or latex barrier if my partner wants. (R)
27. I tell my partner to stop if my partner touches me in a way I don't like.
28. I refuse to have sex if my partner refuses to use a condom or latex barrier.
29. I tell my partner what feels good to me in sex.
30. I refuse to let my partner touch my breasts if I don't want that, even if my partner insists.

Note: The Sexual Assertiveness Scale consists of five subscales which are the average of six items each (after reverse scoring "R" items); subscales are composed as follows: Refusal (items 3,7,11,14,25,30); Birth Control (items 4,9,20,23,26,28); Initiation (not used in this study: items 1,5,12,16,17,18); Communication Sexual Preferences (not used in this study: items 8,10,13,15,27,29); and Communication AIDS Risk (items 2,6,19,21,22,24).

Psychosocial Functioning

Think about yourself in the past 6 months and answer the next questions. Circle the best answer for each question.

A=Never
B=Rarely
C=Sometimes
D=Often
E=Always

1. I know what to do when I have trouble.
2. I feel confused about life.
3. I can cope with big problems.
4. My life is too complicated.
5. I can still get things done when I am stressed-out.
6. The world seems threatening to me.
7. When I have to, I can make a situation better.
8. It takes most of my energy just to get by.
9. I can fix a problem when I have to.
10. I let myself down.
11. I make my own decisions.
12. I feel like there's no way out.
13. I know what to do with my life.

14. My future seems empty.
15. I can make sense out of my life.
16. I feel I am not in control of my life.
17. I succeed because of me, not because of luck.
18. I feel that others are running my life.
19. I can change my life if I want to.
20. Things just happen to me.
21. I can deal with the things I have to do.
22. I felt nervous and stressed-out.
23. I can handle my problems.
24. I felt mad about things I couldn't control.

HIV Risk Measures

Surety of HIV Risk Status

For the next 2 questions, please circle your answer.

A=Not at all sure
B=Slightly sure
C=Somewhat sure
D=Very sure
E=Absolutely sure

1. How sure are you that you have **not** been exposed to the AIDS virus?
2. How sure are you that your sex partners have **not** been exposed to the AIDS virus?

3. Have you ever tested positive on an HIV test (do you have the HIV virus)?

A=No, never had test
B=No, had test but it was negative
C=Not sure
D=Yes

AIDS Risk Behaviors and Attitudes Survey (ARBAS)

The next questions may or may not be true of you. Please say if you think they are true of you or not. Circle your best answer. Thank you for your help.

A=Definitely yes
B=Probably yes
C=Not sure
D=Probably no
E=Definitely no

1. I feel that I am at risk of getting AIDS at this time in my life.
2. I know someone who was tested for the AIDS virus.
3. I sometimes think that I may have been exposed to AIDS.
4. I have had sex with someone in the past 10 years who could have given me AIDS.
5. One of my close friends does things that could lead to them getting AIDS.
6. I believe that I can do things to help protect myself from getting AIDS.
7. I am careful about who I have sex with.
8. I try not to get into situations where I might get AIDS.
9. I make it a point to ask my partners about their sex history.
10. I am not having sex at this time in my life.
11. I use condoms when I have sex.
12. I know someone who was told that he/she had the AIDS virus.
13. Someone that I know has died from AIDS.

Perceived Risk: Mean of items 1,3, and 4
Preventive Behaviors: Mean of items 7 and 8

Partner-Related Risk

Number of Partners

In this survey, a "sex partner" is any person you have done any of these things with:
oral sex: your mouth on your partner's genitals or your partners mouth on your genitals; vaginal sex: a man putting his penis in your vagina; anal sex: a man putting his penis in your rectum.

"Having sex" is doing any of these things with a sex partner.
About how many sex partners have you had in the past 6 months?
_____

The next questions ask about your sex history. We realize that these are difficult questions to answer, but please try to fill in the blanks with your best guess. If the answer is none, please fill in the blank with a zero (0). Please remember that no one will know that these answers came from you. Also, remember that there are no "right" or "wrong" answers in this survey.

About how many sex partners have you had in your life? ———————

Unprotected Sex

Think of each column in this chart as a sex partner you had in the past 6 months. All the boxes below "Partner 1" are about your sex life with Partner 1. All the boxes below "Partner 2" are about your sex life with Partner 2. It might also help to put the partner's initials under each column if you want. Please write in the chart below **how many times** you did each activity in the past 6 months with each sex partner. We understand that it is difficult to give exact numbers for the chart below, but please make the best guess that you can. If you have not done some of these things with your partners, please fill in those squares with a zero (0). If you had more than 3 partners in the past 6 months, you can give information about them at the end of the survey. Extra charts are provided for this. Please remember that no one will know that these answers came from you. Answer as honestly as you can. There are no "right" or "wrong" answers to these questions.

The first 3 columns of this chart are filled in as an example of how one woman might answer. Please write your answers in the three empty columns.

How many times in past 6 mos. have you had	Example Partner 1	Eample Partner 2	Example Partner 3	Partner 1	Partner 2	Partner 3
Partner initials	J.S.	A.B.	T.J.			
Vaginal sex (penis in your vagina) without condom	10	4	2			
Oral sex (your mouth on partner's genitals) with no condom or latex barrier	7	5	4			
Anal sex (penis in your rectum without condom	6	3	4			

Partner Status

Please check all items that describe each of your partners during the last 6 months. If the answer to any of the items is no, please write NO in those squares. If you are not sure, put a question mark (?). Please be sure your partners are listed in the same order as earlier. For example, if Partner 1 is John Smith and has initials J.S. earlier, then make sure Partner 1 is J.S. on this page. If you had more than 3 partners in the past 6 months, you can give information about them at the end of the survey. Extra charts are provided for this. Please remember that no one will know that these answers came from you. Answer as honestly as you can. There are no "right" or "wrong" answers to these questions.

The first 3 columns of this chart are filled in as an example of how one woman might answer. Please write your answers in the three empty columns.

	Example Partner 1	Example Partner 2	Example Partner 3	Your Answers *go here* Partner 1	Partner 2	Partner 3
Please check which are true for EACH partner						
If you want, put partner's initials	J.S.	A.B.	T.J.			
Male?	Yes	Yes	Yes			
Female?	No	No	No			
Has sex with other women	X	?	No			
Has sex with other men	No	?	No			
Is HIV+	No	X	?			
Has AIDS?	No	X	?			
Uses IV-drugs	X	?	X			

Demographics

For the next set of questions, please circle the answer that is best for you or fill in the blanks. If you have comments or anything that you would like to add, please feel free to write them down next to the questions.

1. What is your race or cultural group?

A = White
B = African American

C=Native American
D=Asian American
E=Hispanic American
F=Other _____
                    (please specify)

2. How old are you?   _____ years
3. How long have you gone to school?

A=Did not finish 8th grade
B=Grades 8–12
C=Graduaated from high school
D=Some college work
E=Graduated from college
F=Graduate degree or coursework

4. How much money did you make last year?

A=Less than $10,000
B=$10,000 to 19,999
C=$20,000 to 34,999
D=$35,000 to 50,000
E=over $50,000

5. Are you married now?

A=Single, never married
B=Married
C=Separated or divorced
D=Widowed

In this survey, a "sex partner" is any person that you have done any of these things with:
    Oral sex: your mouth on your partner's genitals or your partner's mouth on your genitals;
    Vaginal sex: a man putting his penis in your vagina;
    Anal sex: a man putting his penis in your rectum.

"Having sex" is doing any of these things with a sex partner

6. Is there a man you regularly have sex with (husband or steady partner)?

A=No
B=Yes

7. About how long have you been involved with your most recent sex partner? (fill in the blanks)

———————— years
———————— months
———————— weeks   (if less than a month)

8. Are you living with a sex partner now?

A=No
B=Sometimes, at least several days a month
C=Yes, all the time

9. How many children do you have? (fill in) ————————
10. Have you been trying to get pregnant in the past 6 months?

A=No
B=Yes

11. What is your religion?

A=Catholic
B=Protestant
C=Jewish
D=Muslim
E=Eastern
F=Other
G=None

12. How religious are you?

A=Not at all
B=Slightly
C=Somewhat
D=Fairly
E=Very

Health Problems

Please think of whether you have any kind of health problem now. Circle the answer that is best for you.

1. Describe your health problem.

I do not have any health problems
very mild
moderate
severe
very severe

2. How long has your health problem lasted?

I do not have any health problems
1 month or less
2–5 months
6–12 months
over 1 year

References

Adler-Cohen, M. A., & Alfonso, C. A. (1997). Women, sex, and AIDS. *International Journal of Mental Health, 26*(1), 99–106.

Aguilar, R. J., & Nightengale, N. N. (1994). The impact of specific battering experiences on the self-esteem of abused women. *Journal of Family Violence, 9*(1), 35–45.

Ajzen, I., & Fishbein, M. (1980). The prediction of behavior from attitudinal and normative variables. *Journal of Experimental Social Psychology, 6,* 466–487.

Aldenderfer, M. S., & Blashfield, R. K. (1984). *Cluster analysis: Quantitative applications in the social sciences.* Beverly Hills, CA: Sage.

Alexander, P. C., & Lupfer, S. L. (1987). Family characteristics and long-term consequences associated with sexual abuse. *Archives of Sexual Behavior, 16*(3), 235–245.

Allers, C. T., & Benjack, K. J. (1991). Connections between childhood abuse and HIV infection. *Journal of Counseling and Development, 70,* 309–313.

Altman, L.K. (1992, July 21). Women worldwide nearing higher rate for AIDS than men. *The New York Times,* pp. C1, C3.

Amaro, H. (1988). Considerations for prevention of HIV infection among Hispanic women. *Psychology of Women's Quarterly, 12,* 429–443.

Amaro, H. (1995). Love, sex, and power: Considering women's realities in HIV prevention. *American Psychologist, 50*(6), 437–447.

American Psychiatric Association (1994). *Diagnostic and statistical manual of mental disorders* (4th ed.). Washington DC: Author.

Anderson, C. (1995). Childhood sexually transmitted diseases: One consequence of sexual abuse. *Public Health Nursing, 12*(1), 41–46.

Aspinwall, L.G., Kemeny, M.E., Taylor, S.E., Schneider, S.G., & Dudley, J.P. (1991). Psychosocial predictors of gay men's AIDS risk-reduction behavior. *Health Psychology, 10,* 432–444.

Bagnall, G., & Plant, M.A. (1991). HIV/AIDS risks, alcohol and illicit drug use among young adults in areas of high and low rates of HIV infection. *AIDS Care, 3,* 355–361.

Bandura, A. (1989). Perceived self-efficacy in the exercise of control over AIDS infection. In V. M. Mays, G. W. Albee, & S. F. Schneider (Eds.), *Primary prevention of AIDS* (pp. 128–141). Newbury Park, CA: Sage Publications.

Bandura, A. (1990). Perceived self-efficacy in the exercise of control over AIDS infection. *Evaluation and Program Planning, 13,* 9–17.

Baron, R. M., & Kenny, D. A. (1986). The moderator-mediator distinction in social psychological research: Conceptual, strategic, and statistical considerations. *Journal of Personality and Social Psychology, 51*(6), 1173–1182.

Bartholow, B. N., Doll, L. S., Joy, D., Douglas, J. M., Bolan, G., Harrison, J. S., Moss, P. M., & McKirnan, D. (1994). Emotional, behavioral, and HIV risks associated with sexual abuse among adult homosexual and bisexual men. *Child Abuse and Neglect, 18*(9), 747–761.

Becker, J. V., Skinner, L. J., Abel, G. G., & Cichon, J. (1986). Level of postassault sexual functioning in rape and incest victims. *Archives of Sexual Behavior, 5*(1), 37–49.

Becker, M., & Joseph, J. (1988). AIDS and behavioral change to avoid risk: A review. *American Journal of Public Health, 78,* 384–410.

Belsky, J. (1980). Child maltreatment: An ecological integration. *American Psychologist, 35*(4), 320–335.

Bentler, P. M. (1990). Comparative fit indexes in structural models. *Psychological Bulletin, 107,* 238–246.

Bentler, P.M. (1995). *EQS structural equations program manual.* Encino, CA: Multivariate Software, Inc.

Bernstein, E. M., & Putnam, F. W. (1986). Development, reliability, and validity of a dissociation scale. *Journal of Nervous and Mental Diseases, 174,* 727–734.

Biddle, B. J., & Marlin, M. M. (1987). Causality, confirmation, credulity, and structural equation modeling. *Child Development, 58*(1), 4–17.

Bond, L., & Semaan, S. (1996). At risk for HIV infection: Incarcerated women in a county jail in Philadelphia. *Women & Health, 24,* 27–45.

Booth, R., Koester, S., Brewster, J. T., Weibel, W. W., & Fritz, R. B. (1991). Intravenous drug users and AIDS: Risk behaviors. *American Journal of Drug and Alcohol Abuse, 17,* 337–353.

Boyer, D., & Fine, D. (1992). Sexual abuse as a factor in adolescent pregnancy and child maltreatment. *Family Planning Perspectives, 24,* 4–11.

Braun, B. G. (1984). Towards a theory of multiple personality and other dissociative phenomena. *Psychiatric Clinics of North America, 7*(1), 171–193.

Briere, J. (1992). Methodological issues in the study of sexual abuse effects. *Journal of Consulting and Clinical Psychology, 60*(2) 196–203.

Briere, J., & Elliott, D. M. (1993). Sexual abuse, family environment, and psychological symptoms: On the validity of statistical control. *Journal of Clinical and Consulting Psychology, 61*(2), 284–288.

Briere, J., & Runtz, M. (1987). Post sexual abuse trauma: Data and implications for clinical practice. *Journal of Interpersonal Violence, 2,* 367–379.

Briere, J., & Runtz, M. (1988). Symptomatology associated with childhood sexual victimization in a nonclinical adult sample. *Child Abuse and Neglect, 12,* 51–59.

Briere, J., & Runtz, M. (1990). Differential adult symptomatology associated with three types of child abuse histories. *Child Abuse and Neglect, 14,* 357–364.

Briere, J., & Runtz, M. (1993). Child sexual abuse: Long term sequelae and implications for psychological assessment. *Journal of Interpersonal Violence, 8*(3), 312–330.

Browne, A., & Finkelhor, D. (1986). Impact of child sexual abuse: A review of the research. *Psychological Bulletin, 99*(1), 66–77.

Burkholder, G. J., & Harlow, L. L. (1996). Using structural equation modeling techniques to evaluate HIV risk models. *Structural Equation Modeling, 3*(4), 348–368.

Butler, J. R., & Burton, L. M. (1990). Rethinking teenage childbearing: Is sexual abuse the missing link? *Family Relations, 39,* 73–80.

Byrne, B. (1994). *Structural equation modeling with EQS.* Newbury Park, CA: Sage.

Caffaro-Rouget, A., Lang, R.A., & Van Santen, V. (1989). The impact of child sexual abuse on victims' adjustment. *Annals of Sex Research, 2*(1), 29–47.

Cahill, C., Llewelyn, S.P., & Pearson, C. (1991). Long-term effects of sexual abuse which occurred in childhood: A review. *British Journal of Clinical Psychology, 30,* 117–130.

Caplan, P. J. (1995). *They say you're crazy: How the world's most powerful psychiatrists decide who's normal.* Reading, MA: Addison-Wesley.

Castro, K. G., Valdiserri, R. O., & Curran, J. W. (1992). Commentary: Perspectives on HIV/ AIDS epidemiology and prevention from the Eighth International Conference on AIDS. *American Journal of Public Health, 82,* 1465–1470.

Catania, J. A., Coates, T. J., Golden, E., Dolcini, M. M., Peterson, J., Kegeles, S., Siegel, D., & Fullilove, M. T. (1994). Correlates of condom use among Black, Hispanic, and White heterosexuals in San Francisco: The AMEN longitudinal study. *AIDS Education and Prevention, 6*(1), 12–26.

Catania, J. A., Coates, T. J., Kegeles, S., Fullilove, M.T., Peterson, J., Marin, B., Siegel, D., & Hulley, S. (1992). Condom use in multi-ethnic neighborhoods of San Francisco: The population-based AMEN (AIDS in multi-ethnic neighborhoods) study. *American Journal of Public Health, 82*(2), 284–287.

Catania, J. A., Gibson, D. R., Chitwood, D. D., & Coates, T. J. (1990). Methodological problems in AIDS behavioral research: Influences on measurement error and participation bias in studies of sexual behavior. *Psychological Bulletin, 108*, 339–362.

Centers for Disease Control and Prevention. (1997). *HIV/AIDS Surveillance Report, 9*(2), 1–44.

Chou, C.-P., & Bentler, P. M. (1990). Model modification in covariance structure modeling: A comparison among likelihood ratio, Lagrange multiplier, and Wald tests. *Multivariate Behavioral Research, 25*, 115–136.

Chu, J. A., & Dill, D. L. (1990). Dissociative symptoms in relation to childhood physical and sexual abuse. *American Journal of Psychiatry, 147*(7), 887–892.

Clark, L. L., Calsyn, D. A., Saxon, A. J., Jackson, T. R., & Wrede, I. A. F. (1992, July). *HIV risk behaviors of heterosexual couples in methadone maintenance.* Paper presented at the Eighth International Conference on AIDS, Amsterdam, the Netherlands.

Cochran, S. D. (1989). Women and HIV infection: Issues in prevention and behavior change. In V. M. Mays, G. W. Albee, & S. F. Schneider (Eds.), *Primary prevention of AIDS: Psychological approaches* (pp. 309–327). Newbury Park, CA: Sage.

Cohen, J. (1992). A power primer. *Psychological Bulletin, 112*(1), 155–159.

Cohen, J. B. (1991). Why woman partners of drug users will continue to be at high risk for HIV infection. *Journal of Addictive Diseases, 19*, 99–110.

Coons, P. M., Bowman, E. S., Pellow, T. A., & Schneider, P. (1989). Post-traumatic aspects of the treatment of victims of sexual abuse and incest. *Psychiatric Clinics of North America, 12*(2), 325–335.

Courtois, C. A. (1988). *Healing the incest wound: Adult survivors in therapy.* New York: Norton.

Cronbach, L. J. (1951). Coefficient alpha and the internal structure of tests. *Psychometrika, 16*, 297–334.

Cunningham, R. M., Stiffman, A. R., & Dore, P. (1994). The association of physical and sexual abuse with HIV risk behaviors in adolescence and young adulthood: Implications for public health. *Child Abuse and Neglect, 18*(3), 233–245.

Deiter, P. J. (1993). *Sexual assertiveness training for college women: An intervention study.* Unpublished doctoral dissertation, University of Rhode Island, Kingston, RI.

du Guerny, J., & Sjoberg, E. (1993). Inter-relationship between gender relations and the HIV/AIDS epidemic: Some possible considerations for policies and programmes. *AIDS, 7*, 1027–1034.

Dutton, M. A., Burghardt, K. J., Perrin, S. G., Chrestman, K. R., & Halle, P. M. (1994). Battered women's cognitive schemata. *Journal of Traumatic Stress, 7*(2), 237–255.

Ehrhardt, A. A., Yingling, S., Zawadzki, R., & Martinez-Ramirez, M. (1992). Prevention of heterosexual transmission of HIV: Barriers for women. *Journal of Psychology and Human Sexuality, 5*(1–2), 37–67.

Ellerbrock, T. V., Bush, T. J., Chamberland, M. E., & Oxtoby, M. J. (1991). Epidemiology of women with AIDS in the United States, 1981 through 1990. *Journal of the American Medical Association, 265*(22), 2971–2975.

Elliott, D. M., & Briere, J. (1992). Sexual abuse trauma among professional women: Validating the Trauma Symptom Checklist-40 (TSC-40). *Child Abuse and Neglect, 16*(3), 391–398.

Fausto-Sterling, A. (1985). *Myths of gender: Biological theories about women and men.* New York: Basic Books.

Finkelhor, D. (1985). The traumatic impact of child sexual abuse: A conceptualization. *Journal of Orthopsychiatry, 55*(4), 530–541.

Finkelhor, D. (1988). The trauma of child sexual abuse: Two models. In G. Wyatt & G. Powell (Eds.), *Lasting effects of child sexual abuse* (pp. 61–82). Newbury Park, CA: Sage.

Finkelhor, D., & Baron, L. (1986). Risk factors for child sexual abuse. *Journal of Interpersonal Violence, 1*(1), 43–71.

Finkelhor, D., Hotaling, G., Lewis, I. A., & Smith, C. (1990). Sexual abuse in a national survey of adult men and women: Prevalence, characteristics and risk factors. *Child Abuse and Neglect, 14,* 19–28.

Finkelhor, D., & Yllo, K. (1987). *License to rape: Sexual abuse of wives.* New York: Free Press.

Flaskerud, J. H., & Nyamathi, A. M. (1989). Black and Latina men's AIDS related knowledge, attitudes, and practices. *Research in Nursing and Health, 12,* 339–346.

Flesch, R. (1948). A new readability yardstick. *Journal of Applied Psychology, 32,* 221–233.

Follingstad, D. R., Rutledge, L. L., Berg, B. J., Hause, E. S., & Polek, D. S. (1990). The role of emotional abuse in physically abusive relationships. *Journal of Family Violence, 5,* 107–119.

Freyd, J. J. (1996). *Betrayal trauma: The logic of forgetting childhood abuse.* Cambridge, MA: Harvard University Press.

Fromuth, M. E. (1986). The relationship of childhood sexual abuse with later psychological and sexual adjustment in a sample of college women. *Child Abuse and Neglect, 10,* 5–15.

Fuller, T. D., Edwards, J. N., Vorakitphokatorn, S., & Sermski, S. (1993). *Using focus groups to adapt survey instruments to new populations: Experiences from a developing country.* Newbury Park, CA: Sage Publications.

Fullilove, M. T., Fullilove, R. E., Haynes, K., & Gross, S. (1990). Black women and AIDS prevention: A view towards understanding the gender rules. *The Journal of Sex Research, 27,* 47–64.

Germano, M. U. (1995). *An investigation of dissociation, attentional focus, affectie responses, and sexual arousal in women.* Unpulished doctoral dissertation, University of Rhode Island, Kingston, RI.

Gershenson, H. P., Musick, J. S., Ruch-Ross, H. S., Magee, V., Rubino, K. K., & Rosenberg, D. (1989). The prevalence of coercive sexual experience among teenage mothers. *Journal of Interpersonal Violence, 4*(2), 204–219.

Gidycz, C. A., Coble, C. N., Latham, L., & Layman, M. J. (1993). Sexual assault experience in adulthood and prior victimization experiences. *Psychology of Women Quarterly, 17,* 151–168.

Glod, C. A. (1993). Long-term consequences of childhood physical and sexual abuse. *Archives of Psychiatric Nursing, 7*(3), 163–173.

Gold, E. R. (1986). Long-term effects of sexual victimization in childhood: An attributional approach. *Journal of Consulting and Clinical Psychology, 54*(4), 471–475.

Gomes-Schwartz, B., Horowitz, J. M., Cardarelli, A. P. (1990). *Child sexual abuse: The initial effects.* Newbury Park, CA: Sage Publications.

Goodman, L. A., & Fallot, R. D. (1998). HIV risk-behavior in poor urban women with serious mental disorders: Association with childhood physical and sexual abuse. *American Journal of Orthopsychiatry, 68*(1), 73–83.

Goodman, L. A., Koss, M. P., & Russo, N. F. (1993). Violence against women: Physical and mental health effects. Part I: Research findings. *Applied & Preventive Psychology, 2,* 79–89.

Greenwald, E., Leitenberg, H., Cado, S., & Tarran, M. J. (1990). Childhood sexual abuse: Long-term effects on psychological and sexual functioning in a nonclinical and nonstudent sample of adult women. *Child Abuse and Neglect, 14,* 503–513.

Gregory-Bills, T., & Rhodeback, M. (1995). Comparative psychopathology of women who experienced intra-familial versus extra-familial sexual abuse. *Child Abuse and Neglect, 19*(2), 177–189.

Groth, A. N. (1979). *Men who rape: The psychology of the offender.* New York: Plenum.

Hamilton, J. A., & Gallant, S. J. (1990). Problematic aspects of diagnosing premenstrual phase dysphoria: Recommendations for psychological research and practice. *Professional Psychology Research and Practice, 21*(1), 60–68.

Harlow, L. L. (1990, August). *Psychometric investigation of a scale to measure demoralization.* Paper presented at American Psychological Association annual meeting, Boston, MA.

Harlow, L. L. (1991). [Unpublished Lifestyle Survey]. University of Rhode Island, Kingston, RI.

Harlow, L. L., Morokof, P. J., & Quina, K. (1991). Predicting HIV-risky heterosexual behavior in Natinal Institute of Mental Health Grant MH47233. Unpublished questionnaire, University of Rhode Island, Kingston, RI.

Harlow, L. L., & Newcomb, M. D. (1990). Towards a general hierarchical model of meaning and satisfaction in life. *Multivariate Behavioral Research, 25,* 387–405.

Harlow, L. L., Newcomb, M.D., & Bentler, P. M. (1986). Depression, self-derogation, substance use, and suicide ideation: Lack of purpose in life as a mediational factor. *Journal of Clinical Psychology, 42,* 5–21.

Harlow, L. L., Quina, K., & Morokoff, P. (1990, August). *Predicting AIDS-risking attitudes and behaviors (ARBAS) in young adults.* Paper presented at American Psychological Association annual meeting, Boston, MA.

Harlow, L. L., Quina, K., Morokoff, P. J., Rose, J. S., & Grimley, D. M. (1993). HIV risk in women: A multifaceted model. *Journal of Applied Behavioral Research, 1,* 3–38.

Harlow, L. L., Rose, J. S., Morokoff, P. J., & Quina, K. (1993, October). *Tests of reasonable solutions in cluster analysis: An AIDS risk example.* San Pedro, CA: Society of Multivariate Experimental Psychology.

Harter, S., Alexander, P. C., & Neimeyer, R. A. (1988). Long-term effects of incestuous child abuse in college women: Social adjustment, social cognition, and family characteristics. *Journal of Consulting and Clinical Psychology, 56,* 5–8.

Herman, J. (1981). *Father-daughter incest.* Cambridge, MA: Harvard University Press.

Herman, J. (1992). *Trauma and Recovery.* New York: Basic Books.

Hernandez, J. T. (1992). Substance abuse among sexually abused adolescents and their families. *Journal of Adolescent Health, 13*(8), 658–662.

Himelein, M. J. (1995). Risk factors for sexual victimization in dating. *Psychology of Women Quarterly, 19,* 31–48.

Himelein, M. J., Vogel, R. E., & Wachowiak, D. G. (1994). Nonconsensual sexual experiences in precollege women: Prevalence and risk factors. *Journal of Counseling and Development, 72,* 411–415.

Holland, J., Ramazanoglu, C., Scott, S., Sharpe, S., & Thomson, R. (1990). Sex, gender, and power: Young women's sexuality in the shadow of AIDS. *Sociology of Health and Illness, 12*(3), 336–350.

Holmes, K. K., Karon, J. M., & Kreiss, J. (1990). The increasing frequency of heterosexually acquired AIDS in the United States, 1983–1988. *American Journal of Public Health, 80*(3), 858–863.

Hoyle, R.H., & Panter, A.T. (1995). Writing about structural equation models. In R.H. Hoyle (Ed.), *Structural Equation Modeling: Concepts, issues, and applications* (pp. 158–176). Thousand Oaks, CA: Sage.

Ickovics, J. R., & Rodin, J. (1992). Women and AIDS in the United States: Epidemiology, natural history, and mediating mechanisms. *Health Psychology, 11*(1), 1–16.

Jackson, J. L., Calhoun, K. S., Amick, A. E., Maddever, H. M., & Habif, V. L. (1990). Young adult women who report childhood intrafamilial sexual abuse: Subsequent adjustment. *Archives of Sexual Behavior, 19*(3), 211–221.

Jemmott, L. S., & Jemmott, J. B. (1991). Applying the theory of reasoned action to AIDS risk behavior: Condom use among Black women. *Nursing Research, 40*, 228–234.

Johnsen, L. W., & Harlow, L. L. (1996). Adult problems in living associated with childhood sexual abuse. *AIDS Education and Prevention, 8*(1), 44–57.

Johnsen, L. W., Harlow, L. L., Morokoff, P. J., & Quina, K. (1994, May). *HIV risk and sexual victimization: A structural equation model.* Paper presented at the American Psychological Association Psychosocial and Behavioral Factors in Women's Health Conference, Washington, DC.

Kalichman, S. C., Hunter, T. L., & Kelly, J. A. (1992). Perceptions of AIDS susceptibility among minority and nonminority women at risk for HIV infection. *Journal of Consulting and Clinical Psychology, 60*(5), 725–732.

Kelly, J. A., Murphy, D. A., Washington, C. D., Wilson, T. S., Koob, J. J., Davis, D. R., Ledezma, G., & Davantes, B. (1994). The effects of HIV/AIDS intervention groups for high-risk women in urban clinics. *American Journal of Public Health, 84*(12), 1918–1922.

Kinzl, J. F., Traweger, C., & Biebl, W. (1995). Sexual dysfunctions: Relationship to childhood sexual abuse and early family experiences in a nonclinical sample. *Child Abuse and Neglect, 19*(7), 785–792.

Kline, A., & Strickler, J. (1993). Perceptions of risk for AIDS among women in drug treatment. *Health Psychology, 12*(4), 313–323.

Kluft, R. P. (Ed.). (1985*). Childhood antecedents of multiple personality.* Washington, DC: American Psychiatric Press.

Koss, M. P., & Dinero, T. E. (1989). Discriminant analysis of risk factors for sexual victimization among a national sample of college women. *Journal of Consulting and Clinical Psychology, 57*, 242–250.

Koss, M. P., & Gidycz, C. A. (1985). Sexual Experiences Survey: Reliability and validity. *Journal of Consulting and Clinical Psychology, 53*(3), 422–423.

Koss, M. P., Goodman, L. A., Browne, A., Fitzgerald, L. F., Keita, G. P., & Russo, N. F. (1994). *No safe haven: Male violence against women at home, at work, and in the community.* Washington, DC: American Psychological Association.

Koss, M. P., & Oros, C. J. (1982). Sexual experience survey: A research instrument investigating sexual aggression and victimization. *Journal of Consulting and Clinical Psychology, 50*, 455–457.

Krueger, R. A. (1988). *Focus groups: A practical guide for applied research.* Newbury Park, CA: Sage.

Kuiper, F., & Fisher., L. (1975). A monte carlo comparison of six clustering procedures. *Biometrics, 31*, 777–783.

Landrine, H., Klonoff, E.A., & Brown-Collins, A. (1992). Cultural diversity and methodology in feminist psychology: Critique, proposal, empirical example. *Psychology of Women Quarterly, 16*(2), 145–164.

Lanktree, C., Briere, J., & Zaidi, L. (1991). Incidence and impact of sexual abuse in a child outpatient sample: The role of direct inquiry. *Child Abuse and Neglect, 15*(4), 447–453.

Lanz, J. B. (1995). Psychological, behavioral, and social characteristics associated with early forced sexual intercourse among pregnant adolescents. *Journal of Interpersonal Violence, 10*(2), 188–200.

Leserman, J., & Drossman, D. A. (1995). Sexual and physical abuse history and medical practice. *General Hospital Psychiatry, 17*(2), 71–74.

Letourneaux, E. J., Resnick, H. S., Kilpatrick, D. G., Saunders, B. E., & Best, C. L. (1996). Comorbidity of sexual problems and posttraumatic stress disorder in female crime victims. *Behavior Therapy, 27*(3), 321–336.

Lewin, M. (1985). Unwanted intercourse: The difficulty of saying no. *Psychology of Women Quarterly, 9*, 184–192.

Lodico, M. A., & DiClemente, R. J. (1994). The association between childhood sexual abuse and prevalence of HIV-related risk behaviors. *Clinical Pediatrics, 33*(8), 498–502.

Loferski, S., Quina, K., Harlow, L. L., & Morokoff, P. J. (1992, February). *Will the pain ever stop? Abuse and AIDS in women.* Paper presented at the annual meeting of the Association for Women in Psychology, Long Beach, CA.

Long, P. J., & Jackson, J. L. (1991). Children sexually abused by multiple perpetrators. *Journal of Interpersonal Violence, 6*(2), 147–159.

Long, P. J., & Jackson, J. L. (1994). Childhood sexual abuse: An examination of family functioning. *Journal of Interpersonal Violence, 9*(2), 270–277.

Lott, B. (1987). *Women's lives: Themes and variations in gender learning.* Monterey, CA: Wadsworth.

Mandoki, C. A., & Burkhart, B. R. (1989). Sexual victimization: Is there a vicious cycle? *Violence and Victims, 4*(3), 179–190.

Mann, J., Tarantola, D. J. M., & Netter, T. W. (1992). *AIDS in the world.* Cambridge, MA: Harvard University Press.

Mays, V. M., & Cochran, S. D. (1993). Ethnic and gender differences in beliefs about sex partner questioning to reduce HIV risk. *Journal of Adolescent Research, 8*(1), 77–88.

Mays, V. M., & Jackson, J. S. (1991). AIDS survey methodology with Black Americans. *Social Science and Medicine, 33*(1), 47–54.

McCormick, N. (1994). *Sexual salvation: Affirming women's sexual rights and pleasures.* Westport, CT: Praeger.

McKusick, L., Hoff, C. C., Stall, R., & Coates, T. J. (1991). Tailoring AIDS prevention: Differences in behavioral strategies among heterosexual and gay bar patrons in San Francisco. *AIDS Education and Prevention, 3,* 1–9.

Meehl, P. (1997). The problem is epistemology, not statistics: Replace significance tests by confidence intervals and quantify accuracy of risky numerical predictions (pp. 393–425.). In L. L. Harlow, S. A. Mulaik, & J. H. Steiger (Eds.), *What if there were no significance tests?* Mahwah, NJ: Lawrence Erlbaum Associates.

Miccio-Fonseca, L. C., Jones, J. E., & Futterman, L. A. (1990). Sexual trauma and the premenstrual syndrome. *Journal of Sex Education and Therapy, 16*(4), 270–278.

Mitchell, J. L., Tucker, J., Loftman, P. O., & Williams, S. B. (1992). HIV and women: Current controversies and clinical relevance. *Journal of Women's Health, 1*(1), 35–39.

Moore, J. S., Harrison, J. S., & Doll, L. S. (1994). Interventions for sexually active, heterosexual women in the United States. In R.J. DiClemente & J.L. Peterson (Eds.) *Preventing AIDS: Theories and methods of behavioral interventions* (pp. 243–265). New York: Plenum Press.

Morgan, D .L. (Ed.). (1993). *Successful focus groups: Advancing the state of the art.* Newbury, CA: Sage.

Morokoff, P. J. (1986). Volunteer bias in the psychophysiological study of female sexuality. *The Journal of Sex Research, 22,* 35–51.

Morokoff, P. J., Harlow, L. L., & Quina, K. (1991, August). *Methodological issues in AIDS research with women.* Paper presented at the American Psychological Association annual meeting, San Francisco, CA.

Morokoff, P. J., Harlow, L. L., & Quina, K. (1995). Women and AIDS. In L. Stanton & S. J., Gallant (Eds.), *Women's Health* (pp. 117–169). Washington, DC: American Psychological Association.

Morokoff, P. J., Quina, K., Harlow, L. L., Whitmire, L. E., Grimley, D. M., Gibson, P., & Burkholder, G. (1997). Sexual Assertiveness Scale (SAS) for women: Development and validation. *Journal of Personality and Social Psychology, 73*(4), 790–804.

Murphy, S. M., Kilpatrick, D. G., Amick-McMullan, A., Veronen, L. J., Raduhovich, J., Best, C. L., Villeponteaux, L. A., & Saunders, B. E. (1988). Current psychological functioning of child sexual assault survivors. *Journal of Interpersonal Violence, 3*(1), 55–79.

Newcomb, M. D., & Harlow, L. L. (1986). Life events and substance use among adolescents: Mediating effects of perceived loss of control and meaninglessness in life. *Journal of Personality and Social Psychology, 51,* 564–577.

Nyamathi, A., Wayment, H. A., & Dunkel-Schetter, C. (1993). Psychosocial correlates of emotional distress and risk behavior in African-American women at risk for HIV infection. *Anxiety, Stress, and Coping: An International Journal, 6*(2), 133–148.

Padian, N. S., Shiboski, S. S., & Jewell, N. (1990, June). *The relative efficiency of female-to-male HIV sexual transmission* (Abstract No. Th. C. 101). Paper presented at the Sixth International Conference on AIDS, San Francisco.

Peplau, L., Rubin, Z., & Hill, C. T. (1977). Sexual intimacy in dating relationships. *Journal of Social Issues, 33,* 86–109.

Peters, D. K., & Range, L. M. (1995). Childhood sexual abuse and current suicidality in college women and men. *Child Abuse and Neglect, 19*(3), 335–341.

Peters, S. D. (1988). Child sexual abuse and later psychological problems. In G.E. Wyatt & G.J. Powell (Eds.), *Lasting effects of child sexual abuse* (pp. 101–117). Newbury Park, CA: Sage.

Peterson, K. E. (1992). Hidden populations at high risk for HIV infection. In M.R. Seligman & K. E. Peterson, *AIDS prevention and treatment: Hope, humor, and healing* (pp. 153–172). New York: Hemisphere Publishing.

Peterson, M. P. (1993). Physical and sexual abuse among school children: Prevalence and prevention. *Educational Psychology Review, 5*(1), 63–86.

Pivnick, A. (1993). HIV infection and the meaning of condoms. *Culture, Medicine, and Psychiatry, 17,* 431–453.

Prochaska, J. O., Norcross, J. C., & DiClemente, C. C. (1994). *Changing for good.* New York: William Morrow and Company.

Prochaska, J. O., Redding, C. A., Harlow, L. L., Rossi, J. S., & Velicer, W. F. (1994). The transtheoretical model of change and HIV prevention: A review. *Health Education Quarterly, 21,* 45–60.

Putnam, F. W. (1993). Dissociative phenomena. In D. Spiegel (Ed.), *Dissociative Disorders: A clinical review* (pp. 1–16). Lutherville, MD: Sidran.

Quina, K., & Carlson, N. L. (1989). *Rape, incest, and sexual harassment: A guide for helping survivors.* New York: Praeger.

Quina, K., Harlow, L. L., Morokoff, P. J., & Saxon, S. E. (1997). Interpersonal power and women's HIV risk. In N. Goldstein & J. L. Manlowe, *The gender politics of HIV/AIDS in women* (pp. 188–206). New York: NYU Press.

Quina, K., Rose, J. S., Harlow, L. L., Morokoff, P. J., Deiter, P., Whitmire, L. E., Lang, M. A., & Schnoll, R. (in press). Focusing in on participants: Feminist process model for survey modifications, *Psychology of Women Quarterly.*

Rainey, D. Y., Stevens-Simon, C., & Kaplan, D. W. (1995). Are adolescents who report prior sexual abuse at higher risk for pregnancy? *Child Abuse and Neglect, 19*(1), 1283–1288.

Rakos, R. F. (1991). *Assertive behavior: Theory, research and training.* New York: Routledge.

Reker, G. T., Peacock, E. J., & Wong, P. T. (1987). Meaning and purpose in life and well-being: A life span perspective. *Journal of Gerontology, 42*(1), 44–49.

Resnick, H. S., & Kilpatrick, D.G. (1996, September). *Rape and HIV risk: An epidemiological study.* Paper presented at the American Psychological Association Women's Health Conference, Washington, DC.

Resnick, H. S., Kilpatrick, D. G., Dansky, B. D., Saunders, B. E., & Best, C. L. (1993). Prevalence of civilian trauma and posttraumatic stress disorder in a representative national sample of women. *Journal of Consulting and Clinical Psychology, 61,* 984–991.

Resnick, H. S., & Seals, B. (1995, June). *Assessment of violence and posttrauma reactions.* Paper presented at NAPWA National Workshop on HIV and Violence, New York.

Rew, L. (1989a). Long-term effects of childhood sexual exploitation. *Issues in Mental Health Nursing, 10*, 229–244.

Rew, L. (1989b). Childhood sexual exploitation: Long-term effects among a group of nursing students. *Issues in Mental Health Nursing, 10*, 181–191.

Roesler, T. A., & McKenzie, N. (1994). Effects of childhood trauma on psychological functioning in adults sexually abused as children. *Journal of Nervous and Mental Disease, 182*(3), 145–150.

Rogers, C. R. (1961). *On becoming a person.* Boston: Houghton Mifflin.

Romans, S. E., Martin, J. L., Anderson, J. C., Herbison, G. P., & Mullen, P. E. (1995). Sexual abuse in childhood and deliberate self harm. *American Journal of Psychiatry, 152*(9), 1336–1342.

Ross, C. A., & Joshi, S. (1992). Schneiderian symptoms and childhood trauma in the general population. *Comprehensive Psychiatry, 33*, 269–273.

Rudy, T. E., Merluzzi, T. V., & Henahan, P. T. (1982). Construal of complex assertion situations: A multidimensional analysis. *Journal of Consulting and Clinical Psychology, 50*(1), 125–137.

Russell, D. E. H. (1983). The incidence and prevalence of intrafamilial and extrafamilial sexual abuse of female children. *Child Abuse and Neglect, 7*, 133–146.

Russell, D. E. H. (1984). *Sexual exploitation.* Beverly Hills, CA: Sage.

Russell, D. E. H. (1986). *The secret trauma: Incest in the lives of girls and women.* New York: Basic Books.

Sanders, B., & Giolas, M. H. (1991). Dissociation and childhood trauma in psychologically disturbed adolescents. *American Journal of Psychiatry, 148*(1), 501–504.

Sarle, W. S. (1983). *SAS/STAT user's guide, version 6, 4th edition.* Cary, NC: SAS.

SAS Institute (1989). *SAS user's guide: Statistics.* Cary, NC: Author.

Saunders, B. E., Villeponteaux, L. A., Lipovsky, J. A., Kilpatrick, D. E., & Veronen, L. J. (1992). Child sexual assault as a risk factor for mental disorders among women. *Journal of Interpersonal Violence, 7*(2), 189–204.

Schaefer, S., & Evans, S. (1987). Incest and chemically dependent women: Treatment implications. *Journal of Chemical Dependency Treatment, 1*(1), 141–173.

Scott, R. L., & Stone, D. A. (1986). MMPI profile constellations in incest families. *Journal of Consulting and Clinical Psychology, 54*(3), 363–368.

Spanos, N. P. (1994). Multiple identity enactments and multiple personality disorder: A sociocognitive perspective. *Psychological Bulletin, 116*(1), 143–165.

St. Lawrence, J. S., Eldridge, G. D., Shelby, M. C., Little, C. E., Brasfield, T.L., & O'Bannon, R. E. (1997). HIV risk reduction for incarcerated women: A comparison of brief interventions based on two theoretical models. *Journal of Consulting and Clinical Psychology, 65*(3), 504–509.

Steckler, A., McLeroy, K. R., Goodman, R. M., Bird, S. T., & McCormick, L. (1992). Toward integrating qualitative and quantitative methods: An introduction. *Health Education Quarterly, 19*, 1–8.

Stein, J. A., Golding, J. M., Siegel, J. M., Burnam, M. A., & Sorenson, S. B. (1988). Long-term psychological sequelae of child sexual abuse: The Los Angeles Epidemiologic Catchment Area Study. In G. E. Wyatt & G. J. Powerll (Eds.), *Lasting effects of child sexual abuse* (pp. 135–156). Newbury Park, CA: Sage.

Stevens-Simon, C., & Reichert, S. (1994). Sexual abuse, adolescent pregnancy, and child abuse. A developmental approach to an intergenerational cycle. *Archives of Pediatric and Adolescent Medicine, 148*, 23–27.

Straus, M. A. (1979). Measuring intrafamily conflict and violence: The conflict tactics (CT) scales. *Journal of Marriage and the Family, 41*, 75–88.

Stuntzner-Gibson, D. (1991). Women and HIV disease: An emerging social crisis. *Social Work, 36*(1), 22–27.

Taylor, E. R., Amodei, N., & Mangos, R. (1996). The presence of psychiatric disorders in HIV-infected women. *Journal of Counseling and Development, 74*(4), 345–351.

Testa, M. (1996, September). *Childhood to adulthood victimization: Role of sexual activity and substance use.* Presented at the American Psychological Association Women's Health Conference, Washington, DC.

Urquiza, A. J., & Goodlin-Jones, B. L. (1994). Child sexual abuse and adult revictimization with women of color. *Violence and Victims, 9,* 223–232.

Velicer, W. F., Prochaska, J. O., Bellis, J. M., DiClemente, C. C., Rossi, J. S., Fava, J. L., & Steiger, J. H. (1993). An expert system intervention for smoking cessation. *Addictive Behaviors, 18,* 269–290.

Walker, E. A., Katon, W. J., Hansom, J., Harrop-Griffiths, J., Holm, L., Jones, M. L., Hickok, L. R., & Russo, J. (1995). Psychiatric diagnoses and sexual victimization in women with chronic pelvic pain. *Psychosomatics, 36*(6), 531–540.

Walker, L. E. (1984). *The Battered Woman Syndrome.* New York: Springer-Verlag.

Ward, J. (1963). Hierarchical grouping to optimize an objective function. *Journal of the American Statistical Association, 58,* 236–244.

Weinstein, N. D. (1993). Testing four competing theories of health-protective behavior. *Health Psychology, 12*(4), 324–333.

Weisberg, D. K. (1984). *Children of the night: A study of adolescent prostitution.* Lexington, MA: Lexington Books.

Wind, T. W., & Silvern, L. (1992). Type and extent of child abuse as predictors of adult functioning. *Journal of Family Violence, 7,* 261–281.

Wingood, G. M., & DiClemente, R. J. (1997). Child sexual abuse, HIV sexual risk, and gender relations of African-American women. *American Journal of Preventive Medicine, 13*(5), 380–384.

Witchel, R. I. (1991). College student survivors of incest and other child sexual abuse. *New Directions for Student Services, 54,* 63–76.

Wyatt, G. E. (1985). The sexual abuse of Afro-American and White American women in childhood. *Child Abuse and Neglect, 10,* 231–240.

Wyatt, G. E. (1992). The sociocultural context of African American and White American women's rape. *Journal of Social Issues, 48*(1), 77–91.

Wyatt, G. E., Guthrie, D., & Notgrass, C. M. (1992). Differential effects of women's child sexual abuse and subsequent sexual revictimization. *Journal of Consulting and Clinical Psychology, 60*(2), 167–173.

Wyatt, G. E., Newcomb, M. D., & Riederle M. H. (1993). *Sexual abuse and consensual sex.* Newbury Park, CA: Sage.

Wyatt, G. E., & Peters, S. D. (1986). Methodological considerations in research on the prevalence of child sexual abuse. *Child Abuse and Neglect, 10,* 241–251.

Zierler, S., Feingold, L., Laufer, D., Velentgas, R., Kantrowitz-Gordon, I., & Mayer, K. (1991). Adult survivors of childhood sexual abuse and subsequent risk of HIV infection. *American Journal of Public Health, 81,* 572–575.

Zierler, S., Witbeck, B., & Mayer, K. (1996). Sexual violence against women living with or at risk for HIV infection. *American Journal of Preventive Medicine, 12,* 304–310.

AUTHOR INDEX

SUBJECT INDEX